The Next Generation

STUDIES IN ANTHROPOLOGY

Under the Consulting Editorship of E. A. Hammel,
UNIVERSITY OF CALIFORNIA, BERKELEY

THE NEXT GENERATION

An Ethnography of Education in an Urban Neighborhood

John U. Ogbu

Department of Anthropology
University of California, Berkeley
Berkeley, California

ACADEMIC PRESS New York and London
A Subsidiary of Harcourt Brace Jovanovich, Publishers

ACADEMIC PRESS, INC.
111 Fifth Avenue, New York, New York 10003

United Kingdom Edition published by
ACADEMIC PRESS, INC. (LONDON) LTD.
24/28 Oval Road, London NW1

Library of Congress Cataloging in Publication Data

Ogbu, John U
    The next generation.

    (Studies in anthropology)
    A revision of the author's thesis, University of
California, Berkeley, 1971.
    Bibliography: p.
    1.   Minorities—Education—Stockton, Calif.
2.   Academic achievement.   3.   Educational sociology—
United States.   4.   Educational anthropology.
I.   Title.
LC3733.S86034   370.19'3   72-13622
ISBN 0–12–785589–0

TO
my father, Ogbu nw'Onu nw'Igbo,
and my mother, Ugo nw'Uzo,
and all Burghersiders,
who so much desire education
for their children because
they themselves never
had the opportunity

Contents

Chapter 9. The Education Rehabilitation Movement:
Taxpayers' Solution to the Problem of
School Failure in Burgherside

Chapter 10. The Silent Minority: What Burghersiders Think
of Taxpayers' "Solutions"

Chapter 11. The Next Generation and the Meanings
of "Equal Educational Opportunity"

Foreword

This is a book written by an anthropologist about a problem that has bedeviled educators, sociologists, psychologists, political leaders, parents, and children: Why is it that some children, and especially minority children living in cities, do so badly in school? John Ogbu went to Stockton, California in 1968 equipped with the anthropologist's most precious tool—the right to be ignorant about the people he was to work among and so the right to ask them about their lives and the way they viewed what was happening to them. He went originally to take part in a project examining community response to a bilingual educational experiment just starting in the schools of "Burgherside" Neighborhood in Stockton. He stayed because he became fascinated with why the people of Burgherside and the educators who taught their children or administered the district schools had such divergent views of what was happening.

Burghersiders are mostly blacks, Mexican-Americans, or Asian Americans, and many of them have immigrated to Stockton from rural areas in the southern United States, Mexico, or Asia; they want their children to do well in school so that they can get good-paying jobs and thus escape the heavy physical toil in the fields or other rough labor to which the majority of their parents have been condemned. The educators identify with middle-class whites, whom Ogbu calls the "Taxpayers," and agree with them that the children must first learn the values of the middle-class world to be able to put forth the effort to learn the skills that good jobs in that world require.

Parents want their children to learn skills. The schools want to reform the children. The children look at the world around them and see little hope that the school work required of them will lead anywhere. School is likely to be classed by them with dead-end jobs and, like such jobs, felt to be unworthy of serious effort. Teachers learn to expect little from the children and reward them with passing marks for minimal performance on work that is often a repetition of what they have done before. Children compare themselves with one another and decide, since all are on much the same level, that they must all be doing as much as is required. Parents are bitter against a system that tells them their children are doing well enough, when they learn that this should be translated "as well as can be expected from a child with this background." They think their children would be able to do much better if they were properly taught, and they deny that children fail to learn because their parents are not interested in their progress or anxious to push them on. They know they *are* interested, although it is sometimes expedient to agree with school officials that their own failures as parents lie behind the difficulties of their children.

John Ogbu got his training in anthropology in the United States, at Berkeley, but he arrived in Berkeley after a childhood and youth spent in West Africa, which has affected his study of Burgherside in a number of important ways. If any American, white or black, had asked the same kinds of questions, informants would have been much less likely to respond with good will because they would have assumed that *Americans* ought to know how their fellow Americans live and the way the schools operate. Ogbu was seen as trying to understand something that was legitimately foreign to him, and the questions he asked were not those for which a routine reply was the accepted standard. He met with the same courtesy that anthropologists have encountered elsewhere in the world when they sought to enter a strange society and understand its ways. Burghersiders and educators (as well as other "Taxpayers") took the same pleasure in his education that Africans have taken in educating me and other American anthropologists who have visited them.

From his African background, Ogbu gained perspective on what is happening in Burgherside and other American cities. He had the built-in standards of comparisons based on experience in another society, which again are an important part of the anthropologist's tool kit. Some questions that might seem vital to investigators who have known only American urban society were irrelevant to him, whereas some they might take for granted were of importance for him. Dr. Ogbu has known many intelligent African adults who are illiterates because schools reached their villages only after they had grown up. He is not likely to make the common Western error of confusing intelligence with literacy, nor is he likely to assume that middle-class American values are a necessary precondition for success in school. He comes from a region in Nigeria where villages compete with one another to see which can build the best schools and send forward the most children to secondary schools and universities. The eagerness of villagers for education and their willingness to sacrifice for it were for him a strong contrast with what he found in Stockton. He saw no reason to believe that the black people of Stockton, whose ancestors may well have come from his own part of Africa, had become less intelligent simply because they lived in the United States. Although he writes about all the children of Burgherside, whatever their origin, and compares their progress, implicitly throughout this book he is asking himself, "If black children can succeed so brilliantly in African schools, why should they fail so miserably in American schools?" He argues that it is because in the latter situation they are encouraged to fail and taught that effort does not bring the same rewards for the Burgherside child that it does for the child in the more prosperous sections of the city dominated by "Taxpayers."

Others who have looked at children and the schools they attend may have come to the same conclusion before Dr. Ogbu tried to understand what anthropologists call "the folk systems" of the various groups in Stockton, that is, the way they perceive the world and so create the reality to which they respond. Few have documented the effect upon the children as thoroughly as he has done.

Inevitably Dr. Ogbu's conclusions will be challenged. One of the most fascinating aspects of his book is the extent to which his own assumptions about the nature of man, derived from his Nigerian childhood, are similar to those with which many of his "Taxpayers" operate. He believes that human beings can do whatever it is they decide they want to do and that it is natural for people to work hard and with enthusiasm to gain their ends. He expects parents to "push" their children and the children to face the future with zest as a game which challenges their resources. Naturally enough, then, he writes his book to explain what it is that is thwarting the natural bent of human nature to succeed. This is where he departs most firmly from much that has been written by educators, sociologists, psychologists, and others who assume that children must be taught to learn and trained to will success.

E. COLSON

Acknowledgments

This book is a revised version of my Ph. D. dissertation, presented to the Department of Anthropology at the University of California, Berkeley, in June 1971. I am grateful to the department for teaching me anthropology, a field I scarcely knew existed until I arrived here from my village in Igbo-land, Nigeria, more than 10 years ago. I am most grateful to Professor Elizabeth F. Colson, who made my graduate training an intellectually exciting and rewarding period of my education, who supervised the prep-aration of my dissertation, and who encouraged its revision for publication. I wish also to thank Professor Eugene E. Hammel for his encouragement while I was preparing the manuscript for publication and Anne Brower for her many valuable comments on earlier versions of this work. Others who provided helpful suggestions include Professors George DeVos, Mazi O. Ojiaku, and William Simmons.

Stockton Unified School District financed the first 10 months of the re-search, employing me as an ethnographer in Burgherside neighborhood in connection with a bilingual educational demonstration project in Burgher-side elementary school. In the summer of 1969 the school district also provided computer services for the tabulation of the quantitative data collected from school records and other sources. Thereafter, the district supported my research in many other ways that made its completion possible. I am grateful to the school district and its various personnel. Among others I wish to thank the following school officials for their special assistance: Mr. Arthur G. Becker, then Associate Superintendent for Instruction, and Mr. James L. Shannon, Director of Research and Evalua-tion. I also want to thank Dr. Theodore Parsons, formerly of the School of Education at the University of California, Berkeley, who first suggested the research in Stockton, who introduced me to Stockton Unified School District, and who thereafter provided helpful advice.

The University of California provided a grant-in-aid, which I used for collecting quantitative data from school and other local documents and for coding these and other quantitative data for computer analysis. A University of California Summer Faculty Research Fellowship has made possible completion of this book for publication. I wish to thank the University for its support.

I am indebted to Jan Rice, Nancy Selman, Cordie Sims, Victoria Wilson, Harrison Hun, Robert Roe, the Reverend Richard Litherland, and the Robert Byers for the various forms of assistance they provided me in the field. I also wish to thank many individuals who have helped to prepare the materials for this book by typing, map-drawing, and the like—especially Barbara Andersen, Linda Andersen, Jane McGary, Carolyn Rohrer, and Mary Jane Tyler.

Finally, my greatest gratitude is to Burghersiders for teaching me what I have learned about their neighborhood, themselves, and their education. It was their understanding, tolerance, friendship, and support that made this research possible. I wish to thank the leaders of Burgherside Neighborhood Improvement Association and the staff of the neighborhood center for their special assistance.

I have not attempted to conceal the name of the city in which this study was done. It would have been difficult to do so since I have made an extensive use of written sources bearing references to Stockton. I have, however, used the name Burgherside in place of Boggs Tract, purely out of convenience. I often pointed out to my informants, especially members of the school district personnel, my desire to represent as accurately as possible the facts about Burgherside education. On this basis I requested and received access to many documents from which I collected both qualitative and statistical data. At the same time I pointed out that my interpretation of these data would not necessarily represent the official position of the school district. In this book there are many instances where I have expressed my disagreement with the official position. I have not, however, presented my own interpretation of events in Burgherside education as absolute truth. Others will undoubtedly disagree with me. As in most anthropological studies, individual Stocktonians, except for public figures, remain anonymous.

I am entirely responsible for all errors, misinterpretations, and other blunders that may be found in the present work.

CHAPTER 1

School Failure: An Adaptation to Education with Limited Opportunity

Introduction

This book is about education in Burgherside, a low-income neighborhood in Stockton, California. The majority of the residents are blacks and Mexican-Americans: They make up about 92% of the elementary school population. The study reported here probes into the reasons for many children from the neighborhood failing in public schools. From the elementary grades through high school their schoolwork is generally poor. Many of them do not complete high school, and those who graduate do so with the average grade of "C" or lower. Very few go to college or get useful vocational training after high school. Many take up unskilled jobs for wages as low as those of their less educated parents. Some remain unemployed for a considerable length of time. The only major alternative for the unemployed young men is to go into the military service; the young women get married or have children out of wedlock and become welfare recipients.

Current literature of educational problems in the cities tends to lump different types of people under such terms as lower class, the poor, ethnic minorities. In this book I shall define more precisely the population studied. Not all children from a background of poverty fail in public schools; nor do all those who fail come from such a background. For example, it is possible that white and black children from backgrounds of poverty do poorly in school for different reasons. This book is concerned with school failures among ethnic minorities rather than among the poor in general. However, not all children from ethnic minorities do poorly in public school. In Stockton, for example, Chinese, Filipino, and Japanese children do better than black and Mexican-American children even when all groups come from a similar socioeconomic background. Some informants in the Stockton school system stated that Chinese and Japanese children who arrive from China and Japan learn to speak English and adjust faster than do Mexican-American children entering public schools at the same time with a similar language handicap. In general, the same "educational handicap" does not appear to affect all ethnic minority groups to the same degree.

I shall distinguish between two types of ethnic minorities that I encountered in Stockton, designating one group as *subordinate minority* and the other as *immigrant minorities*. By subordinate minorities I mean those minority groups who were incorporated into the United States more or less against their will. Subordinate minorities include the American Indians who were already here before the dominant whites arrived and conquered them, the Mexican-Americans of the Southwest and Texas who were similarly incorporated by conquest, and blacks who were brought here as slaves. Immigrant minorities include Arabs, Chinese, Filipinos, Japanese, among others. These groups came to the United States for the same reasons as the dominant whites—for political or religious asylum, but especially for economic betterment. Subordinate and immigrant minorities appear to differ in the way they perceive American society and in how they respond to the educational system. The present study deals primarily with the educational problems of subordinate minorities, that is, blacks and Mexican-Americans.[1]

---

[1] I am aware that a large portion of the Mexican-American population today either came from Mexico or are descended from those who immigrated to the United States from Mexico since the early 1900s. I base my classification of Mexican-Americans as a subordinate minority on the grounds that some Mexicans were already in the Southwest (including California) and Texas before the Anglo-Americans arrived, conquered, and displaced them from power (see Burma 1970). The pattern of relationship which later emerged between the conquered and displaced Mexican-Americans and the dominant whites was largely extended to those who later immigrated from Mexico. Furthermore, the two groups of Mexican-Americans have tended to develop similar attitudes toward the dominant whites and, at least in recent years, a common feeling of peoplehood. Some of my Mexican-American informants in Stockton, especially those from Texas, expressed their resentment toward the dominant whites partly because of the discriminations against them and other minorities and partly because, as they pointed out, the whites had taken their territory and displaced them by deceit and conquest. I have not completed my comparative study of the subordinate and immigrant minorities in American society, and I therefore regard my statements here as tentative. At this stage it appears to me that the attitudes of subordinate minorities toward American society are shaped not only by the prejudice and discrimination of the dominant whites toward minority

A survey of current studies of school failures among the subordinate minorities will show that certain important questions are rarely raised or answered. For example: Can we adequately explain the high proportion of school failures among the subordinate minorities without taking into account the historical basis for their association with the dominant whites and their experiences in that association? If a high proportion of school failure is characteristic of each subordinate minority group, can we adequately explain the reasons for this and devise effective programs to solve the problem by focusing our analysis on the characteristics of individual pupils, their parents, and teachers in the public schools? Can we adequately explain the high proportion of school failure without taking into account the functions that public school education serves for the subordinate minorities? In what ways are the present theories of school failures of subordinate minorities different from "theories" that purported to explain the school failures of eastern and southern European immigrants in the past?

Questions like these imply that the high proportion of school failures among subordinate minorities cannot be explained by such contemporaneous factors as the home and neighborhood environment, hereditary endowment, the influence of the school, or a combination of all these. American public schools are an institution established by the society to serve the specific needs of the entire society, the needs of its segments, and the needs of individual Americans. Society maintains the schools as long as they serve those vital functions for which they were established or which in the course of time have developed. The participation of each segment of the society also largely depends on the functions that the public schools serve for that segment; consider, for instance, the case of the Amish(Hostetler and Huntington 1971). In the same way, individual Americans participate in the school system to the extent that their needs are served by this institution. In this chapter I shall argue that (*a*) the public-school institution in America has not adequately served the needs of subordinate minorities; (*b*) the high proportion of school failure among subordinate minorities constitutes an adaptation to their lack of full opportunity to benefit from their education in contrast to dominant group; (*c*) the present situation cannot be changed merely by changing the home and neighborhood environments, by changing or abolishing the traditional school organization, by applying eugenics, or even by all of these. Above all, an increase in the opportunity of the subordinate minorities to benefit socially and economically, *on an equal basis with whites*, from their educational achievements is required.

---

groups but also by their deep feeling that their initial incorporation into the society had somehow been accomplished through treachery and injustice on the part of the dominant whites.

The Meaning and Purpose of Public School Education in the United States

The orientation of the present study requires that we state the meaning and purpose of education as institutionalized in American public schools. This means both how education is conceptualized by Americans and how it is practiced in the public schools. In this sense, education does not include all experiences, as some writers imply (Henry 1971:274), but is essentially what Cohen (1971:22) has described as the teaching of "standardized and stereotyped knowledge, skills, values and attitudes by means of stan-, dardized and stereotyped procedures." Thus, education is essentially formal, and it is with this kind of formal education in Burgherside that the present study is concerned.

In American society the main function of formal education is to prepare the young to assume adult roles in the economic, political, and social organization of society. But Americans usually place emphasis on the school's role in preparing young people for desirable occupational roles; this emphasis accounts for the close association between the schools and the business community (Callahan 1962:1). Katz (1971:xviii) has even suggested that the American public school system arose primarily to serve the needs of the American economy, which has developed a vast array of divisions of labor that often require highly specialized training obtained through formal education in the schools. That people will go through such training is ensured by the existence of an elaborate belief system in which "success" or "failure" in any "enterprise" is attributed to individual responsibility. This belief in individual responsibility originated initially from Puritanism and the frontier situation but is now incorporated into the folklore of modern, specialized, industrial economy. People who are successful are praised as being ambitious, imaginative, industrious, persevering, talented, and the like; those who are not successful are blamed as lacking in these qualities. It is also believed that every American has equal opportunity and that any individual with ability can succeed not only in school but also in society. To seek to "upgrade" oneself is held to be morally good and the proof of this "upward orientation" lies in success. Conversely, it is morally bad not to seek to "upgrade" oneself and failure is the proof that one has not (Cloward and Ohlin 1960:106, 125; Sexton 1970:19).

Thus far I have looked at the relationship between formal education and the American economy from the standpoint of society at large. What is the function of formal education for the segments of American society? America is a plural society that is stratified along lines of birth-ascribed status (racial, ethnic, religious) as well as social classes in terms of acquired status (education, occupation, income, life styles, and the like). There are prescribed means by which each segment based on birth-ascribed status, through the accomplishments of its members, can "move up" in the class system (Berreman 1972), and education is one of the principal means by which such social mobility is achieved.

Finally, formal education serves some important functions for the individuals. Since almost every occupation in the society, particularly those carrying greatest prestige and financial rewards, requires specific "credentials" or "qualifications," people go to school to obtain these "credentials." Americans, as Berg points out (1969:1), therefore, have become "education-conscious to extra-ordinary degree." They are preoccupied with formal education for utilitarial rather than intellectual reasons. Berg (1969:1-2) goes on to say that this

> ... helps to explain the considerable rise in the educational attainment of the work force and the boom in what has been termed, somewhat infelicitously, the knowledge or educational industry. The well-publicized concern of parents, young people, and a variety of social commentators with education and academic performance is more than matched by the concern of researchers, educators, government policy-makers and businessman. Thus we quote a phenomenal increase in interest in education—that is, in schooling and related training programs—among economists, manpower experts, foreign-aid officials, marketing specialists, publishers, and even investment analysts in the nation's financial centers. In each of these circles, education, generally equated with years of formal schooling, is seen as a major factor affecting productivity, economic growth, income shares, and the array of other phenomena that corporations consider in decisions regarding plant location, advertising, and production planning.

Americans of all ranks send their children to school to prepare them to get good jobs and high wages, as well as to achieve fine life styles and to be able to live in better neighborhoods when they grow up. Parents from the subordinate minorities I studied in Stockton, like other Americans, do not send their children to school because they want them to become intellectuals. Their children, however, do not succeed in school. Let us review some of the explanations that have been offered for their failure.

Three Current Explanations of School Failures

Three types of explanations have emerged in the last decade to explain why subordinate minorities and the poor fail in public schools. The most influential of these explanations (in terms of the social policy it generated) is based on the concept of the "culturally deprived" (Riessman 1962). Under criticisms, this concept was often renamed "culturally disadvantaged," "culturally different," "socially rejected," and the like, but the basic meaning has remained unchanged. This explanation views the school as a victim forced to take on the additional burden of removing the "resistance to learning" that the children from poor and minority backgrounds bring with them. According to Sexton (1970:59):

> The total impression transmitted to many educators by the concept [of cultural deprivation] is that the "rejected," "disadvantaged," or "deprived," child is handicapped, not by the school or society, but by their own culture and behavior, and that he is so different and "crippled" that he cannot be expected to achieve as others. Many educators point to the culture of the child and family as total explanation of school failure.

One version of this explanation holds that the subordinate minority children fail in public schools because they are "retarded" in their language and in their psychological and social development. This retardation is said to be caused by their home and neighborhood environments, which do not provide them with the "stimulation" for normal development (Ausubel 1964; Hunt 1964, 1967, 1969a; Deutsch 1967). The proponents of this view argue that the way to reduce school failures among such children is to develop "remedial programs" within the schools that will "provide an antidote for what they have missed" at home (Hunt 1969b:39). This explanation and the solution proposed come from experimental and developmental psychologists who assume, unconsciously and erroneously, that the homes and neighborhoods where these children grow up are comparable to experimental laboratories. They also erroneously assume that the early experiences of the children are just like those of rats, monkeys, and other animals in their laboratory. Thus they think that the children have been deprived in the same way that they have sometimes "deprived" their animals in experiments (see Deneberg 1970:1-2).

Another version of the "cultural deprivation" explanation is that the children from subordinate minorities fail in public schools because they grow up in cultures that are different from that of the white middle class or "the mainstream" (Cloward and Jones 1963; Inkeles 1966; Riessman 1962). The argument goes somewhat like this: There are many cultural variants in the United States, that of the white middle class being the best. This culture embodies those qualities of life valued most by Americans such as future orientation, desire for success in life, initiative, good work habits, talent, perseverance, and the like. This culture is also the one on which education in public school is based, so children from middle-class background bring with them values, attitudes, and learning skills that are similar to those found in the schools. Children from subordinate minority background, however, have different values, attitudes, and learning skills; consequently they do not succeed in school (Taba 1967:2).

Tremendous efforts have been made to document the ways in which the "cultures" of subordinate minorities "cause" school failures (see

Frost and Hawkes 1966; Katz 1967; Webster 1966). I seriously doubt, however, that cultural differences account for the school failures of these children. Other groups like Arabs, Chinese, Filippinos, and Japanese have retained their different ethnic ways of life and yet their children still do well in school. Moreover, in Asia and Africa people with radically different cultures also do well in Western-type schools, although many did not have traditions of formal education in the past. Furthermore, as some social scientists have pointed out, what is often described as the "culture" of subordinate minorities may be a distortion of their life styles based on unrepresentative statistical studies (Leacock 1971; Sexton 1970; Stein 1971; Valentine 1968). Other studies support the finding of the present author that the poor and subordinate minorities want the same things middle-class people want, including good education, good jobs and good wages, and better living conditions (Cloward and Ohlin 1960; Ginzberg 1967; Goldstein 1967; Hyman 1953).

The second type of explanation for the school failures of children from poor and subordinate minority background blames the schools. The idea that schools might contribute to failures for some children is not new (see Brookover and Gottlieb 1964; Hollingshead 1949; Lynd and Lynd 1937; Warner et al. 1944). But this explanation has gained increasing attention from social scientists and reformers only recently (Baratz and Baratz 1970; Guthrie et al. 1971; Hentoff; 1966; Rosenthal and Jacobson 1968; Katz 1971; Kohl 1967; Leacock 1969; Moore 1967; Rist 1970; Reimer 1971; Sexton 1961; Silberman 1970; Stein 1971). Many school critics now question the appropriateness of the traditional classroom arrangement as a setting for effective learning. Some argue that children from poor and ethnic minority background fail to learn as others do because they receive inferior education and because their teachers are mere disciplinarians and custodians who do little actual teaching (Guthrie et al. 1971; Leacock 1969; Moore 1967; Sexton 1961).

To reduce school failures created by the deficiencies of the schools critics have proposed several reforms, two of which will be examined here. One reform is called the "performance contract system". Here a contract is signed with an educational firm to teach children and the firm is paid only if the children improve in their learning. The performance contract system does not reject the notion that the children are failing in school because they are "culturally deprived"; it simply assumes that educational firms know better how to overcome the effects of "cultural deprivation" on school learning than does the traditional school. This type of reform has now been tried in many school districts and the results are dismal (see *The Stockton Record* Dec. 14 1971 :5; Janssen 1972; Hey 1972).

The other proposed reform would replace the traditional school or the traditional classrooms with "alternative schools," "open classrooms," "free schools," "schools without walls," and the like (Hertzberg and Stone 1971; Illich 1970; Kohl 1969; Kozol 1972; Reimer 1971; Silberman 1970). These reformers, influenced by the British informal classroom and the Montessori Methods, want to replace a "formal" with an "informal" approach to education. Within the last few years hundreds of "free schools" have sprung up all over the United States and the concept has acquired many meanings (Cooper 1971; Kozol 1972). Some of these "free schools" have been carefully planned and founded by people with thorough knowledge of the British or the Montessori systems, but others have been established by people whose only credential is their disaffection with the public school system for various reasons. This contrasts sharply with developments in England where, as Silberman (1970:213) tells us

> The trend toward informal education . . . is not a sudden departure from the past. [It] has developed gradually over the last half a century, out of the insights and experiments of inumerable teachers, "heads" [principals], local and national school inspectors and advisors, and college and university professors.

The relevant question for us is whether "alternative" or "informal" education can solve the educational problems of the children from ethnic minority backgrounds in the United States. I see no reason to think that it will. In England this approach has not reduced the problems of school failures among West Indian and other ethnic minority children; nor has it solved the problems of school failure among the British lower class (Bernstein 1970; ILEA Report 1967; The Newson Report 1963).

Furthermore, educational reform that seeks to substitute "informal" for "formal" education constitutes a redefinition of the function or purpose of public school education. I think that this redefinition can be properly understood when viewed in the context of current changes in the American economy rather than in the context of assumed deficiencies of the traditional school organization. Formal education in America is now available to more people than the American economy can absorb in its present state. Americans, as I pointed out earlier, believe that the achievement of various levels of education—grammar school, high school, four years of college—and similar "credentials" *qualifies* them to assume various occupational roles in their economy and receive different rewards. In recent years, however, the experiences of many "qualified" people indicate that these "credentials" have lost some of their values: People with good "credentials" are finding it increasingly difficult to get the jobs they desire. Furthermore, developments in the industries have caused more or less temporary unemployment among highly qualified people in engineering and similar fields. These occurrences have had both economic and psychological consequences that have led critics to question the traditional functions of the school. The traditional school organization and formal education are viewed as obsolete by the critics because the products of formal education, the "credentialed graduates," are no longer being absorbed by the economy at an adaptive rate. Thus we now hear educational reformers and social scientists saying that education should be "informal," "humanistic," "for creativity," and "for personal development."

This raises other serious questions, especially with respect to the subordinate minorities. What do these people see as their educational needs? Will informal education satisfy these needs? I think that some advocates of informal education have neither consulted the poor and subordinate minorities nor do they really understand their needs. The subordinate minorities still believe that formal education *can* help them "upgrade" themselves. They blame their present marginal position in the economic system on their lack of adequate education as well as on the institutional barriers that prevent them from receiving full benefits for their education. This is the position of the blacks and Mexican-Americans I studied in Stockton. They would not, I believe, endorse the idea of "free" or "alternative school" **if they understood what it really means.**

The third explanation for the school failure of subordinate minorities postulates that blacks do less well than whites in public school because they have inferior genetic endowment for intelligence (Jensen 1969a, see also Eysenck 1971; Harvard Educational Review 1969; Herrnstein 1971; Scarr-Salapatek 1971a,b).[2] This is an old explanation that has recently reappeared perhaps because "remedial educational programs" (compensatory education) based on the concept of "cultural deprivation" failed to reduce school failures, especially among black children. Jensen argues that compensatory education failed because it tried to "boost IQ and scholastic achievement," which are determined primarily by genetic inheritance. He reports that the consensus among psychologists is that blacks are on the average about 15 points lower than whites in measured intelligence IQ. Herrnstein adds that people who occupy the upper levels of a society usually can be shown to have higher intelligence than those below them. It follows, he argues, that even when all the external (social and legal) barriers to upward mobility are removed for all groups in the society those occupying the lower levels will continue to retain their relative positions because "Actual social mobility is blocked by innate human differences (Herrnstein 1971:63)."

---

[2] Much of the controversy about IQ has centered around black-white differences. It should be noted, however, that other subordinate minorities generally score lower than whites in IQ and scholastic achievement tests. My argument in this section applies to both blacks and Mexican-Americans.

As a social anthropologist I am not technically qualified to debate with psychologists on their conclusion that IQ as determined by test scores is genetically based, or that blacks in the United States are 15 points below whites in IQ scores. Furthermore, I accept their conclusion that there is a correlation between how people perform on intelligence tests and how they perform on scholastic achievement tests (Jensen 1969a; Herrnstein 1971). But does such a correlation imply a causal relationship between the performance on the two types of tests? If the low IQ of blacks is established by how they perform on one test and their low scholastic achievement is established by how they perform on another test, then the real problem to be explained is *why blacks do poorly on both tests*. Psychologists like Jensen and Herrnstein would reply that both are determined by "heredity", and it is with this explanation that I disagree. From my own observation of black children and from my discussions with them and with teachers and parents, I think that these children do not take their schoolwork and their tests seriously; *they do not, therefore, try to maximize their test scores*, whether for IQ or scholastic achievement. These test scores simply do not represent the real potential of black children. The question that has rarely been asked is: Why do black children not compete vigorously in school and work for the highest scores when they take intelligence or scholastic achievement tests?

The argument that blacks do less well than whites in school because of genetic inferiority is unsatisfactory for other reasons. First, through miscegenation a large percentage of black Americans have inherited white genes, presumably including those for intelligence and scholastic achievement. But it has not been shown that blacks with more white genes are more intelligent than those with fewer, nor that black Americans with white genes are more intelligent than black Africans without them. Comparisons of this type are needed if we are to accept the hypothesis that blacks fail more often in school because they are genetically less intelligent than whites.

Second, the United States is one of many plural societies with domination-subordination stratification based on birth-ascribed status. Other such societies include Britain (the English versus West Indians, Pakistanis, and so on), British Guyana (blacks versus East Indians), Fiji (East Indians versus Native Fijians), India (Brahmins versus Untouchables), Nationalist China (Mainland Chinese versus Taiwanese), New Zealand (Pekeha vesus Maori), Northern Ireland (Protestants versus Catholics), South Africa (Boers versus Zulus), Burundi (Watusi versus Wahutu), to name just a few. A worthwhile psychology project would be to conduct a comparative study of intelligence differences between dominant and subordinate groups in these plural societies. If such a comparative study confirms Herrnstein's hypothesis that the dominant group is always the more intelligent, then we might rephrase the hypothesis to read that in a stratified society, level of intelligence is always a function of social position. We would also hypothesize that where a subordinate group supplants the dominant group it develops a superior intelligence to correspond to its new dominant position.

Third, the "scientific proofs" of unique and inferior genetic or racial characteristics of eastern and southern European immigrants in the early part of this century provide a good basis from which to judge similar "proofs" about the genetic inferiority of blacks as put forward today (see Grant 1970; Kraus 1966). In 1910 the Dillingham Commission compiled a 42-volume report with many "scientific assumptions" confirmed by selective statistics to prove that, among other things, the high rate of illiteracy among eastern and southern European immigrants was due to "inherent racial tendencies." Today these groups, for all purposes of scientific "proofs" of racial differences, are considered "white" and are shown to have superior genetic endowment over blacks.

In the following pages I shall present an alternative explanation of the high rate of school failures among the subordinate minorities. As stated earlier, children from subordinate minorities do not seem to work hard in school or attempt to maximize their scores in examinations. The problem to be explained, therefore, is why they have adopted this attitude: Why do black and Mexican-American children not work hard in school? Why do they not compete vigorously in the classroom? This problem is both historical and contemporaneous.

The Conceptual Framework

The works of Durkheim (1951), Merton (1957), and Cloward and Ohlin (1960) suggest that when the behavior of a large number of people within a society or any segment of it departs from the "normal," then the problem to be explained is the behavior of the group, not that of its individual members.

In his study of suicide Durkheim (1951) showed the condition under which social control breaks down and deviant behavior occurs. Merton extended the analysis. He distinguished between two aspects of the social order: first, the *culture* structure, which consists of both *the goals* that society encourages its members to seek and *the methods* by which they may legitimately reach those goals, and, second, the *social* structure, the various kinds of relationships among members of the society (e.g., social class, ethnic groups). He states that a society regulates its goals so as to reduce conflicts and frustrations among its members and ensure that people will use legitimate means to reach these goals. And he argues further that if people are unable to reach these goals through the methods prescribed by society they are likely to develop anomie (Merton 1957:134).

Cloward and Ohlin (1960) carry this analysis further by showing how frustrations generated within the social structure for a given segment of society may lead to some form of adaptation as a solution to that problem. Basing their analysis on Merton's work they point out that (*a*) "pressures" that lead to deviant behavior can exist in the absence of a breakdown of social order and (*b*) such "pressures" vary in severity at *different points* in the social order. That is why, they suggest, lower class youth are apparently more likely than middle-class youth to engage in extreme law-violating behavior (Cloward and Ohlin 1960:85). These authors argue that delinquent subcultures are adaptations representing solutions to collective problems facing the lower-class youth, namely, "the disparity between what the lower class youth are led to want and what is actually available to them (Cloward and Ohlin 1960:86)." They then go on to suggest how a group develops an adaptation to solve their common problem generated by the social structure.

Of particular relevance is the evolution of what these authors call "a retreatist subculture" or "a retreatist adaptation." This kind of adaptation develops when a group of people fail to reach their goal through the methods prescribed by society or by any other. People with this kind of experience tend to become alienated from society, "abandoning both cultural goals and efforts to achieve them by any means (Cloward and Ohlin 1960:186)." This theoretical orientation may be applied to the study of the problem of massive school failures among subordinate minorities. In many respects their behavior in the public school system represents a departure from the norm. In a society that stresses hard work and success this group is marked by apathy and failure in the school system.

The main thesis of this book is that the high proportion of school failures among subordinate minorities is both a reaction and an adaptation to the limited opportunity available to them to benefit from their education. This limitation exists even though Americans believe that a person should be employed, paid, and granted other benefits according to his or her education.

There are three ways by which American society has traditionally prevented subordinate minorities from receiving full benefits from their education. First, subordinate minorities have generally received inferior education, especially at the elementary and secondary levels. This ensures that when they are "tested" for higher education or jobs they will fail. Second, they are forced to terminate their education sooner than members of the dominant group, partly because of earlier inferior education and partly because of social and economic hardships. This ensures that many members of subordinate minorities will not reach levels of education that qualify them for the most desirable occupational roles and wages (see Crossland 1971). Finally, members of subordinate minorities who attain equal education (quantitatively and qualitatively) with members of the dominant group are forced to accept occupation and wages below those given to whites. Evidence indicates that until recently this discriminatory treatment was practiced more intensely against blacks who had a college education than those who did not (see Ginzberg 1956).

The educational dilemma of subordinate minorities is that their children are expected to work as hard as whites in school for fewer ultimate rewards from society; this is not an individual but a group problem. Consequently, the solution that has evolved, a high proportion of school failure, is a group rather than an individual solution. Faced with this educational dilemma, subordinate minorities apparently chose to stop working hard in school since they could neither expect more for their hard work nor force society to change its discriminatory practice. They have thus reduced their anxiety about having to work hard for little by adjusting their efforts downward to a level commensurate with what they think they will actually get for their education. This is the type of reaction that experimental psychology would lead us to expect: In a competitive situation in which people find themselves consistently "unfairly" rewarded for their accomplishments they sooner or later adjust their efforts to fit the expected rewards (Clayton 1965; Hill 1963; Hull 1943).

Two belief systems—one that of subordinate minorities, the other that of the dominant whites—have emerged to explain the school failure of subordinate minorities as it relates to their marginal position in the socioeconomic organization (see Figure 1.1).

Subordinate minorities, therefore, justify their lack of serious competition in school by saying that it is useless trying to work as hard as whites in school when school success would not qualify them to succeed in society *because they are blacks or Mexican-Americans.* Consequently many of them do not try to learn how to succeed in school; they do not take their school work seriously; they do not persevere when their school work appears difficult; some give up, believing that their school work is hard without actually trying to find out if it is or not. These are responses to the first half of the self-fulfilling prophecy in the education of subordinate minorities: the belief that it is hard for subordinate minorities to "make it" in the white world (including the school) discourages them from trying and results in their failure to make it, that is, in school failure.

The white belief system, which contributes the other half of the self-fulfilling prophecy in the education of subordinate minorities, consists of both folk and "scientific" definitions of the subordinate minorities as intellectually and culturally inferior to whites. Whites confirm their folk beliefs and "scientific" theories by pointing to the high proportion of school failures and low scores on intelligence tests (IQ) among subordinate minorities. These beliefs and theories form the basis on which the schools

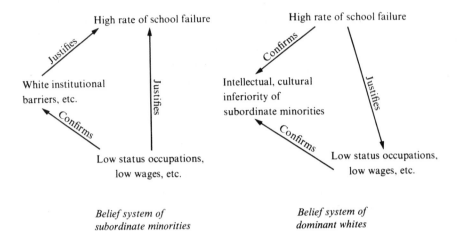

Figure 1.1 Belief systems of subordinate minorities and dominant whites to explain high rate of school failure among subordinate minorities. [Source: Author's interviews with Burghersiders and members of the dominant white group in Stockton, 1968–1970.]

sort and classify children from subordinate minorities, a classification that often marks the children as failures *before* the school actually teaches them anything. It is important to remember that teachers participate in the belief system of the dominant whites rather than that of subordinate minorities, and that their definition, classification, and treatment of the children are determined by that belief system. The major function of the white belief system is to justify the low position of subordinate minorities in the socioeconomic structure of society by ensuring that subordinate minorities do poorly in school. Their low position in turn reinforces the white belief system.

The high proportion of school failure among blacks and Mexican-Americans in Burgherside is the result of this type of adaptation. The dominant perspective on education that appears to exist among Burghersiders may be summarized as follows: Education is a very valuable thing to have; it brings all kinds of economic and social rewards. But the society does not permit blacks and Mexican-Americans to enjoy these rewards on an equal basis with whites. First, society sets many institutional barriers to prevent blacks and Mexican-Americans from getting a good education; second, those who get a good education do not receive its full benefits because of discrimination. In short, it is hard for blacks and Mexican-Americans (like Burghersiders) to "make it" (that is, to succeed) in Stockton and elsewhere in America. In competing with whites for occupational placement, promotion, wages, and the like, blacks and Mexican-Americans *lose just the same* whether they have education or not. There is, therefore, no reason for them to work as hard as whites in school: *They will eventually lose anyway.*

The development of this attitude has probably been unconscious. It remains largely so, although it is verbalized in many contexts. But the belief that it is hard to succeed in the "white world" (that is, America) has come to serve both as an explanation for actual past and current experiences of discrimination and as a justification for not trying very hard to succeed in school. If one believes that one will not "make it" in the wider society because of external institutional barriers, then one may feel that it serves no purpose to try to "make it" in school, preparing oneself for opportunities that will not be available after graduation.

How the Study Was Done

I went to Stockton in 1968 to take part in a bilingual education demonstration project in Burgherside neighborhood. My position was that of an ethnographer: I was to describe the way of life of Burghersiders as it existed at the time. I eventually focused my study on the nature of formal education in Burgherside. That is, I studied educational beliefs and practices of Burghersiders, of various categories of people involved in Burgherside education, and of the schools attended by Burghersiders. I also studied the functions of education in Burgherside.

The assumption a student makes about causes of school failure in a place like Burgherside largely determines the research approach he adopts in the field. Some students, for example, assume that they know what American education is, or should be. They further assume that subordinate minorities are failing in school because their language, family structure, genetic endowment, and the like are different from those of the dominant group. These students, therefore, attempt to "discover" how these factors *cause* school failure and what can be done to eliminate the problem.

In the present study I have used a somewhat different approach. As an African, I could not claim to know from the start what American education is or should be, nor the appropriate behavior that leads to success in school. Instead, I set out to study education in Burgherside as a cultural institution. The school is merely a mechanism through which this institution serves the needs of society, its segments, and its individual members. My goal was to study how the people in Stockton, including Burghersiders, conceptualize their educational system and their place in it, and how these conceptualizations influence the way they behave within the institution. I felt that understanding this would throw some light on why Burghersiders behave the way they do in school, why they have such a high proportion of failures.

In order to achieve my objectives I found it useful to employ what Bohannon (1957:4, 1965, 1968, 1969) has called the "folk system" and which he describes as "the core of anthropological studies." A people's folk system greatly influences its behavior in any area of its culture. The folk system is built up through perceived experiences and the interpretations of these experiences. According to Bohannon(1957:4):

> Events that occur within a social field (however defined) can only be perceived in company of an interpretation. Obviously, the human beings who participate in social events interpret them: they create meaningful systems out of the social relationship in which they are involved.

The folk system is similar to Berger and Luckman's (1966) concept of "social reality". From this perspective the behavior of any group of people in schools, churches, or political rallies, is not governed by an "objective reality out there," but by the "reality" they experience and interpret. Most studies of causes of school failure among the poor and subordinate minorities often attempt merely to document the middle-class interpretation of the universe of these people. Although the theories that emerge from such studies may be self-consistent and satisfactory to the researchers and their school of thought, they need not represent accurately the "realities" they attempt to explain or describe.

When I went to Stockton to study education in the Burgherside neighborhood I expected that the behavior of Burghersiders would be determined largely by their own conception of what education really is, that is, determined by how they perceive and interpret education and the school in the light of their own experiences. These experiences include both those of individual Burghersiders, their collective experiences as residents of one neighborhood, and their collective experiences as members of ethnic minorities in time and space. Home environment and genetic endowment certainly influence the way in which children behave in school, but their influence on the school failures of subordinate minorities appear to be exaggerated. An equally important factor, one that is often neglected, is the people's notion of what education "really" is, their folk system or folk theory of education and its concomitant behavior. It is this folk system that I regarded as the starting point of the present study.

In a plural community like Stockton all segments do not share an identical folk system of education—each ethnic, socioeconomic, and neighborhood group views education differently—and various segments participate in education in various roles. In order to understand the behavior of Burghersiders in the educational institution, I found it necessary to study not only the relationship between Burghersiders and these Stockton groups, but also what the latter think about education in Burgherside and how their perspectives influence their behavior.

1. *Field Techniques.* I spent a total of 21 months (September, 1968 to May, 1970) doing the study. I lived in Stockton during the first 16 months and then visited the city every other week for interviews lasting from two to three days. The research was planned to cover the following segments of the community: (*a*) Burghersiders, as the principal group of the study; (*b*) residents of adjoining neighborhoods attending the same junior and senior high schools with Burghersiders; (*c*) organizations and leadership representing the interests of the subordinate minorities in the wider community (i.e., their spokesmen); (*d*) school personnel; (*e*) Taxpayers, principally the middle-class Stocktonians and the organizations they formed to assist with "problems" of Burghersiders and similar groups.

Burghersiders were the focus of the study. I had no particular difficulty in establishing rapport with them, but neither did I take it for granted. My major acquaintance with the people began soon after my arrival. I was introduced at a meeting of the board of directors of the Neighborhood Center and in a few weeks was coopted as "one of the representatives of the school." Throughout my study, my association with this board, the Neighborhood Association, and the Neighborhood Center proved very helpful. The association even organized a fund-raising program to aid the refugees of the Nigerian civil war and gave a farewell party in my honor at which time, among other things, I was made a life member.

Because of a housing shortage, I did not live within Burgherside, but spent most of my time there, visiting families, interviewing, or just observing and participating in activities. Early in my study I began systematically to build rapport with a cross section of the neighborhood: (*a*) I visited churches and other groups to explain that I had come to study their education. (*b*) I made myself known to as many people as possible by participating in various activities and talking with people. (*c*) During the second month of the study, I wrote to families with children at the elementary school to ask if I could visit them to explain the nature of my study (because of my earlier contact with the children at school this request generally met with favorable responses and my reception in these families was very warm). After these initial contacts I was able to visit many families informally whenever I was in the area and I attended religious services and other social events with some of them. I also exchanged dinner invitations with a few others.

In a neighborhood like Burgherside it is not possible to rely on only a few informants for the description of any aspect of the local culture. Therefore I tried to obtain information about education from as many informants as possible, although some informants were interviewed more than others because they had unusual knowledge or a better ability to describe the situation in Burgherside. I was not able to interview some potential informants either because of a language barrier or because I never had the opportunity.

In keeping with my theoretical orientation, I attempted to obtain as much information as possible not only about the education of Burgherside children but also about that of their parents and of their parents' siblings and their parents. During the first phase of fieldwork (October, 1968 to January, 1969), I carried out an intensive survey of more than 100 households, that is nearly all the households in the area with children in the elementary school and whose members were English-speaking; some were not interviewed for reasons of illness, work, and so on. This study covered, among other things: (a) place of origin and childhood experiences; (b) education of informant, informant's parents and siblings; (c) history of informant's migration; (d) educational and occupational experiences of informant, his parents and siblings; (e) marital history; (f) political, social, and religious affiliations, and participation in Stockton and Burgherside; (g) kinship, household compositions, and so on.

In the spring and summer of 1969 I interviewed the same parents again, that is, those who still lived in the neighborhood. This interview was by means of a questionnaire in the form of "forced choice" and covered: (a) background information; (b) attitudes towards a bilingual demonstration education program at the elementary school; (c) participation in school programs; (d) school integration and other issues being debated within the school district.

During the last four months of 1969 I conducted a final interview with Burgherside parents (and sometimes children) in 40 families from my earlier samples, chosen because we had exceptionally good rapport. This was an intensive interview about education in Burgherside. I had spent a part of the previous summer (1969) analyzing the data collected during the prior nine months. The intensive interviews with these 40 families consisted mostly of discussions of some of the points I derived from the preliminary analysis of my data. Interviews with individual informants were tape-recorded and lasted from one to four hours.

I interviewed approximately 225 Burgherside students in the fifth through twelfth grades mainly by means of questionnaires that dealt with (a) family background; (b) educational and occupational goals; (c) influence of parents, teachers, and peer groups as perceived by the children; (d) the extent to which the children saw themselves or others as responsible for for the type of work they did in school. During the last few months of the study about 75 black and Mexican-American eighth, ninth, eleventh, and twelfth graders were interviewed individually and intensively. As in the case of the 40 families mentioned above, these interviews consisted of discussion of some of the salient points about education in Burgherside derived from a preliminary analysis of earlier data.

Other data from Burgherside included those from the Neighborhood Improvement Association, namely, (a) interviews with leaders and members of the association and the staff of the Neighborhood Center about education, jobs, and related matters; and (b) written documents from the files of both the association and the Neighborhood Center dating back several years as well as during the period of my study.

2. *Southsiders and Ethnic Minorities.*[3]   Some residents of neighborhoods close to Burgherside belonged to the same voluntary associations with Burghersiders and often thought they had common problems in education. I was able to participate as a member of some of these voluntary associations, such as the credit union set up by the Council of Neighborhood Associations. I attended meetings in these other neighborhoods, especially those dealing with education, and I also attended meetings organized by blacks and Mexican-Americans to deal with specific issues affecting the education of their respective groups. A number of leaders of both these ethnic groups were interviewed about education during the course of the study.

3. *Taxpayers.*[4]   I extended the study to include "Taxpayers" for two reasons. First, I discovered early in the fieldwork that important decisions affecting Burghersiders are usually made by those who call themselves "Taxpayers," and who live outside the neighborhood. These people control Burgherside education as teachers, administrators, and the like. It was essential to study their folk theory of education and how it affected Burgherside education. I developed good rapport with Taxpayers of all types, attended their meetings, especially those concerned with the education and welfare of Burghersiders and similar groups. I interviewed some Taxpayers intensively on education and related matters in Burgherside. Although I interviewed Taxpayers with divergent viewpoints, I relied heavily on those whom I had come to know very well. The interviews were carried on in their homes, usually on weekends, and most were done after I had completed the study in Burgherside. Taxpayers' organizations supplied valuable documents about education and related matters including (a) statistical data on education, occupation, and the like; (b) position statements of formal Taxpayers' organizations on educational issues; (c) reports of activities of these organizations on behalf of Burghersiders and Southsiders; and (d) studies of some educational problems in Southside and the entire community.

4. *The Schools.*   Throughout the study I spent considerable time at the elementary and junior and senior high schools. I had fairly good rapport

---

[3]Southsiders refer to the residents of the three districts in the southern part of Stockton (see Map 2 in Chapter 3).

[4]See Chapter 3, pp. 49–51 for the definition of "Taxpayers."

with the teachers and other school personnel. I interviewed some of them systematically, but I relied on my own observations and verbal and nonverbal interactions during my visits to the schools. However, during the last five months of the study I selected a number of teachers, counselors, and other school officials whom I knew very well and interviewed them on education in the community, especially in Burgherside and Southside.

While I was employed by the school district during the first nine months of the study, I examined relevant school records on students, including all Burgherside children from kindergarten through twelfth grade as well as the 300 junior and senior high students from adjoining neighborhoods. The information obtained about all these children include: (a) school and class attendance for a period of two years, 1967–1969; (b) family background; (c) school progress as indicated by letter grades given to students in various classes; and (d) discipline problems. I also studied the comments that teachers make each year on the elementary school schildren in their classes. These comments were very revealing of the teachers' conceptions of Burgherside children. Other information from the school system include data from the minutes of the Board of Education meetings and annual reports of the elementary and junior and senior high school principals over a number of years. These reports contained a good deal of information on curriculum, staff, community relations, guidance, and discipline problems, as well as the children's academic progress. Other reports commissioned by the school district, such as that on pupil personnel services, were studied, as were reports of state–mandated tests and the state evaluation of the compensatory education programs. Bulletins and memos from the central administration and related sources also provided useful data on education in the community. Finally, I attended several meetings at each of the schools serving Burgherside as well as at the central administration where the problems of education in the area were discussed.

The field situation was on the whole relatively "open," that is, many formal groups in Burgherside and elsewhere in the community that dealt with education were easily accessible. Furthermore, throughout my study there were several educational crises that led to open debates between people of divergent views in the city. These crises not only provided opportunities to observe the various forces influencing education in Stockton but also provided occasions on which people with different views formulated and stated their positions lucidly.

CHAPTER 2

Burgherside Neighborhood, Stockton

Physical Layout and History

Burgherside is a 30-square-block area located west of the Mormon Slough (see Map 1) and west of Pershing Avenue. The area between the slough and Pershing Avenue has paved sidewalks and belongs to the city. When the War on Poverty began in San Joaquin County in 1965, Burgherside became one of the county's nine "target areas" and was designated as Target Area A, together with the surrounding city areas. Burgherside holds less than half the population and constitutes about two-fifths of Target Area A. However, the entire area, especially that west of the slough, is commonly referred to as Burgherside, and the Burgherside Neighborhood Center is designated the "Area Outpost" in the War on Poverty.

The present research covers that part of Target Area A west of the slough and corresponds roughly to the neighborhood served by Washington Elementary School. This school's attendance area is bounded on the north by the Port of Stockton, on the south by the Sante Fe Railroad and the fiberboard factory, on the east by the slough and the railroad yard and on the west by vacant lands, which have been zoned for industrial development, interspersed with factories and warehouses.

Burgherside came into being because of housing shortage and discrimination during both the Second World War and the Korean War. Many laborers who came to Stockton to work in agricultural and defense-related

Map 1 Burgherside Neighborhood.

industries began to build shacks here because housing specifications were less stringent than in the city. Families that saved up enough money were later able to replace the shacks with better structures. Several families I visited proudly described how they built their own houses, some of them "according to books" on "how to build your own home," and usually with the help of friends skilled as plumbers, carpenters, and the like. At least two men, one Mexican-American and one black, were building their own homes during my study. The Mexican-American had bought a shack and lot for $3,000 and began to rebuild it with the assistance of his children and friends. The black man built a good-looking two-bedroom house from scratch; it took him more than a year and he worked on it every day except Saturdays, when he did not work because he is a Seventh Day Adventist. The majority of the families either have built or are buying their own homes (see Table 2.1). Families who own their homes keep them in much better condition than do those who rent.

TABLE 2.1

Home Ownership and Rental among Burgherside Families Interviewed between October, 1968 and January, 1969[a]

Ownership/ rental status	Black (76)	Mexican-American (56)	Other (13)
Homeowner	59.21	66.07	56.15
Renter	40.79	33.93	53.85

[a]Source: Author's interview with Burgherside families.

Burgherside is not a compact neighborhood. Some blocks are completely filled with residences, but there are many with vacant lots. Houses vary in size and quality, especially in the "real Burgherside," that is, the unincorporated area. One visitor in 1963 reported that although Burgherside had some "modest, neat dwellings," 50% of the houses in the neighborhood were "substandard shanties."[1] In some areas, particularly in the northern portions of the neighborhood, houses are built on double lots and so situated as to have large fenced front and back yards. Table 2.2 gives the value of houses situated in Burgherside in 1960, values which had not significantly changed by 1969.

In 1960 Burgherside had a population of 2,103; in 1969 the population was only 1,764 because about 130 families to the east of South Fresno street had been relocated outside Burgherside between spring 1965 and summer 1968, owing to construction of the new freeway.

The streets in Burgherside are extensions of those in the city but they are not as well maintained. Sidewalks are not paved; many are dusty during the summer and full of gullies and puddles when it rains. The neighborhood

TABLE 2.2

Values of Homes Occupied by Owner in Unincorporated Burgherside According to 1960 Census[a]

Values of homes	Number of units	Percentage of units
Less than $5,000	104	49.28
$5,000 to $9,900	102	48.41
$10,000 to $14,900	5	2.37
$15,000 and over	0	0.0

[a]Source: U.S. Census Bureau, 1960.

[1]The visitor was Joan Johnson, a reporter for a Catholic newspaper. A member of the Neighborhood Association gave me a clipping of her article on Burgherside.

became a water district in 1960; but its streets were not lighted until 1967, following a petition signed by 17 taxpaying residents. Lighting was installed at six locations, but most of the neighborhood remains unlighted.

In the early 1960s Burgherside had a reputation for its bars and "gambling houses," but by the time I arrived only two bars were operating. "The Chism" is the gathering place for blacks, especially on weekend evenings; patrons of this little bar come from this and other neighborhoods, and some are former residents of Burgherside who probably come to meet with their old neighbors and friends. Mexican-Americans patronize the "Mexican Canteen," where the music, dance, food, language, and indeed everything except the police patrolman are Mexican. A second Mexican-American bar was soon to be opened; the prospective proprietor was waiting for a license. In addition, Burgherside has one restaurant and one grocery store, the latter leased by a Chinese family from its black owner. There are 5 churches and 11 ministers in the neighborhood; most Burgherside ministers have their churches in other neighborhoods or even outside Stockton, and churches within Burgherside belong to outside ministers. Similarly, many Burghersiders often attend religious services elsewhere and many outsiders come to Burgherside for the same purpose.

A park and neighborhood center were established in 1967 and now constitute the service and recreation centers. Previously the community used the local elementary school facilities. Major events such as the annual queen ball and the Halloween and Christmas parties are still held in the school auditorium. The parties are sometimes co-sponsored by the school and the Neighborhood Association.

The city has made several attempts to annex Burgherside, arguing that annexation would enable Burghersiders to "enjoy the services provided by the city." But Burghersiders reject this, believing that they would have more to lose if they joined the city. A long-time resident and local leader explained that Burghersiders would like to have sewage and sidewalks but that they can't afford it:

> The city does not give you these things for nothing. Take me, for instance, with two streets by my house, I would have two streets to pay for the sidewalks and the pavements and the curbs. This would cost me at least $2,500. And if the sewer line passes your place, it is $13 a year. Then there are city taxes.

Burghersiders feel that they are fighting annexation:

> like those rich people that live in the north part of Stockton. They fight the same for their independence because they don't want to pay the heavy cost of city government. And we are doing the same thing.

Economic Life

How do Burghersiders make their livings? A large number are employed
in unskilled and semiskilled jobs, especially as farm laborers. Some work
for the government at the Defense Depots or Navy Annex near Stockton.
Others have independent businesses and operate stores, gas stations, car-
repair shops, hotels, and restaurants, or contracting work in construction
and farm labor. Many are unemployed or depend on public assistance.
In 1960 the 452 families in the area had an average annual income of $3,778;
17 families had less than $1,000 per year (see Table 2.3). The figures I obtained
on annual income for 105 households in the fall of 1968 indicate that the

TABLE.2.3

*Income of Families in Burgherside according to the 1960
Census*[a][b]

Income	Spanish surname (170)	Nonwhite (225)
$1,000 or less	—	7.56
$1,000–1,999	7.06	12.89
$2,000–2,999	7.65	11.11
$3,000–3,999	17.65	27.11
$4,000–4,999	7.06	20.89
$5,000–5,999	9.41	9.78
$6,000–6,999	8.82	8.89
$7,000–7,999	2.94	1.88
$8,000–8,999	—	—
$9,000–9,999	—	—
$10,000 or more	8.24	—

[a]Source: U.S. Census Bureau, 1960.
[b]Values expressed as percentages.

situation has not changed significantly. Twenty-one households have an
income of less than $2,000 per year; only 17 have an income of $6,000
or more.

Besides the "ministers," one teacher and one draftsman constitute
Burgherside's professional class. The "ministers" themselves are blue-
collar workers and may be out of work for as long as six months in the year.
Only 51 of the 82 working parents whom I interviewed in the fall of 1968
had permanent jobs all year round. Men and women work whenever possible, although some men do not want their wives to work (see Table 2.4).
In some families the teenagers also work "to help out," especially in the
summer and on weekends.

During the summer peak of farm work, a man with a regular nonfarm job takes a second job at the cannery, working night shifts at the cannery and days at his regular job, often getting little sleep. His income from the cannery is usually about twice his earnings on his regular job. His wife may also work at the cannery at least part of the season, depending on her seniority on the job. The teenaged children may work in the fields picking tomatoes, cherries, and the like.

TABLE 2.4
Wage Earners in Burgherside Households[a][b]

Wage earners	Black (75)	Mex.-Amer. (51)	Other (18)
Man only	29.33	49.01	30.77
Woman only	26.67	17.65	30.77
Man and woman	37.33	25.53	38.46
Man, woman, child(ren)	6.67	9.80	—

[a]Source: Occupational Survey of Burgherside Families by Anthropologist, October, 1968 to January, 1969.
[b]Values expressed as percentages.

Some families drive to distant farming areas over the weekends "to glean the fields" and often come back with large quantities of peaches, apricots, and other fruit. These discards are made into all kinds of preserves, which the families store for use during the year.

In the winter months when farmwork is finished, only a few people— those with seniority—continue to work at the cannery. At this time farm laborers may try to get nonfarm jobs, but this is usually difficult because the winter season is the peak of unemployment in Stockton. Furthermore, farm laborers may not have the qualifications for other jobs or for unemployment benefits. To conserve what they earned during "the season," some Mexican families return to Mexico where they can live cheaply for a few months. Others try to manage with what they have until the next season. Some of those who worked at two jobs during "the season" may have made enough money to buy a few more things for their homes, for their children, and for themselves.

Burghersiders

It is possible to divide Burghersiders into *permanent* and *transient* residents. The permanent residents can be further divided into migrants and nonmigrants. Most of the permanent nonmigrants are black and many are women and children; they include a few white-collar and skilled workers, the teacher and the draftsman, the "businessmen," and retired people. Some work at the cannery most of the year because they have seniority and others are domestic workers in Stockton. What all permanent non-migrants have in common is that they spend the entire year in Burgherside, except when they go on vacation or to visit the "folks back home" in the South or in Mexico. Other permanent residents are, in fact, migrants. For them, Burgherside is a home to return to during their off seasons. Most of the migrants are men who leave their families in Burgherside when they go to work in Salinas, San Jose, and elsewhere. A few sometimes take their wives and teenaged children to work with them in the fields. At the end of the harvest season, some of these men travel to Alaska under contract to work in the fishing industry until the next farming season.

Transient residents of the neighborhood fall into several categories. One group is made up of people who own property in Burgherside, but who, for most of the year, do not live there. At the beginning of harvest season they move out with their families; when the season is over they return to Burgherside for a few weeks and then proceed to spend the winter in Mexico, returning again just before the next farm-labor season begins. Another group of transient families lives in Burgherside only during the farm-labor season. When they arrive each year at the beginning of the season, they may stay with relatives or friends, or rent a place of their own. A man may leave his wife and children in the home of a relative or friend while he and his host either commute daily to their place of work or take off for several weeks at a time. The wives are sometimes in the work parties if they do not have little children. At the end of the farm-labor season, these families return to their own permanent bases.

Thus, there is a sort of exchange of population in Burgherside during the farm-labor season. Some families move out and return at the end of the season; others move in and leave at the end of the season. These non-permanent residents probably constitute only a small portion of Burgherside's population. According to 1960 census, more than 50 % of the residents had been living in Burgherside since 1955. But Burghersiders operate within an economic niche that creates an ecological time perspective different from that of the white middle class. For example, the latter have their vacations during the summer months whereas Burghersiders often have their vacations during the winter, which, as will be pointed out in Chapter 6, leads to some conflict with school authorities over school attendance.

A domestic group with both parents present is the commonest family form in Burgherside. However, many households have only one parent, usually the mother, as Table 2.5 shows. These figures, based on school records, are not entirely accurate; for reasons I did not discover, many children from single-parent homes outside Burgherside's elementary school district were assigned to Washington School. Furthermore, other children from single-parent homes may live in other districts but attend school in Burgherside if their grandparents live there, especially if their mothers are working.

TABLE 2.5
Percentage of Burgherside Schoolchildren Living with One or Both Parents, or with Parent Substitutes[a]

Child lives with	Elementary (259)	Jr. and Sr. High (145)
Both parents	71.43	63.45
Mother only	21.62	25.52
Father only	0.39	5.51
Other relatives	5.02	2.07
Nonrelatives	1.54	3.45

[a]Source: Stockton school records.

My survey of more than 100 households and data from my survey of students' backgrounds show that the basic residential, social, and economic unit in Burgherside is the nuclear family, consisting of a man, his wife, and their children, and including other consanguineal and affinal kinsmen: aged parents of one of the spouses, grandchildren, a young son- or daughter-in-law, and the like (see Figure 2.1a). This type represents more than 65% of the families. The second type of family structure (Figure 2.1b), representing more than 20%, consists of a woman and her children. The absence of a male spouse may result from several factors: unwed motherhood, desertion, separation (including deportation of aliens), divorce, or widowhood. Such a family may include the woman's aged parent(s), her boyfriend, her own grandchildren, and a son- or daughter-in-law. Type III consists of a man and his children but may include other relatives (Figure 2.1c). Households of this type may result from death or desertion of the female spouse. About 6% of the families are of this type. Finally, there is a pattern (Figure 2.1d) consisting of grandparents and grandchildren. This occurs when old people whose children have grown up and left home more or less adopt their grandchildren.

Many households include three generations of Burghersiders (see Table 2.6). There appear to be several reasons for the existence of many three-generational households. Burghersiders prefer to take care of their aged parents in their homes rather than send them to homes for the aged. Perhaps the reason for this is economic; on the one hand, Burghersiders cannot afford the cost of supporting their aged parents in convalescent homes; on the other hand, social security or other public assistance payments to these parents may bring additional income to the family. Three-

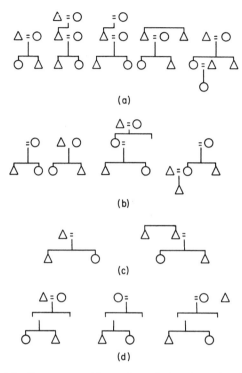

Figure 2.1 Types of family structure: (a) type I—variations in nuclear households; (b) type II—structures of households headed by women; (c) type III—households headed by men without spouses; (d) type IV—households and grandchildren.

generational households also occur because young unwed mothers often remain in their own parents' homes, and because separated or divorced couples may return to their parents with their own children.

Grandparents play a very important part in the rearing of Burgherside

TABLE 2.6
Generational Composition of Informants' Households by Ethnic Groups[a][b]

No. of generations in home	Black (76)	Mex.-Amer. (57)	Other (13)	Total (146)
Two	60.53	73.68	76.92	67.12
Three	30.26	26.32	23.08	28.08
Other	9.20	—	—	4.79

[a]Source: Anthropologist's survey of composition of Burgherside households between October, 1968 and January, 1969.
[b]Values expressed as percentages.

children, whether or not both parents are present in the household. Some couples may "loan" their children to their own parents. Sometimes, however, parents and grandparents disagree about the "proper way" to bring up the children. In one case there was a dispute between the parents and the maternal grandmother of an eleven-year-old girl as to *who really owns her*. The grandmother contended that the child belonged to her because she had taken care of her *ever since she was a baby*. The parents argued, however, that they should take back the girl because her grandmother was "spoiling" her.

Whether Burgherside children have one or two parents they are part of the social networks of kinship, marriage, and neighborly relationships existing in the neighborhood. Many children have grandparents, uncles, aunts, cousins, older siblings, and godparents who live in Burgherside or in other neighborhoods in Stockton. Playmates in the school and in the community may be mostly relatives.

TABLE 2.7
Birthplaces of Burgherside Children[a][b]

	School level of children		
Birthplace	Elementary (253)	Jr. High (66)	Sr. High (80)
Stockton	64	62.12	61.25
Other Calif.	15	9.09	20.00
Other U.S.	15	13.64	15.00
Mexico	6	15.15	3.75

[a]Source: School records, Stockton Unified School District.
[b]Values expressed as percentages.

At eight or nine years of age, Burgherside children begin to help in the home—running errands, taking messages from one family to another, accompanying parents or older siblings to the stores, and babysitting their younger brothers and sisters. From about the fifth grade, the children whose parents do not speak English begin to interpret for their parents, especially when they go shopping. Older girls assist in food preparation and housework and the boys mow lawns and do general yard work.

Training in responsibility also takes place in the church. Only 15.7% (16) of the adolescents interviewed attend church services regularly; 72.5% (72) do so occasionally, and 11.8% (12) never go to church. Of those who do go to church, very few are *active*, that is, sing in the choir, go to Sunday school classes, or belong to youth fellowships or other church clubs. Those who are active in church begin to assume responsibility quite early. In one church the superintendent of the five Sunday School classes, ranging from kindergarten to adults, is a tenth-grade boy; the general secretary is a high-school girl, and an eighth-year boy conducts the choir during the period of offerings.

In migrant households teenagers may join the work force during the farm-labor season. Thus children learn very early that their households depend on income from seasonal labor. If teenagers work, they usually give their earnings to their parents, who give them a small amount for their personal needs.

Unemployment is high among Burgherside adults and finding jobs is even harder for Burgherside children. Many children, therefore, experience the frustration of unemployment before they "finish school." Like their unemployed parents and other Burgherside adults, they interpret this inability to get jobs as the result of racial discrimination. Burgherside people rarely discuss their problems in getting jobs in the context of Stockton's total unemployment. One young man who was unable to get a job decided to go to college so that he could tell the black man one day what the white man did:

> *Well, me, I wanted to get ahead, that's why. See! Like the job I'm going to have to get I tried to get it you know. When I got there they say, "Well we don't have any opening at the moment. We'll call you." The same thing every place I went, "We'll call you." So I came out here and I said, "I'm going to get me a job, and I can't do it because of the white man."* I mean—this is the way I feel. *And that is not the only reason. I wanted to get ahead so I can tell the black man that the white man did that.*

Burgherside is drawn together by its residents' many kin ties, a kinship network that extends beyond the domestic group. My initial survey of more than 100 households in the neighborhood showed that Burghersiders have parents, siblings, uncles, aunts, cousins, and affinal relatives living either in Burgherside or in Stockton. A later study of the ownership of house lots in the neighborhood confirmed that many of the residents are related by birth or marriage (see Figure 2.2).

The formation of the kinship network results partly from the pattern of migration into the neighborhood. Many Burghersiders came initially because they had a friend or relative already living there. An Arkansas immigrant in 1969, for example, came because her uncle *thought it would be good for her,* and, like her relatives who preceded her, she came with her children.

The children of such immigrants, after having grown up in Burgherside, often set up their own households there or in other parts of Stockton. I was repeatedly told that people do not live in Burgherside merely because

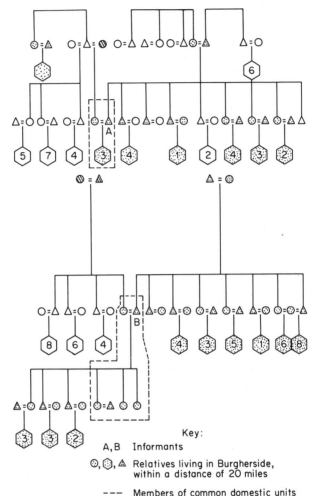

Figure 2.2 Kinship network of two informants in Burgherside.

they are poor; they choose to live there because they like it. As one informant explained: *To the people in Burgherside, it is a home, a real home.*

The kinship network is also built through marriage. Interethnic marriages are few, but marriages among people who have grown up together in Burgherside or Stockton are common. Sometimes such marriages are initiated by parents or grandparents who wish to *keep the young people out of trouble,* but nowadays young people want to choose their own spouses. Parents and grandparents are more strict about dating with their daughters than with their sons. Many Mexican-American parents, for instance, refuse to allow their daughters to go out by themselves or with a date. When a girl is given permission to go out, she is often asked to take one or more of her siblings along. Many girls dislike such surveillance and may marry a neighborhood boy *just to escape from home.* If parents approve of their marriage, the young couple may be encouraged to settle in Burgherside, or at least in Stockton.

Burghersiders are involved in other networks of relations as neighbors and friends. One visitor to the neighborhood in 1963 mentioned the "defensive, isolationist outlook" of the residents as exemplified by the predominance of fences, unfriendly dogs, and "No Trespassing" signs. However, these are protective devices against "outside intruders" rather than symbols of an "isolationist outlook." On two occasions during my study, Burghersiders were worried about a "suspicious character" who was driving around their neighborhood. Once a member of the board of directors of the Neighborhood Center and the Neighborhood Improvement Association was called home from work so that he could track down the suspicious character. The people say they are afraid their children will be kidnapped or their women raped by such intruders. They do not make the same remarks about their neighbors. Neighbors are often seen talking "across the fence" or visiting one another. They visit friends and neighbors who are sick, giving advice about health or bringing some food to the sick. Burghersiders say that they like to behave *like we did back home,* in the South and in Mexico. People become friends because they are neighbors, work together, marry into the same households, or for a number of other reasons. Neighbors and friends may also choose one another as godparents for their children.

Outsiders, particularly middle-class Anglos, picture Burghersiders as rather lonely people. Some even go further, saying that Burghersiders suffer from all kinds of "psychological problems" because they are poor and lonely. Every neighborhood, be it Burgherside or any other, has its "lonely" people. But Burghersiders cannot be characterized as lonely or isolationist. I have already described the kinship and other networks within which all kinds of interaction take place. Interviews with families were often punctuated by visits from friends and relatives, phone calls, greetings to and from passersby. One evening, for example, during a two-hour interview, the following interactions took place: my informant's ex-husband called from out of town; two of her girl friends phoned; a male acquaintance stopped by for a few minutes with his girlfriend, who was visiting from out of town; the informant's boy friend called; a neighbor stopped by for a brief visit; the informant's uncle phoned to tell her that he was not going out of town, as he had previously said he would; later, I took the informant and her two children to see one of her girl friends in another neighborhood. Needless to say, our interview was not completed that evening.

In Burgherside these relationships occur both within and between ethnic
groups of blacks, Anglos, and Mexican-Americans. There are no serious
conflicts between members of the various groups, as the people themselves
repeatedly point out:

> *The Negro and the Mexican people in this community live together and*
> *they are friendly with one another. No, we have had no conflict here.*
> *That's one thing I'm very glad of. Your neighbor is your neighbor and*
> *you have that. They visit one another; they are very well intermingled.*
> *When we used to have the Fire District meetings, we had just as many*
> *Mexicans, if not more, than we had Negroes. The same as when we first*
> *organized the Fire District* [showing me a photograph of Burgherside
> Fire-District Volunteers]. *You can see it, we had just as many Mexicans*
> *as we had Negroes.*

However, a few quarrels and fights among children were interpreted as
occuring along ethnic lines. In one fight involving a black and a Mexican-
American pupil at the elementary school, the Mexican parents threatened
a court action. It was alleged by some people that the Mexican family was
prodded to do this by "outside agitators." The matter was later dropped.
Normally such difficulties will be settled by the Neighborhood Improvement
Association, which may call an open meeting of parents "to talk things
over."

In addition to these social bonds growing out of kinship, friendship,
marriage, and neighborhood relations, Burghersiders also share other
characteristics that distinguish them as a separate community. The majority
of the permanent residents share certain notions about Burgherside—its
location, its history, and its people, that are not shared by outsiders.
Similarly, outsiders have certain notions about Burgherside that are not
shared by Burghersiders. For instance, Burghersiders regard their neighborhood with much affection, whereas some outsiders regard the neighborhood
and its people in very negative terms. This may be illustrated by what
happened after Burgherside and its surrounding city neighbors were lumped
together in 1965 as "Target Area A" in the War on Poverty. The Area
Outpost, located inside Burgherside, is supposed to serve a target population
of 4,000 people. All efforts to induce the population outside Burgherside
to participate in the governance or activities of the Outpost have generally
failed. The Neighborhood Center Aides who canvass for community
participation tell of doors being *slammed in our faces as if we did something
wrong.* Even other poor people do not wish to be identified with Burgherside and its residents.

But Burghersiders, especially within the 30-square-block area, who
participate in certain common community activities and programs have a

sense of sharing problems such as poverty, unemployment, poor streets and lighting, and school dropouts and "push-outs," and they also share certain antagonisms toward the dominant Anglo group.

The earliest unsuccessful attempt to establish a neighborhood organization for self-improvement in Burgherside was in 1954. The effort, repeated in 1957, resulted in the founding of the Burgherside Fire District. In that year an old woman in the neighborhood burned to death in her home in one of the area's frequent fires. Until that time, Burgherside had had no fire protection. Residents say that the city Fire Fighting Unit, located near the neighborhood but on city property, made no attempt to save homes from burning: *It would only try to protect the electric poles and other government and commercial installations. It was gloomy to watch a home burn down,* said one informant. The morning after the incident of the old lady's death, a group of black and Mexican-American residents met to organize a Fire District. They obtained advice and other forms of assistance from some businessmen and politicians and received a charter of incorporation in September, 1958. The Stockton Fire Department helped to train Burgherside volunteer fire fighters, who also received some training at the local Junior College and elsewhere. A long-time leader of the Fire District explained: *Everybody helps you when you are trying to do it as you should—not begging, not demanding, but as man-to-man. Sure we got cooperation, and that was long before the Civil Rights Law was passed.* Burgherside's Fire District was the first in the state to have a black man as fire chief. After it was incorporated, a "mutual-aid agreement" was signed with the rest of the city and county districts. This was an accomplishment to which Burghersiders still point with much pride, because they were now in a position: *to do something to help the city. At one time the city would not cooperate with us, but after they had a series of fires and we had to help them, then they did. Now they, of course, belong to the Mutual Aid, too.*

The neighborhood organization of the Fire District became the effective voice in Burgherside. Its leaders became the spokesmen of Burgherside. They succeeded in barring from the area certain industries that they did not consider to be in its interest, including an auto-wrecking yard. Ever since the Fire District was organized, men have dominated it as members of the Board of Directors and volunteer fighters. The women formed the Fire District Auxiliary to assist the men. The Fire District enjoyed wide community support:

> *Well, we had the support of every section of the community, not all, but practically. We had the majority of the district behind us. And of course we had closed meetings, and when we got a lot of people together they discussed the problems of the community. So therefore the Fire District was in a position to help the community as a whole.*

In the early 1960's Catholic and Protestant clergymen working in the area encouraged Burghersiders to form a Community Council that met each week to discuss the problems of the neighborhood and how to organize "clean-up campaigns." Since the leaders of the Fire District could not act as leaders of the new council because of "conflict of interest," community leadership was shared between the two organizations. The leaders of the council (later called the Burgherside Neighborhood Improvement Association) encouraged the participation of the entire community in its membership and activities. They organized clean-up campaigns, Red Cross classes, Boy Scouts, youth clubs, and, with the help of volunteers from Stockton's colleges and churches, they organized individual tutoring and study-hall for Burgherside students.

The War on Poverty brought a new era of community participation. Each Target Area formed a Neighborhood Service Center with a paid staff and a Board of Directors appointed by the people. Burgherside Neighborhood Improvement Association provided the organizational structure through which Burgherside Community Center operations were established. The leaders of the Association became the Board of Directors of the Community Services Center. With a paid staff of center director, neighborhood aides, center secretary, the association built a center and a park for the neighborhood. As in the case of the Fire District, men dominated the leadership and women formed an Auxiliary.

Community feeling in Burgherside is reinforced by both the Neighborhood Annual Parade and the selection of Burgherside Queen in June. The Annual Parade is a community-wide event and is preceded by the Queen Contest, in which Burgherside girls between the ages of fifteen and twenty-one may compete. Tickets for the Queen Ball, at which the winner is crowned the "Queen of Burgherside," sell for five cents each and the girl who sells most is declared the winner. In 1969 the winner had sold more than $400 worth of tickets. Residents participate in the parade as planners, members of the parade team, organizers, or spectators. Many groups from other neighborhoods or from agencies such as the police also participate in the parade, which takes place on a Friday afternoon and is followed by two days of a neighborhood fair at the park.

Today, community spirit in Burgherside is probably on the wane. The relocation of about 130 households to make way for the new freeway not only reduced the population of the area, but also deprived Burgherside of some of its leaders and brought a sort of disorganization to the community. Many Burghersiders are now uncertain of their own futures in the area, which they feel they are powerless to determine. At a community meeting in 1969, participants decided that they wanted Burgherside zoned a residential–commercial neighborhood. They made a representation to the

County Planning Commission, which appeared to concede to this request. But shortly after I completed my studies, it was reported in *Stockton Record*, a local newspaper, that in the general plan for the city development Burgherside could be annexed and zoned for industrial development by 1985. The rumor that this would happen had, of course, been circulating in Burgherside for a long time. A number of the households have already begun to build new homes in other "city fringes" or are considering doing so.

CHAPTER **3**

Taxpayers and Burghersiders in Patron-Client Relationship

Ethnic and Residential Stratification

In order to comprehend more fully *why* Burghersiders behave the way they do in school and elsewhere it is necessary to describe their relationship to the rest of the Stockton community. Stockton, like the rest of American society, is stratified both by birth-ascribed status (race and ethnicity) and by achieved status (social class). Birth-ascribed status largely determines the opportunity individuals and groups have to achieve social mobility within the class system. In addition, there is a residential stratification that tends to coincide with the social class and ethnic stratification systems. Stockton is divided by natural and man-made barriers into geographical and residential districts (see Map 2). Stocktonians say that a new west-east freeway, when completed will reinforce the north-south demarcation of the city. Three of the residential districts are in North Stockton and are occupied by the more affluent and powerful white middle and upper classes. The three districts in South Stockton, including Burgherside, are occupied by the lower class and by ethnic minorities.

The population of Stockton from its earliest days included members of various ethnic groups. American Indians of the Miwok tribe were the origi-

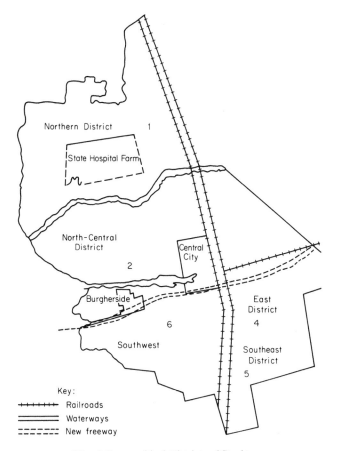

Map 2 Geographical Districts of Stockton.

nal inhabitants of the area. Soon after the arrival of non-Indian settlers in the late 1840s most of the Indians died from a disease called "recurrent fever" and from other causes. Whereas in 1852 the Indians were the second largest ethnic group (379 of the total 5,092), in 1960 they numbered only 88 of a total population of 86,226.

There are two "white" groups in the city, according to the official classification of the population. The first is currently officially designated as "white with Spanish surname," consisting mostly of people of Mexican descent; they have been in the city from the beginning and have at various periods in the city's history been designated as "whites." They were first reported as a separate ethnic group in 1910, when they numbered 188. In 1920 they had increased to 731. They were not reported separately again until 1960, when they numbered some 11,881. The other "white" category, designated "other whites" and consisting mainly of people of European descent, has been the most dominant ethnic group in the city from the beginning; the German immigrant who founded the city belonged to this group. In 1960 they numbered 72,648 of the total population of 86,226.

Blacks were also among the earliest settlers. In 1852 there were 81 of them, all of whom were "free." In 1854, they organized two churches, one Methodist and one Baptist. No large wave of immigrant black people reached Stockton until the Second World War; since then, there has been a relatively rapid increase in their population, numbering 7,312 in 1960.

The Chinese came during the gold rush to work in the mines and on railroad construction, and later they were employed as farm laborers. At the time of this study, the Chinese population was in decline (2,291 in 1960) primarily because of the "out-migration of the second and third generations . . . who have achieved higher education and have migrated elsewhere for greater employment possibilities [MCCP 1967:52]." The same decline in numbers, and for the same reason, is also true of the Japanese (1,523 in 1960), who as a group have had a much shorter stay in Stockton than the Chinese. In 1890 there were only six Japanese in the city; four years later there were enough of them to support the first Japanese store, and in 1906 the first Buddhist church was organized in Stockton.

The Sikh Indians probably came to Stockton after 1900. A Stockton historian says of this group, "At one time a large number of these Hindus worked in the island country, but at the present time, a Hindu is a rare sight in Stockton [Martin 1959:183]." Their temple, constructed in 1919, now serves only a very small number of people.

The most recent ethnic group to appear in the Stockton census is the Filipinos, who first appeared in the official census in 1960, numbering 2,364. However, interviews and case histories reveal that many of them have been in the city much longer than that.

Thus far I have used the ethnic categories, "negro," "oriental," "white with Spanish surname," "other white," and the like, that are used by the school and other agencies, as well as by the community, to designate certain segments of the population. These conventional categories often form the basis of official and community attitudes and behavior toward such segments, but these categories differ from the somewhat finer distinctions on which members of these groups base their own attitudes and behavior.

Members of the "other white" group sometimes distinguish themselves according to the homeland of their ancestors in Europe, but in general they regard themselves as "whites," a term they often use as though it were synonymous with "American." They feel that Stockton was founded by "Americans" (that is, whites), who brought "the American heritage" and the values that have been passed on to the present "Americans" of the city. Whites make up more than 80 % of the population and are the most powerful group economically, politically, and socially; most of them live in the northern half of the city. The term "Anglo" is sometimes used by whites to refer to themselves and the term is frequently used by Burghersiders for all whites of non-Mexican descent. Throughout this book I shall use "Anglo" in the same way as Burghersiders use it.

The category "white with Spanish surname" presents special problems in both external and internal classification, since it includes many persons whose only common characteristic may be Spanish surnames. It includes Mexicans, Mexican-Americans, Spanish-Americans, Portuguese-Americans, and some Anglos. Mexicans are people of Mexican nationality, according to informants; a Mexican may become a permanent resident, a citizen, or he may remain a foreigner living in Stockton. The term "Mexican" may also be used to designate anyone of Mexican ancestry, although the more common designation for such persons is Mexican-Americans if they were born in the United States. Mexicans and Mexican-Americans both usually have Spanish surnames. Other persons with Spanish surnames do not necessarily identify with Mexicans and Mexican-Americans. Thus, some people from the southwest United States who have Spanish surnames prefer to be called Spanish-Americans. Their ancestors, they say, came from Spain just as the ancestors of the "other white" groups came from various European countries; they are not of Mexican ancestry and do not identify with Mexico. The ancestors of some Spanish-Americans were here before the Anglo came. Most Spanish-Americans regard themselves as members of the "other whites" category. Many Portuguese-Americans who regard themselves as whites also have Spanish-sounding surnames; for example, the name "Salazar" is found among Mexicans, Spaniards, and Portuguese, as is the name "Mendoza." Finally, through marriage, many Anglo women come to be classified as "white with Spanish surname." As can be seen in Table 3.4, most Mexicans and Mexican-Americans reject the designation "white with Spanish surname," as being imposed on them by Anglos.

In recent years some people of Mexican ancestry have preferred to have their group called "Chicano," although this is opposed by the members of the older generation and the middle class, who regard the term as derogatory. In a series of articles used in a history class at Burgherside Junior High School, Macias has defined "Chicano" as follows:

A chicano is a living representative of the concept of *"La Raza."* His social stratification may be *"bato loco"* (dude in the ghetto), or that of a university professor of anthropology. As to his feelings of his racial heritage, he is more apt to be proud of his Indian side than his Spanish. This is so because he sees the Spaniard as an *entremetido* (intruder) who came and destroyed a people who conquered astronomy, and produced a calendar that is beyond marvel; a people who developed pumpkins, squashes, potatoes, sweet potatoes, chocolate, tomatoes, peanuts, chile, corn, and avocados, that were added to the world's food supply [Macias, n.d. :2].

Members of the older generation in Stockton have not in great numbers embraced this new way of thinking about their group, though they reject the label "white with Spanish surname." The middle-class-oriented organization, Mexican-Americans United for Action (MAUFA), petitioned the Stockton Board of Education in June of 1969 not to label their group as "Chicanos", "Browns", and the like because these are "demeaning titles" (SUSD 1969b:4586)[1]:

> That the Board take the necessary steps to eliminate the labeling of Mexican-Americans as "Browns," "Chicanos," etc. This minority is first of all "Americans" of the Caucasian race and proud of their Mexican culture and heritage. We feel it is demeaning to use any other labels other than "Mexican" when the need arises to describe our ethnic origin.
>
> Furthermore, we respectfully request that any nomenclature given by the school district to the study of our culture and history be labeled by its correct name—"Mexican History and Culture" or "Mexican Ethnic Studies"—and not the demeaning titles of "Chicano History," "Brown Studies," and the like. We are proud of our ethnic origin but even more proud of being "American citizens," wishing to be treated as any other normal American.

A few years ago most people of Mexican ancestry in Stockton would have defined themselves as "'Americans' of the Caucasian race and proud of their Mexican culture and heritage." Today there is a substantial disagreement regarding their racial identity—Caucasian or Indian. There is, however, an agreement that their culture is Mexican and most people regard the term Mexican-American as an appropriate designation. I shall therefore use this term to refer to people of Mexican ancestry.

Because of the terminological confusion discussed earlier it is difficult to place Mexican-Americans in Stockton's stratification systems. In 1957 they were reported to be living mainly in South Stockton (southwest, southeast, and south of Main Street); in 1960 they were found as "whites with Spanish surnames" widely dispersed throughout the city. It seems, however, that most Mexican-Americans still live in South Stockton; they constitute the largest ethnic minority in the community but their political and economic power is quite small.

The term "Negro" is no longer acceptable to all members of this ethnic group, some of whom prefer to be called "black," arguing that "Negro" was imposed on them by the dominant Anglo. Although "black" is becoming widely accepted it is still opposed by many people of the older generation and by the middle-class members of the group. For example, when Negro teachers formed their Black Teachers Alliance in 1969 they could not recruit more than 45% of the Negro teachers because many did not wish to be identified with the term "black." Some considered it "too radical."

---

[1]Stockton Unified School District is henceforth abbreviated as SUSD.

TABLE 3.1

Ethnic Identity of Stockton Residents as Reported by Informants Themselves, Compared with Their Official Classification by the Public School System,[a][b]

| Self-Classification | Official classification in public school | | | | | |
	Anglo (49)	Black (136)	Filip. (24)	Mexi. (125)	Orien. (36)	TOTAL (370)
Mexican	20.41	—	—	73.60	—	27.57
Mex.-Amer.	2.04	—	—	6.40	—	2.43
Spanish	2.04	—	—	5.60	—	2.16
Latin-Amer.	2.04	—	—	.80	—	20.54
Filippino-Amer.	8.16	—	41.67	3.20	8.33	5.68
Filippino-Mex.	—	—	33.33	3.20	2.78	3.51
Negro	2.04	82.35	—	.80	—	30.81
Black-Amer.	—	1.47	—	—	—	.54
Afro-Amer.	—	11.03	—	—	—	4.05
Black & Brown	—	—	4.17	1.60	—	.81
Black & White	—	.74	4.17	—	—	.54
White & Brown	2.04	.74	16.67	.80	—	1.89
Japanese	—	—	—	—	19.44	1.89
Chinese	—	—	—	—	61.11	5.95
Chinese-Jap.	—	—	—	—	5.56	.54
Caucasian	.74	—	2.40	—	—	5.95
Anglo-Amer.	2.04	—	—	—	—	.27
Italian-Amer., Irish-Amer., etc.	16.32	—	—	—	—	2.16
American	6.12	.74	—	1.60	2.78	1.89
Irish, French, etc.	—	2.21	—	—	—	.81

[a]Source: Anthropologist's survey, and students' cumulative folders at junior and senior high schools.
[b]Values expressed as percentages.

In some households, parents may be referred to as Negroes while their children are called black. During an interview a 31-year-old woman referred to her parents and older siblings as Negroes, but referred to herself, her husband, and her younger siblings as black. I then asked, "Now, could you tell me why you call yourself a black person and call your parents Negroes?" She explained the difference as follows:

Oh, I think it has to do with attitude. And most of the older generation are "colored" or "Negro" to me because the . . . Well, things are changing too fast now that they wanted to deny that they were black. That was the only way they found that they could get along with . . . you know, just get along. And so now we are saying, "We want," you know, not so much "even though I'm black" but even "because I'm black, I want the same opportunities." And so a lot of times I just think that as for the younger generation, most of it is being black, once we are doing things. But you still have the ones who are colored, you know. They allow themselves to be colored, to be called "colored," without saying, "Wait a minute. I want to say what I want to be called. I want to be called 'black'."

Some members of the older generation—this informant's uncle, for example—now call themselves black, but in general, the young blacks feel that the older ones do not share the new attitudes. I will use the term *black* to designate this group because even those who do not use the term to identify themselves often permit others to use it to identify them and their group.

In 1957, blacks were reported to be restricted to residential areas in South Stockton. In the early 1960s the situation had not changed substantially; they were still being excluded from the best residential districts in Stockton. (See census tracts 9, 10, 11, 14, 15, 16, 18, 32, and 33 in Table 3.2; see Table 3.5) According to the 1960 census, more than 40% of the Anglo population and only 0.1% of the black population lived in these areas. In 1963 the average cost of houses in these areas was $16,500. The blacks who tried unsuccessfully to move in there were professional people, teachers, social workers, and a medical doctor (Meer and Freedman 1966). Their average income was $12,000 per year, and in many cases both husband and wife had at least a high school education or one college degree.

Real estate agents had unwritten laws which barred blacks and other minorities from living in certain parts of the city, especially in the northern and north-central districts. When questioned about this, Stockton's real estate agents would reply: *We have to go slow, the whites aren't ready. We wish they were ready.* Furthermore, local loan firms normally refused to make loans to blacks who wished to buy homes in the exclusive white area. By 1963, however, twenty families had been able to "cross the line" by buying directly from property owners. In the mid-1960s Stockton, like most of the nation, became more civil-rights minded so many more black families and other minorities have been able to move north of Main Street into some of the exclusive areas. This movement has coincided with the period in which governmental agencies and the schools have actively sought to recruit more educated and professional members of minority groups. These newcomers have generally moved into the northern and north-central portions of the city. In another development, the Federal Housing Authority, through its subsidized-housing program is placing some low-income households of ethnic minority background in areas that are predominantly Anglo.

Chinese and Japanese prefer to be so called rather than to be called Orientals. In 1957, the Chinese lived mainly in South Stockton but by

TABLE 3.2

Distribution of Ethnic Groups in Stockton by Census Tracts[a]

Census tract	Anglo	Spanish-surname	Black	Other	TOTAL
1	4,536	883	305	1,217	6,941
2	1,051	439	486	385	2,361
3	974	119	—	51	1,144
4	6,969	220	9	220	7,418
5	2,216	228	5	40	2,489
6	1,551	753	318	78	2,700
7	3,816	1,304	1,177	1,352	7,649
8	1,200	113	10	7	1,330
9	5,199	256	—	198	5,653
10	4,502	—	—	17	4,519
11	9,871	71	—	42	9,984
12	5,586	176	17	93	5,872
13	5,336	354	10	34	5,734
14	3,772	181	—	42	3,995
15	5,574	111	—	17	5,702
16	2,356	42	—	2	2,400
18	3,241	168	—	—	3,409
19	3,459	1,926	7	25	5,417
20	2,724	779	1,488	157	5,148
21	1,178	157	950	22	2,307
22	5,021	1,090	62	82	6,255
23	2,681	964	1,397	308	5,350
24	4,025	474	227	942	5,668
25	1,569	377	202	511	2,659
29	2,448	262	302	239	3,251
30	1,172	118	189	97	1,576
31	6,871	59	97	111	7,138
32	4,953	31	—	32	5,016
33	6,599	358	1	1	6,959

[a]Source: U.S. Census Bureau, 1960.

1969 a sizable number of them were living in North Stockton; for example, the number of Chinese students at Stagg High School (North Stockton) was the same as those in Edison High School (South Stockton). Similarly most Japanese lived in South Stockton in 1957; in 1969 a good many were living in North Stockton. These two groups have also been more successful economically than either blacks or Mexican-Americans, and residential restrictions against them have also been breaking down since the late 1950s. The Filipinos refer to themselves as Filippinos in dealing with other groups or official agencies, but among themselves they tend to identify with their respective language groups. Most Filipinos live in South Stockton, especially in the southwest. Like the blacks and Mexican-Americans of South Stockton they have not been economically or politically successful.

Occupational Stratification and Persistent Unemployment

In the last century Stockton's agricultural industry was boosted by the completion of the transcontinental railroad and the arrival of cheap Chinese labor. Stockton benefited greatly from the growth of this industry and of the region's population, and as an inland port it became a trade, service, and manufacturing center. During the Second World War and the Korean War, Stockton also became an important center for "food production and processing to support the soldiers and military installations" (MCCP 1967). In recent years Stockton's economic base has been changing toward service economy and manufacturing industries, but the city retains the "middleman" position in the agricultural industry, "purchasing primary products from outside the metropolitan area and then canning, packing, shipping and distributing these products from local industries to other parts of the state, the nation, and the world [Little 1964 :3]." A large number of Stocktonians are still employed in some aspect of agriculture within the city, and Stockton also supplies a large amount of farm labor to the surrounding areas of primary agricultural production.

There is an occupational stratifications along ethnic lines, with the Anglos dominating the economy. The descendants of the pioneer Anglo families now constitute the upper stratum of the community. These people formerly controlled the agricultural land but in recent years have begun to invest in manufacturing industries located in the city. Most business and professional people in Stockton are also Anglos, as are those in skilled and craft jobs. Through their labor and craft unions Anglos manage to keep to a minimum the members of other ethnic groups entering into these occupations.

Mexican-Americans are found in many areas of the economy but rarely in managerial or supervisory positions. A survey of their employment situations in the 1950s showed that Mexican-Americans made up 29.2 % of the employees of selected firms but only 0.3 % of those in supervisory positions (U.C. Extension 1957:9). The situation had reportedly improved at the time of this study, but there are no accurate figures to support this. Beginning in the middle 1960s certain agencies, such as the school district, that received money from the federal government have been required to make some effort to increase the number of Mexican-Americans and other ethnic minorities on their staffs. Since this increase in the hiring of minorities depends on federal funding, when there is "a serious cutback in federal funds" it results in a cutback of minority personnel. This happened within the school district in the 1968–1969 school year, when the number of classified personnel with "Spanish surnames" was reduced from 134 to 104.

An important point for the present study is that most of the Mexican-Americans who live in South Stockton, including those in Burgherside, are blue-collar workers and farm laborers. This is also true of the blacks, most of whom are in blue-collar jobs, although a few are farm laborers. Blacks are not found in business or skilled crafts in any significant number. However, the number of black teachers and other professionals has appreciably increased in the past few years. As they did in the case of Mexican-Americans, the school system and other agencies "receiving federal funds" "actively and aggressively" began in 1965 to recruit blacks with professional qualifications from other states, especially from the South, in order to "achieve racial balance" of their staff. Immigration from the Philippines has also increased the number of Filipino professionals in the city, but the vast majority of this ethnic group are migratory farm laborers using Stockton as a base.

Orientals came to Stockton originally to supply cheap farm labor. They have now been displaced in this role by Mexican-Americans and Filipinos. Most second- and third-generation Orientals have become businessmen and professionals, with many of the third generation moving from Stockton to places having better employment opportunities.

Stockton has persistent unemployment problems, as Table 3.3 shows. In addition to the high rate of unemployment the area experiences a high seasonal variation in employment, stemming primarily from the role of agricultural industry in the local economy. Informants at the local Department of Human Resource Development repeatedly point out that other

TABLE 3.3

Monthly and Annual Rates of Unemployment in Stockton Metropolitan Area, 1959–1969[a][b]

Month	Year				
	1959	1961	1963	1965	1969
January	11.5	13.6	11.2	11.3	8.4
February	12.6	14.8	13.2	10.7	10.3
March	11.8	13.3	11.5	10.1	9.3
April	9.0	9.6	9.3	9.1	7.0
May	6.5	8.6	8.1	8.0	6.7
June	7.0	9.1	8.7	7.3	6.5
July	5.5	8.4	9.0	7.1	6.2
August	4.0	6.0	6.0	5.6	4.3
September	3.0	5.1	4.8	3.9	3.6
October	4.2	5.1	5.1	4.2	5.6
November	7.2	8.6	8.6	6.4	6.7
December	9.1	9.5	9.3	7.6	7.7
Annual Average	7.5	9.2	8.6	7.6	6.9

[a]Source: State of California, Department of Human Resource Development, 1966, 1969.
[b]Values expressed as percentages.

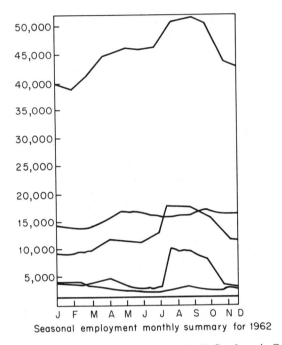

Seasonal employment monthly summary for 1962

Figure 3.1 Seasonal employment summary for months of 1962, San Joaquin County. [Source: Stockton Metropolitan Economy (Little 1964).]

sectors of Stockton economy are dependent on the agricultural sector. For instance, in the winter months when employment in agriculture is at its lowest level, agricultural workers and those in related industries "generally have less money to spend so that this affects most businesses in town, many of which lay off some employees, thus compounding the unemployment problem."

Figure 3.1 shows the proportion of seasonal employment in various sections of Stockton's economy.

The people who are most affected by both the seasonal employment changes and the unemployment situation are the blue-collar and farm-labor workers, people often locally described as "marginally qualified and unskilled workers." These workers are mainly blacks and Mexican-Americans living in Burgherside and South Stockton. Their position in the local economic structure can be summarized as follows: First, most of them are in blue-collar occupations and agricultural jobs; second, their jobs are often seasonal and therefore many residents of neighborhoods like Burgherside do not have year-round employment and, because of discrimination, the rate of unemployment among blacks and Mexican-Americans is higher than among the Anglos who are similarly "marginally-qualified and un-

TABLE 3.4

Unemployment Rate among Blacks, Mexican-Americans, and the Entire City in 1960 [a] [b]

Ethnic group	Male	Female
All	7.7	8.3
Spanish surname	13.8	28.2
Negro	13.4	41.0

[a]Source: U.S. Census (quoted in South Stockton Parish, 1967).
[b]Values expressed as percentages.

skilled workers." Table 3.4 shows that in 1960 unemployment among blacks and Mexican-Americans was almost twice that for the entire city.

The reasons for the unemployment of blacks and Mexican-Americans in Stockton are complex and the situation cannot be adequately explained simply in terms of lack of training. As I pointed out earlier, these people have not been allowed equal opportunity for training in skilled jobs and crafts by the Anglo unions. Second, there are blacks and Mexican-Americans in the area with "qualifications" for "clean jobs" who are not hired. (This was particularly true until 1967, when blacks organized boycotts of certain businesses in the city, and recently both blacks and Mexican-Americans have applied pressure on some firms and agencies to hire "qualified" members of their groups.) Third, educated minority youths tend to leave the city because of their inability to find desirable employment there. This accounts for the decrease in the population of Chinese and Japanese groups, as shown by the census of 1960, and to some extent applies also to blacks and Mexican-Americans. The Stockton economy has expanded and become more industrial since the 1950s; but blacks and Mexican-Americans have remained largely in the role of unskilled laborers in all sectors of the economy.

Taxpayers and Burghersiders in Patron–Client Relationship

These differences in the residential locations and in the social and economic status of Anglos and of the ethnic minorities, especially the *subordinate minorities* of South Stockton (blacks and Mexican-Americans), influence to a large extent the way the two groups view themselves in relation to one another and the way they behave toward one another. Burghersiders, like other Southsiders (that is, residents of South Stockton), see the city as divided into two unequal parts, Northside and Southside. This inequality is reflected in the differences in the economic, social, and political power of residents of the two sides. Northsiders are mostly rich, powerful, and often prejudiced Anglos, according to Burghersiders; and they maintain that in contrast to Southside the Northside has: *all the beautiful houses and money and things*. It is an unfriendly, "foreign territory," where one may work but may not live. This attitude toward Northside is illustrated by the concern about a Burghersider who had married an Anglo and moved North. His friends advised him to move back to Southside where he could get some help *any day they* [the Anglos] *decide to get him*. Burghersiders speak of the Southside and Burgherside as if they were one and the same thing. The residents are *mostly poor blacks and Mexicans who are trying to upgrade themsleves*. They blame *those people up North* for the problems of Southside, such as unemployment, poverty, inadequate housing, and "school push-outs."

Those whom Burghersiders refer to as "the people up North" are the ones who commonly regard themselves as the "Taxpayers" of Stockton. Most of them are Northsiders, but some live in other parts of the city. Most Taxpayers do not want to live as neighbors with people they regard as "Nontaxpayers," such as Burghersiders. When a Stocktonian achieves the status of a Taxpayer he tends to move away from those he now regards as Nontaxpayers and uses both institutional and informal means to prevent such people from moving into his neighborhood.

Everyone who owns a house with any market value, whether he lives in Northside, Southside, or Burgherside, pays a property tax, the amount of the tax varying according to the assessed value of the house. Most Burghersiders pay lower taxes on their houses than do Northsiders, partly because their houses are assessed at lower values than houses on Northside and partly because they live outside the city and do not have to pay for some services provided only within the city. Similarly, all residents of Stockton pay income tax on their annual wages. Theoretically this income tax varies according to one's annual income, so that Burghersiders, who are often only seasonally employed and work in low-paying jobs, probably pay lower income taxes than do people permanently employed on higher paying jobs.[2] However, Burghersiders *do pay property and income taxes* as well as sales tax, but they are often publicly described and treated as Nontaxpayers.

In Stockton, then, the distinction between Taxpayers and Nontaxpayers is one of social classification. A Taxpayer is anyone who not only pays

---

[2]It does not necessarily follow that people who have higher income pay more taxes in Stockton or elsewhere in the United States. I heard over the radio during the second week in April, 1971 that in 1970 there were 56 millionaires in the United States who paid "no taxes." A friend of mine once described an acquaintance, still in his twenties, who has over three million dollars but has never paid taxes. On the other hand, I know of a family of nine in Stockton where both parents work, making a combined income of some $7,200 a year, who had to pay about $500 in tax in 1971.

taxes (property, income, or both) but also is publicly acknowledged as a Taxpayer. To be so recognized, a person must live in a neighborhood (*1*) with few or no welfare recipients, particularly those receiving Aid to Families with Dependent Children or AFDC, and (*2*) with high assessed property values. Conversely, a person is not acknowledged as a Taxpayer if he lives in a neighborhood (*1*) with many welfare recipients, particularly those on AFDC, (*2*) with low assessed property value, and (*3*) if he is himself a welfare recipient.

Public acknowledgement of the status of Taxpayers takes various forms: (*1*) Public officials, especially those elected, speak of Taxpayers as the final arbiters of public policies and are careful to avoid offending them. (*2*) Taxpayers are the ones usually appointed to serve on various public boards and commissions, to act in the role of citizens. (*3*) When citizens are invited to express their views on public issues, the opinions of Taxpayers are considered more seriously than those of Nontaxpayers; this is true whether Taxpayers and Nontaxpayers speak as individuals or as representatives of their respective organizations—the organizations of Taxpayers having more influence on public policies than the organizations of Nontaxpayers. (*4*) Interests and opinions of Taxpayers receive elaborate coverage in the local newspapers, radio, and television, whereas news coverage of Nontaxpayers occurs frequently—only in relation to "their problems" with particular emphasis on their violation of the law and the various ways in which Taxpayers are helping them.

Taxpayers and Nontaxpayers are not distinguished by their own terminology in class identification; both Taxpayers and Nontaxpayers tend to refer to themselves as "middle class" or "working class." Thus when I asked students from Burgherside and other Southside neighborhoods about

TABLE 3.5
Southside Placement of their Families in the Social Class System [a][b]

Identifying groups	Upper	Middle	Lower	Working	Do not know
All Burgherside (76)	—	53.95	13.16	30.26	2.63
Anglo (53)	1.89	56.60	15.09	18.88	7.55
Black (86)	3.49	58.14	10.47	24.42	3.49
Mexican-American (106)	1.89	62.26	8.49	23.58	3.77
Filipino (26)	3.85	61.54	7.69	26.92	—
Oriental (33)	3.03	60.61	12.12	18.18	6.06
Unspecified (7)	—	71.43	—	28.51	—
Total (311)	2.57	60.13	10.29	22.51	4.51

[a] Source: Author's survey of social-class placement of junior and senior high school students in Southside schools, 1969.
[b] Values expressed as percentages.

the social class of their households, most said that they came from "middle class" families (see Table 3.5). Although these people are regarded by others as lower class, they do not so regard themselves.

Taxpayers distinguish themselves from Nontaxpayers on various grounds. First, they see themselves as bearing the cost of running the city government and its social services, including education. They are very unhappy about this responsibility; their protest against "high and unjust taxation" dates back to the year Stockton was incorporated as a city: Compare the notice of a protest meeting that appeared in 1850 with a similar notice appearing in 1970:

July 13, 1850:   GRAND MASS MEETING!!
The People of Stockton are requested to meet *EN MASSE* ON SATURDAY EVENING The 13th inst., at 7 o'clock, on the PUBLIC SQUARE, Near Mr. Wood's Church, for an expression of views upon the unjust and oppressive TAX which has recently been imposed on them by the courts of Sessions; and to decide upon what course to pursue in reference to the same. MERCHANTS AND MECHANICS ARE SPECIALLY REQUESTED TO ATTEND. *Vox Populi.*

October 31, 1970:   PROPERTY TAXES TOO HIGH?
Property Owners—Farmers—Businessmen. You are invited to attend a Public Meeting, to be Held Monday Night, Nov. 2nd, at the Stockton Ballroom. Help set a Plan of Action to Lower Taxes Now! Attend this Vital Meeting Monday Night.

Second, most Taxpayers regard themselves as the true representatives of the society and its culture. They are the bearers of Stockton's "right" culture, often referred to as the "mainstream." The contemporary members of the "mainstream culture" were either born into it or "have been assimilated," even though their forebears came from different cultures. In the minds of the Taxpayers there is a strong relationship between Nontaxpayer status and resistance to assimilation into the mainstream; those who "resist" assimilation are seen as unwilling to adopt values that can transform them into Taxpayers and more "useful" citizens of Stockton. A recent study of church-oriented Taxpayers sums up their attitudes toward Nontaxpayers as follows:

...62% of the Stockton Churchmen think that people of lower socioeconomic groups are stupid, narrow in their view, intolerant, lacking in imagination, lacking in curiosity and lacking in ambition. Some people said that they were immoral and dirty. Others said that they were concerned only with their own well-being but were not willing to improve their own situation. Among the people who said these things were teachers, professional men, housewives, secretaries, and young people [Hutchinson 1965:4].

Taxpayers are not unanimous in expressing such views, and the study points out that 15% of them said that they were sensitive to lower socioeconomic groups. In any case, the views expressed by the overwhelming majority of the Taxpayers about "the problems" of lower socioeconomic groups, like Burghersiders, differ from how the latter see themselves.

Informal relationships between Taxpayers and Burghersiders are few, and when they occur they are colored by the mutual definitions and expectations described above. A few Burghersiders have kinship and marriage relationships with Taxpayers. One Burgherside parent said she has a brother, a teacher, whom she described as a Taxpayer. In two Burgherside households arrangements were under way at the time of this study to marry daughters to sons of Taxpayers living on the Northside. These Burgherside parents and others in similar situations expressed reservations about such marriages but said they were unable to stop their daughters from marrying whom they chose. So they told their daughters: *It's up to you. We can't stop you.* One mother went so far as to tell the prospective son-in-law that she wished he were a Nontaxpayer:

My daughter has a boyfriend from Northside. Oh, I wish I could talk her out of it. [Laughter] *The boy's father is a doctor or maybe a psychiatrist. And he is Anglo. But he is just as young as her. He's very smart. He gets all "A"s and "B"s in school. He's in college now, and he's a good worker, you know. Nice kid. He comes here all the time. I tell my daughter, "How does this boy feel? He lives in a beautiful house up in Northside, how does he feel about you?" This is what gripes me. This is what gets me. And I tell the boy, "I like you. You're real nice." And I said, "I just wish you were one of us."* [Laughter] *And he says, "Well, I can't help that."*

Intimate social interactions on a friendly basis are few. Burghersiders do not visit the homes of Taxpayers as much as they visit their friends on the Southside, nor do they share social activities such as parties and outdoor hobbies. Exceptions occur when such activities are formally organized at the school and the Neighborhood Center. School parties are open to teachers and neighborhood people, and Taxpayers who have specific interests in Burgherside usually attend the activities at the Neighborhood Center, as do representatives from certain agencies.

When a Burghersider moves to the Northside and becomes a Taxpayer, he may find his old social ties ruptured so that he has to make a new set of friends. One parent described the case of a former neighbor and classmate, who is now a doctor and a Taxpayer in North Stockton. The doctor once met my informant and asked:

Why don't you come to visit me any more? We are still friends, aren't we? Nobody visits me no more. None of my friends visits me no more. My informant went on to explain: *It is true. Like I says to myself, "Golly, I hate to go and visit him. Maybe he has got a beautiful home like that." You feel low. But any time I meet him he'll start talking about old times and things like that. You can't erase that. So I told my wife, I says, "Now I don't even like to talk about those old times."*

Burghersiders give as reasons for this lack of intimate contact between themselves and their friends who become Taxpayers: (*1*) jealousy on the part of Nontaxpayers, which leads to rejection of Taxpayers; (*2*) difficulty in communicating with educated Taxpayers; and (*3*) a feeling that the Taxpayer may regard the person as "dumb" and may not treat him with respect.

Economic relations also exist between Taxpayers and Nontaxpayers. Taxpayers employ Burghersiders as housemaids, "garden boys," and other domestic servants. In both public and private business, Taxpayers often work alongside Nontaxpayers as supervisors or "bosses." In industries, farming, and other forms of business Taxpayers are the employers. Taxpayers own or manage the businesses located in or near Burgherside; Burghersiders do not own any businesses in which they employ any Taxpayers. Burghersiders are customers in local stores, never proprietors; and they often feel that they are not getting "a fair deal" in these stores and may travel to the Taxpayers' neighborhoods to buy what they need. They also frequently complain that they are not employed in businesses in their neighborhood. They point out, for example, that although the city calls Burgherside "Port Neighborhood," very few Burghersiders are employed at the Port. The economic interests of Taxpayers often come in conflict with what Burghersiders consider their own interests. Burghersiders fought the establishment of an auto-wrecking industry in their neighborhood, and also, unsuccessfully, fought the establishment of a liquor store. They view the attempt to zone their neighborhood for industrial development as an attempt on the part of Taxpayers to take advantage of them.

These conceptions that Stocktonians have as Taxpayers and Nontaxpayers influence the way they behave toward one another in school and elsewhere. The relationship between those who call themselves Taxpayers and those whom they regard as Nontaxpayers (e.g., Burghersiders) is often defined by the former in terms of clientage; that is, taxpayers regard themselves as patrons and expect Burghersiders to behave like clients. A patron–client relationship exists as the model that guides the actual behavior of the two groups toward each other, even though the "conscious model" of the community is that all the citizens are equal regardless of "race, religion, or national origin," economic status, or place of residence.

The model of the patron–client relationship was originally employed by Foster (1961, 1963, 1967) and later by Whitten (1965) to analyze the processes of social organization in a peasant village and a semiurban community respectively. Dyadic contracts exist in modern industrial societies like the United States, although we do not yet know the extent to which these ties fit in the model of patron–client relationship. The situation in Stockton provides an opportunity to explore the utility of the model in studying social behavior in urban America.

Foster (1967:217) makes a distinction between two types of dyadic contracts:

> "Colleague" contracts . . . tie people of equal or approximately equal socioeconomic positions, who exchange the same kinds of goods and services. Colleague contracts are phrased horizontally, and can be thought of as symmetrical, since each partner, in position and obligations, mirrors the other. . . . "Patron–client" contracts . . . tie people . . . of significantly different socioeconomic statuses (or orders of power), who exchange different kinds of goods and services. Patron–client contracts are thus phrased vertically, and they can be thought of as asymmetrical, since each partner is quite different from the other in position and obligations.

Colleague ties exist among Taxpayers as they do among Burghersiders, but not between the two groups. There is social interaction among taxpayers, who, for example, invite one another to dinner, cocktails, and the like. Married couples among the Taxpayers often organize themselves into a "club," rotating their meetings from one household to another; the hosting couple is expected to provide food, drinks, and other forms of entertainment for the group, although sometimes the other couples are expected to bring food and drinks with them. Similar exchanges exist among Taxpayers in other areas. For example, Taxpayers "make deals" like those between defense lawyers and the district attorneys or even judges. And sometimes Taxpayers help one another or their relatives to secure desirable jobs in return for political or other support.

Colleague ties also exist among Burghersiders. Neighbors and friends visit one another when there is illness, death, or birth in a household—often taking food and other gifts, which are reciprocated in due course by the receiving parties. A Burghersider may assist his neighbor or friend to repair a car, and the friend at some later date may assist him to repair his fence or paint his house. When Burghersiders give birthday parties for their children, they usually invite the children of their friends and neighbors. Among Burghersiders, as among Taxpayers, people are expected to reciprocate in the ways defined by each group and according to the means of the parties in the dyadic contract; and the purpose of the exchanges of goods and services is to maintain the existing relationship as colleagues (Foster 1967:218).

The ties between Taxpayers and Burghersiders involve a different kind of exchange because the two groups occupy different positions in status, power, influence, and authority. In their analyses both Foster (1963, 1967) and Whitten (1965) state that it is the clients who initiate patron–client relationships because of their own needs. Foster (1967 :229–30) writes that:

> Tzintzuntzenos, recognizing their humble position and lack of power and influence, are continually alert to the possibility of obligating a person of superior wealth, position, or influence, thereby initiating a patron-client relationship which, if matters go well, will buttress the villagers' security in a variety of life crises that are only too uncertain: illness, the sudden need for cash, help in legal dispute, protection against various forms of possible exploitation, and advice on the wisdom of contemplated moves.

The situation in Stockton is slightly different; it is would-be patrons, the Taxpayers, who initiate and insist on maintaining patron–client relationships where none need exist. Many functions or services performed by the patron, as described by Foster, have been taken over in Stockton by local, state, and national "public" agencies such as the County Health District, Department of Human Resource Development, Department of Public Assistance, Housing Authority, and the Public School System. Theoretically, asymmetrical contracts between individual professionals in these public agencies and Burghersiders should not exist because the professionals are adequately paid for their services from public funds. For example, the ideal relationship between teachers and parents in the schools would be one of colleagues, since parents are part of the public that provides the funds to pay teachers for their services. Usually, every attempt is made to pay teachers adequately; when there is a discrepancy between their services and their wages and fringe benefits (payment), the contract is renegotiated so that either the payment is increased or teachers take on additional duties. In this way the reciprocity between teachers and parents of the public as colleagues is "expressed in continuing exchange of goods and services [Foster 1967:218]."

Teachers, however, do not define their relationship with all parents as a colleague relationship; they thus define their relationship with parents who, according to them, are Taxpayers. They define their relationship with Burghersider parents, whom they regard as nontaxpayers, as a patron-client relationship. They reason that although their services are paid for with public funds, Burghersiders do not contribute to such funds because they are nontaxpayers. The public funds, they argue, come from their own taxes and those of other Taxpayers. From the perspective of teachers the flow of goods and services in their relationship with these two kinds of parents may be sketched as follows:

1. Colleague relationship with Taxpayer parents:

Teachers
Education of taxpayers'children
$\xrightarrow{\hspace{3cm}}$ Taxpayer-Parents
Wages, Fringe Benefits from taxes
$\xleftarrow{\hspace{2cm}}$

2. Patron–client relationship with Burghersiders:

Teachers
Education of Burgherside children
$\xrightarrow{\hspace{3cm}}$ Burgherside parents
Deference expressed in specific forms
$\xleftarrow{\hspace{3cm}}$
of behavior determined by teachers

From the teachers' point of view, the treatment of Burghersiders as colleagues would mean a one-way flow of services. They therefore require that Burghersiders exchange deference in behavior for the services they receive. They do not merely *request* that Burghersiders act like clients; they *demand* this role explicitly and may insist on compliance on threat of witholding services.[3] The few Burghersiders who insist on colleague relationships with teachers or Taxpayers in other agencies may be called "trouble-makers," and even denied the services they need. Therefore, in general, most Burghersiders tend to conform to Taxpayers' expectations; at least, they pretend to accept the patron–client relationship and behave accordingly.

The patron–client relationship that characterizes the interaction of Taxpayers with Burghersiders has some important implications for the way that Burghersiders behave at school. Taxpayers define Burghersiders not only as Nontaxpayers, but also as "people with problems" that keep them as financial burdens to Taxpayers. Therefore, Taxpayers regard the transformation of Burghersiders into Taxpayers through education and job retraining as their primary responsibility. They achieve only a partial success and many Burgherside children grow up to become "wards" of the community, maintained by "public assistance" or "welfare." Those who become recipients of "public assistance" are rarely resocialized to become Taxpayers. Thus the second major function of Taxpayers as patrons is "taking care of those who become stratified" as welfare recipients.

A significant feature of the patron–client relationship between Taxpayers and Burghersiders is that the two groups have almost mutually exclusive definitions of the "problems" Burghersiders have at school—their genesis and their solutions. Since Burghersiders have no power, the views of Taxpayers generally prevail—whether they affect education, employment, or housing.

---

[3]For example, a mother on AFDC would be asked to see to it that her child attends school more regularly or lose her welfare payment; a parent whose child has violated some school rule may be ordered to appear before the principal and promise that the child would never repeat the same offense or face some penalty specified by the education code (see Chapter 7).

CHAPTER **4**

Educational Attitudes and Aspirations of Burghersiders

Introduction

In Stockton, teachers and Taxpayers generally believe that children from Burgherside do poorly in school because their parents neither value education nor encourage them to achieve. The weight of this belief can be seen in the emphasis both teachers and other school officials place on the need for parents to become "involved" in the schools. I shall deal with this particular point in a later chapter.

In the present chapter I shall describe the educational values of Burghersiders. In studying parents' attitudes toward education, social scientists administer questionnaires either to children (Bordua 1960; Kahl 1953) or to parents (Cohen 1965). I collected data for the present chapter with a variety of techniques: questionnaire interviews of Burgherside parents and children, informal intensive interviews, and observations in many households and in the neighborhood for a period of several months. Furthermore, to understand more fully the attitude of Burghersiders toward education I carried out a three-generational study of the educational values and experiences of (*1*) grandparents of Burgherside children, (*2*)Burgherside parents, and (*3*) Burgherside children.

58

Except in a few cases, my data on Burgherside grandparents came from interviews with Burgherside parents since many of the grandparents lived and died in the rural southern United States or in Mexico.

Analysis of the data on the education of three generations of Burghersiders shows that when the oldest generation was growing up, education was not regarded as important as it was for the second generation; for the third generation, good education is generally viewed as indispensable. Three factors account for this development. The first is the trend toward urbanization. More than 90% of Burgherside grandparents grew up in the rural southern and southwestern United States or in rural Mexico, where their social and economic life demanded little or no formal education. But, as their children were growing up, changes began to occur in their rural communities that created the need for either more education or emigration. Some Burgherside parents remained in these changing rural communities until they migrated to the cities as adults; others left for the cities as adolescents. In the cities, both groups generally recognized the need for more education than had been necessary in their rural homelands. Burgherside children at the time of the present study were almost all urban born, and are growing up at a time when they and their parents recognize the need for more education than their parents had.

The second factor is that more education has been made available for each subsequent generation of Burghersiders. When Burgherside grandparents were growing up, their rural communities generally had schools that went no farther than the sixth grade or less. The rural schools attended by Burgherside parents went farther, although usually not up to the twelfth grade; most Burgherside parents who grew up in the cities, of course, could attend four-year high schools. Today, Burgherside children are growing up in a community with a number of colleges.

The third factor that accounts for the increase in educational aspirations is the relative increase in the opportunities available for blacks and Mexican-Americans to benefit from their educations in terms of good jobs and better wages. For Burgherside grandparents education did not seem "profitable" because in those days they would not be employed or paid on the basis of their education. When Burgherside parents were growing up, blacks and Mexican-Americans were still being rigidly excluded from good jobs and wages based on education, although the situation had slightly improved relative to the time of their own parents. Moreover, Burgherside parents who eventually moved to the city found that education was relatively more useful there than in their rural communities. At the time of this study, both parents and children in Burgherside said that more opportunities are becoming available for blacks and Mexican-Americans with good educations. Therefore they feel that there is a greater need for education today than ever before (see Ginzberg 1967). This attitude, although widespread, is not yet shared by everyone in Burgherside. There are, for example, a few Mexican households that have come to Stockton mainly to make money through farm labor and plan to return to Mexico. For such people, it is more important to put their adolescent children to work than to encourage them to succeed in American schools. There are a few other parents regarded by Burghersiders as "uneducated";[1] these are said to feel that blacks and Mexican-Americans will never or do not yet have the opportunity to succeed in America even if they have good educations. These parents do not encourage their children to work hard to succeed in school. And there are some Burgherside children who feel the same way, that it is no use working hard to succeed in school because society still discriminates against blacks and Mexican-Americans.

The Last Generation: Education and Burgherside Grandparents

Some Burgherside grandparents never had any formal education; others had only a few years. None of them completed college, as can be seen from Table 4.1.

Many adult informants in Burgherside knew very little about their own parents' education. Some of them remembered only that their parents *couldn't read or write*, or that they could only sign their names. For example, one informant said: *Yea. My father knew how to sign his name and count.* This probably means that his father had sixth grade education or less.

TABLE 4.1

Grandparents' Education in Years[a]

		Percentage reaching various levels of education			
	None	Grades 1–6	Grades 7–9	Grades 10–12	Grades 12 plus
Grandfathers					
Black (57)	19.3	61.40	8.77	5.26	5.26
Mexican (52)	28.85	59.62	5.77	5.77	—
Other (13)	15.38	38.46	17.69	30.77	7.69
Grandmothers					
Black (62)	14.52	46.77	14.52	20.97	3.23
Mexican (51)	26.0	46.0	14.0	10.0	4.0
Other (12)	—	50.0	33.33	38.33	

[a] Source: Author's interviews with Burgherside parents.

[1] Burghersiders define an "uneducated parent" as (*1*) one who has no common sense or (*2*) one who does not have much formal education. Speakers usually mean the latter.

One black informant told me: *I don't know if my mother went to school at all. But she knew how to read and write. She had a pretty good memory.* A Mexican-American father reported that both his parents were born in Mexico, and he didn't know just how far they went in school. His father could read and write in Spanish. His mother, who died in Stockton at the age of 105, could read in Spanish, but did not know how to write it. I also interviewed some grandparents who had no formal schooling. However, one grandmother reported completing eighth grade in Stockton at the age of 48 and "finishing school" at 53.

Burgherside grandparents were not school dropouts, even though they did not have much education. Most of them "finished school"; that is, they completed the highest level of formal schooling locally available.

Some parts of rural Mexico and the southern United States had no schools when Burgherside grandparents were growing up, and some local schools went only to the sixth grade or less. Those who wanted more education had to move to a small town or city, and since they were mostly children of peasants (Mexico) or sharecroppers (the rural South) this was difficult. In fact, Burgherside grandparents left school when they "finished school" locally.

Burgherside parents, therefore, do not consider their own parents dropouts. One Mexican parent reported that his father: *went as far as the sixth grade in Mexico—which was the farthest he could go there.* He does not know if his father ever went back to school, but: *He worked as a clerk; and mother was a housewife but she could read and write.* In some parts of Mexico and the rural southern United States the local school might go as far as the eighth, ninth, tenth, or eleventh grade. As one Mexican informant explained, to go beyond this point *would mean going to learn some trade.* A black woman also reported that her mother "finished school" at eleventh grade, because: *That was considered finishing school in Texas when my mother was coming up. They didn't have no twelfth grade and she went on to a vocational school to study nursing.*

Burgherside grandparents grew up in communities where formal education was not considered necessary either for social status or for the operation of the local economy. That many Burgherside grandparents did not finish high school or go to college was not because they lacked the motivation or the intellectual ability. They grew up in communities where neither the cultural values nor the social system included formal education. They grew up expecting to carry on the same rural economic activities as had their own parents, who were not educated: farm labor, sharecropping, domestic service, and homemaking.

But some Burgherside grandparents *actually* dropped out of school, mainly to go to work to help support the family. As peasant farmers, sharecroppers, or farm laborers, their parents found it difficult to "come out even" unless the entire family was employed. Take for instance one informant born in 1890 in North Carolina, but raised in California. He went as far as the fifth grade and then had to stop to help his parents take care of the younger children. He explained that: *In those days older children had to help by working to raise the younger ones.*

A few Burgherside grandparents went through twelfth grade or beyond. One grandfather attended college because his own father was: *a smart man, a minister with a large congregation,* [who] *also owned a large farm in Texas.* This grandfather had two brothers and six sisters, all of whom went to college. He himself did not graduate, but left to become a schoolteacher, then a farmer, and then a railroad worker and motor mechanic.

Burgherside parents say that their own parents encouraged them to go to school and get a good education, but they did not *push them real hard.* One Mexican father said: *My father wanted me to get an education, but I didn't like school.* A black mother said: *My parents didn't have much education either. They only went to grammar school. But they definitely encouraged me to go on.* Another woman was born in a place where *there was no Negro school.* Her father, born in Waco, Texas, in 1892, had only a sixth-grade education and worked as a farm laborer, but he taught the informant "to read and write" before they moved to a place where she could go to school.

The "Lost Generation": Education and Burgherside Parents

Burgherside parents call themselves the "Lost Generation", primarily because they are "uneducated." They have a little more education than their own parents, but they are not educated enough "to make it" now in the city where they have migrated. In Burgherside, good education is nowadays considered as an avenue to good jobs.

Burgherside parents say that when they were "coming up" the jobs available to them were the same whether or not they had an education. Even those who grew up in Stockton point to people who, they say, had college educations but worked as laborers *with their degrees in their pockets.* Many parents grew up in the rural South or Mexico, where formal education was not necessary in order to "make it." But now Burgherside parents say that the situation is changing. More and better opportunities are opening for blacks and Mexican-Americans with good educations. Furthermore, the jobs that formerly were open to people without education, such as farm labor and semiskilled factory work, are disappearing. *The machines are taking over,* Mexican parents repeatedly said after they saw a movie at St. Benedict's church titled *The Work Crisis.* Burgherside parents therefore say they are "lost" (*1*) because they did not prepare them-

TABLE 4.2

Rural and Urban Birthplaces of Burgherside Parents[a]

Ethnic membership	Percentage born in rural areas, small towns, or cities		
	Rural areas	Small towns	Cities
Fathers			
Black (24)	79.0	—	—
Mexican-American (24)	58.0	4.0	38.0
Other (3)	100.0	—	—
Mothers			
Black (48)	75.0	—	25.0
Mexican-American (32)	56.0	—	44.0
Other (10)	70.0	—	30.0

[a] Source: Author's interviews with Burgherside parents.

selves by education for the opportunities now opening up and (2) because "the machines" are taking over their jobs. Like their own parents, most Burgherside parents were born in rural areas (see Table 4.2). Some moved to the city as children with their parents. Others moved to the city as adults. About 90% of the black parents came from the rural South; two or three were born in Stockton. About 20% of the Mexican-American parents were born in Stockton, but some of those who were born in Stockton and in other urban centers later returned to Mexico with their parents and were educated in rural, rather than urban areas, and in Mexico, rather than in the United States. This explains in part why some parents born in Stockton do not speak English. Whereas eleven more blacks grew up in urban areas than were born there, only four more Mexican-American parents did.

Of Burgherside parents nearly 50% attended school in rural areas and

TABLE 4.3

Location of Schools Attended by Burgherside Parents[a] [b]

Location	Fathers		Mothers		
	Black (23)	Mexican (22)	Black (48)	Mexican (30)	Other (12)
Rural U.S.A.	57	—	54	29	50
Urban U.S.A.	43	59	46	55	33.32
Rural Mexico	—	41	—	13	8.33
Urban Mexico	—	—	—	3	8.33

[a] Source: Author's interviews with Burgherside parents.
[b] Values expressed as percentages.

50% went to school in urban areas; more than 90% of Burgherside grand-parents who had any education attended rural schools (see Table 4.3).

Table 4.4 shows the amount of formal education Burgherside parents have had. Some Burgherside parents, like their own parents, never had any formal schooling, but most parents had more education than their own parents. Parents who grew up in urban centers have had more education than those who grew up in rural areas.

Table 4.4 represents the present level of parents' education, not the level attained when Burgherside parents first left school. Most Burgherside parents, like the grandparents, were *not* school dropouts when they left school. They, too, had "finished school," completing the highest level of schooling available in their community. For example, a 74-year-old grandmother, who had no formal education, told me that her son "finished school" at ninth grade because, *the school only went that far.*

Some Burgherside parents "did not finish school." Some dropped out because they did not like school, but the majority who "did not finish school" said that they went to work to help support their families. Others left school because of illness.

In the parents' generation, the younger children often had better op-portunities to continue their education than the older ones, who left school earlier to work. Table 4.5 shows that younger siblings tend to go further in school than the first born. As I indicated earlier, formal education was not regarded as an asset in the peasant or sharecropping economy, and so older children were pressed into economic activities at an early age. In later years, however, the rural economy itself began to change, the need for formal education was perceived, and this enabled later siblings to continue their education.

Table 4.4

Education of Burgherside Parents [a][b]

	Fathers		Mothers		
Amount of schooling	Black (23)	Mexican (22)	Black (48)	Mexican (30)	Other (11)
None	4	8	—	3	—
K–6	25	50	29	34	18.18
7–9	13	13	19	41	36.36
10–12	42	21	42	19	36.36
12 plus	17	8	10	3	9.05

[a] Source: Author's interviews with Burgherside parents.

[b] Values expressed as percentages.

TABLE 4.5

Education of Oldest and Youngest Siblings [a][b]

Years of school	First born (59)	Last born (60)
0	10.17	—
K–6	27.12	31.67
7–9	22.03	18.33
10–11	23.73	11.67
12 or more	16.95	38.33

[a] Source: Author's interviews with Burgherside parents.
[b] Values expressed as percentages.

Farm-labor migration was disruptive to the education of some parents when they were young. When their families moved, the purpose was not to give the children a better educational opportunity but to seek employment in migratory farm labor. Such families might not always return to their "permanent" homes in time for the children to enter school at the proper time. Children tended to lag behind in their school work, and eventually they left school, *because they couldn't keep up.* This was often true in families with Mexican-American parents whose parents came from Mexico. Their families came to the United States to accumulate capital through farm labor and then to return to Mexico to invest their savings in "businesses" or in developing their "ranches." It was important for these families that everybody who could work did so; formal schooling for their children was incidental and their stay in the United States temporary.

I have so far in this section mainly considered Burgherside parents whose educational background is rural. Those who were born in rural areas but came to urban areas as children experienced some difficulty in adjusting to the urban educational system, especially if they came to the city in their adolescent years. Adjustment to rural schools, whether in the U.S. or in Mexico, differed from adjustment to urban schools. Take for example the case of a black informant who went to school in rural Arkansas; her teachers were all members of her community and, perhaps, her church. Parents with such a background often say that their teachers were more concerned about their education than teachers in Stockton are for their children's education. Their teachers and parents knew one another as neighbors, friends, relatives, and members of the same churches. Teachers identified with the schools where they taught in contrast to Burgherside teachers (see Chapter 7). *Back home,* they say, *teachers really want to educate the children and are not there just because of the money, and the parents and the whole community would support the teachers even when they were very strict.* It was rapport between teachers and parents rather than the involvement of parents in the schools that was the important factor. The "uneducated parents" were not involved in the schools and were not required to be for their children to be able to learn.

The rural school was also different in another respect. The "school year" was determined by the agricultural cycle. Burgherside parents who grew up in the rural South attended school for from three to five months instead of nine months in the year because they had to get out early and pick cotton. Children with this kind of background did not adjust easily to the urban school system, which often made no provisions for pupils with rural backgrounds. Their parents did not understand the urban system and did not fit into the school's image of "parents who value education." The Mexican's adjustment difficulties were further compounded by the fact that parents and children might not speak or understand English well. Therefore, many people who came to the city as adolescents "did not finish school." Such people assert that they were "pushed out."

There is another reason for not "finishing school," often mentioned by Burgherside parents who were born and educated in urban centers. They say that when they were growing up education did not offer black and Mexican people the "occupational and financial rewards that are supposed to go with it." As I have already pointed out, Burgherside parents can name people they know who had a college education but *didn't get a good job.* One man with a college degree is said to have worked as a garbage collector when he first came to Stockton. Another man who almost qualified as a lawyer ended up working as a janitor. A Mexican-American father said he was an "A" student until he got to the junior high school where he was told he could not take "print-shop." The "print-shop" was only for those whose parents were printers. His own parents reacted to this exclusion by pulling him and his brothers out of school and putting them *to work in the fields*:

> *My parents felt that because of prejudice that they went through that you're not going to go up there and make it. This is what my mother used to tell me and I carried it in my conscience. "You are going to school and your father didn't go to school. And eventually you are going to have the same job as your father but he never had no education. So what good is your education? To go and work in the fields?" You see! This is what is embedded in my conscience. And this is what I try to overcome all the time.*

The appeal of education in urban centers lies in its greater potential economic reward there than in rural areas. But many soon reached the conclusion that perhaps *going to school was not worth it* since they would end up with poor jobs and poor income, like their own parents who had no education. One informant, for instance, chose *to make the Navy a career* rather than go to college because: *more education did not promise to pay.* He had finished high school *with good grades,* but there were few things he could do as a black man. He could have gone to college after he got out of the Navy, but he reasoned that he might not get a good job when he graduated. So he re-enlisted in the Navy *to make it a career.* The pay is not very good, according to the informant, but: *at least it would provide me with some security,* that is, when he retires after 22 years of service he will have a secure income for the rest of his life.

In the past, then, Burghersiders were discouraged from seriously pursuing education because there were no strong social and economic incentives for them to do so. They did not get the jobs they qualified for or the promotions they deserved; and they encountered many other discouraging "racial problems" in the course of their work. As one woman said:

> *Take for instance my husband. When he is working he should get a promotion. Well, they will not promote him on the job. They will take some other,* [sic] *white guy and give him a promotion. Well, that works on his* [my husband's] *mind. He knowed that he should have earned a promotion and he is not getting it and then he just sinks further and further down in depression, you know. And in time he just becomes nonfunctional because of his experience . . . And this is still true up to the present time. We are the last hired and the first fired on any job. And we also have to go through the problem of being harrassed a lot of times. Because whereas you could be doing your work correctly but maybe your foreman has racial problems and they take this out on you. And actually it's just the total state of mind sometimes that you have to work with and that destroys the learning process too. It's not that you can't do it. It's just what you have to endure, you know, mentally. It's what it does to you psychologically that takes hold upon us here.*

These experiences must be taken into account for any realistic analysis of the problems of education in Burgherside. Burgherside parents and their parents did not consider formal education as learning for learning's sake, and they take the same attitude toward the education of their children today.

The probable effect of lack of postschool opportunity on children's behavior in school has been recognized by a few social scientists. Miller (1967:2) notes that for children of ethnic minorities the "school is likely to be a meaningless way station to nowhere" because of the restricted "opportunity structure of the postschool world." In explaining why they did not "finish school" those Burgherside parents who grew up in urban areas usually made it clear that they were discouraged by what they saw as this restricted opportunity.

Some parents who grew up in the city dropped out of school because of conflict with their own parents. When their families moved into urban centers the parents continued to interpret their children's behavior in terms of rural values, maintaining rural attitudes toward life while their children developed more urban outlooks. Burgherside parents said that as adolescents they wanted to date, go to parties, wear certain types of clothes, and choose their own spouses, but such behavior was met with strong opposition from their parents. Today, some of the older parents, especially those from Mexico, still complain that their children disobey them and do as they like: *They will usually have their own way if they are grown up. If the parents refuse they will elope. So we have tried not to make our daughters elope*, one grandmother explained. Her two daughters, aged 27 and 25, but still living at home, nodded in agreement. Other parents reported that they dropped out of school to get married in order to do what they liked because their parents did not understand. Take for example the case of a mother who dropped out in tenth grade, although she later "finished school" and went to college:

PARENT: *Yea. 18 years old and they don't let you go out. 18-year-old girls —they will never let their daughters go out.*

ANTHR.: *And how do they end up marrying so young?*

PARENTS: *They sneak around* [laughing]. *I used to do that. My Mom and Dad never let me go out. When I was 18 years old I wanted to go to the dances, you know. And I would beg my mother, "Oh, please let me go out with the girls to the hall." "Oh, heaven forbid! No!" And she never let me go out, and to go to the show I had to take all my brothers and my sisters with me* [laughing]. *And I quit school. I just quit school when I was 16. I just got fed up with school. I didn't have good clothes and I was ashamed. I didn't want to take the bus, I didn't like the girls around here. Why do you think I understand? I felt like this myself. I said, "Mom, I'm quitting school." I was 16 years old and the next day I quit school.*

Even after she left school her parents would not let her go out. So she eloped and got married.

Migration into urban centers enabled many Burgherside parents to return to school for more formal education (see Table 4.6). In Burgherside, slightly more Mexican-American women than Mexican men, and more black men than black women have gone back to school for more education. Mexican-American men tend to send their wives back to school *to learn English* so they can get jobs. One man explained this by saying that he already has a job and *can speak English very well* but that his wife needs to go to school in order to learn English to get a job. In the black community,

TABLE 4.6

Burgherside Parents Who Reported Having Gone Back to School to Get More Education[a][b]

Response	Fathers		Mothers		
	Black	Mexican	Black	Mexican	Other
Yes	42	25	39	40	23
No	58	75	61	60	77

[a] Source: Author's interviews with Burgherside parents.
[b] Values expressed as percentages.

it is the wife who sometimes persuades her husband to return to school "to get more education." The blacks believe that the physical labor done by black men makes them too tired to think about getting more education. So black women have to persuade their husbands to get more education. One informant recently successfully talked her husband into going back to school: *At first I started school and I pushed my husband in because he was a good student, you know.*

Burgherside parents go back to school for the following reasons: (*1*) to learn English, for the non-English-speaking parents; (*2*) to "finish school," that is, to complete the equivalent of junior high (ninth grade) and senior high school (twelfth grade); (*3*) to learn about their ethnic heritage—black history, Mexican-American history, and the like; and (*4*) to get vocational training, which is the reason most Burghersiders go back to school. The men train to be painters, plumbers, dental technicians, carpenters, electronic technicians, and so forth. The women train to be typists, secretaries, electronic technicians, nurses' aides, licensed vocational nurses, and registered nurses. Recently some Burgherside women, one or two of whom have now moved out of the neighborhood, started training as teachers through the Teachers' Corps program.

Some Burgherside parents have many "skills" but often don't have "the little certificate" to prove that they actually trained for a particular job. For such a person it is necessary to go back to school to get the "certificate," unless he considers himself too old to do so. The following is a typical comment from those *who know things but don't have no diploma.*

PARENT: *I know all kind of trade and work but I don't have nothing, you know, no diploma, no certificate for these things. Say, for instance, like truck-driving and "half-way" mechanical work. . . when any kind of machinery stopped I can go and put it back to work. But I don't have, you know, the schooling.*

ANTHR.[2]:   *Well, you're just like my father. He could do a lot of things although he didn't have any schooling. Of course in his day in Africa people didn't have to have diplomas to do things.*

PARENT: *Well, that's me. Take putting to work a boatsman. Because during the Army when I rode round the water there I paid the strictest attention to it. I take my boat, I realized if there is fault or what not. So I got a little scale to check it and made it to safety and what not. And some things as that—something go wrong with the motor and I go right into it and find out what is wrong with the motor and me and the boatsman would kneel down and look something wrong and knowed what it is, solve the problem that came along and in a little while have it in operation, going on.*

That is, during his military service the informant became skilled in repairing boats and other machines, but he never got certificates (diplomas) to show that he learned to do these things. Since he does not have these certificates no one is willing to employ him as a skilled workman in these trades.

The amount of education attained by grandparents and parents in Burgherside cannot be explained wholly on the basis of individual psychological makeup or ability. Their education was both culturally and structurally determined. In the rural South and rural Mexico, people did not need much formal education to adjust socially and economically. Urban cultures made education a priority, but structurally the people saw it as essentially nonrewarding. However, now Burgherside parents are a "lost generation" because (*1*) many did not have a chance to get an education in the first place; (*2*) those who got some education did not have job opportunities; (*3*) the only jobs available to them as "uneducated" are now being taken over by machines (automation); and (*4*) now that "better" job opportunities are opening up they *don't have any papers* to get the jobs.

The Educational Goals of Burgherside Parents for Their Children

In 1967 Burghersiders showed their attitudes toward education when they in many ways publicly expressed their concern about their children's failures in the public schools. They said that their children were not only failing in school, but also had become almost antischool. One informant estimated that by 1967 Burgherside children were causing property damage at the neighborhood elementary school "amounting to about $300 a year."

To correct the situation, Burgherside Neighborhood Improvement

---

[2]Anthr. in dialogues represents Anthropologist throughout.

Association did two things. First, it petitioned the school district to open the school for the use of the young people during the summer. Burghersiders felt that *this would give the kids something to do and reduce the amount of damage being done to the school.* This proved to be a successful approach because the children began *to feel that the school was theirs.* A year later the annual damage was reduced to $30–$40. Burghersiders were so pleased that at a Board of Education meeting in the summer of 1967, the Neighborhood Association presented the schools superintendent with a flower plaque for letting the children use the school.

Second, the Association sponsored a neighborhood meeting on school dropouts. It invited representatives of community agencies, including the school district, the District Attorney's Office, the Sheriff's Office, and the Probation Department. Burghersiders proposed to these representatives that: *There really wasn't a dropout problem but a "push-out" problem in Burgherside and elsewhere in the county.* Their children were being *suspended or expelled from school for trivial offenses such as chewing gum in class, running in the hallway, having bad attitudes.* Furthermore, they pointed out that *push-out is a dead and useless way of encouraging children to stay in school and work hard.*

A week later Burghersiders took as the theme of their annual parade, "A Dropout is Dead!" The teenage girls carried a banner bearing the theme at the head of the parade, followed by some teenage boys carrying a coffin on which was written: "A Dropout is Dead!" As the banner and the coffin passed, the watching residents nodded in agreement. They explained that the theme meant that their children should "finish school" because if they dropped out of school they would not be able to get good jobs, good wages, support themselves and their families, and pay taxes.

Today Burghersiders still insist that a "dropout" or a "pushed-out" is "dead," and this describes their general attitude toward their children's education. Most Taxpayers, including some school personnel assured me that Burghersiders do not value education and are not concerned about their children's success in school. For example, a teacher asked me: *Don't you think, Mr. —————, it's because these people don't value education? I mean, it doesn't really mean much to them how their children do in school?* Taxpayers say that since Burgherside parents do not have much education themselves they cannot value education for their children, or that Burgherside children are dropping out of school because their parents are also dropouts, or that *It is a case of generations of welfare recipients.* Taxpayers' logic about education goes like this: A child does well in school *because* his parents and his grandparents did well in school; every child behaves as his parents behaved, and this imitation is deliberately encouraged by the parents. Yet many Taxpayers boast that they have done better than their parents both in education and in occupation. Many teachers, for instance, had parents who were not of middle-class background, who did not have college educations or "whole lots of money." Thus, although Taxpayers are "proud to have made it," they rarely concede that Burghersiders can "make it."

Taxpayers say that Burgherside children come from homes where there are no books, where parents neither read nor encourage their children to read. It is said that Burgherside parents do not provide their children with "models." Many Burgherside parents do not read because they are "uneducated," but there are books in many homes, books that parents have bought specifically for their children. Fourteen households have one or two sets of encyclopedias, and one household has spent as much as $600 on such books. Some Burgherside parents buy these expensive books because they think their children will use them for their homework. Sometimes they buy books rather than encourage their children to use the public or school library for fear they will lose the library books. These parents want their children to read and their solution is to buy books including encyclopedias, for them.

Burghersiders want their children to "finish school," that is, to complete twelfth grade. Beyond this they are somewhat vague in stating what they want for their children. Most parents do not know what it costs to send a child through college; they know very little about scholarships and other financial aids, and they assume that college education is so expensive that they "can't afford it." Therefore parents who would like to have their children go to college do not intend to send them. They usually say that they want their children to "go as far as possible," which often means that they "should graduate" from high school. They do not want their children to drop out of school. When a child drops out, Burghersiders suspect that he has been "pushed out."

Educational Goals of Burgherside Children

Burgherside children do not want to grow up to do the same kinds of jobs now done by their parents—farm labor and other unskilled and semiskilled work. They feel that their parents have these jobs and receive low wages partly because they did not have a good education when they were growing up, and partly because of occupational discrimination against blacks and Mexican-Americans in Stockton. Therefore, although they reject their parents' occupational status, they do not reject their parents themselves because of their low socioeconomic status. This rejection does not involve psychological conflicts because Burgherside children blame society rather than their parents for the latter's low status. As one Mexican-American youth in twelfth grade said: *My parents didn't have an education but they saw how much they suffered without one, and they didn't want me to grow up like they did. I feel that's how other parents feel. They want me to have the things they didn't have.*

Burgherside parents are one reason, and a very important reason, that children want to "finish school." Even the few surviving Burgherside grandparents encourage children to finish. A 69-year-old woman said of her eighth-grade granddaughter: *I've told her why she's going to school and she should know. I told her she's going to get her education and to learn to be able to get a good job.* Parents "push" their children more than their own parents "pushed" them. Burghersiders distinguish between "telling" and "pushing" a child. To "push" a child means (*1*) to assist him in his studies; (*2*) to supervise his homework and study at home; (*3*) to ask frequently how he is doing in school and if he needs any help; (*4*) to reward the child, usually with money, when he does well in school and punish him when he does poorly; and (*5*) generally to stress the importance of a good education. Burgherside parents who "push" their children often use their own experiences as examples of the hardships their children can expect to go through if they fail to get a good education. As one father explained:

> *I realized that if I had had the prompting and pushing that we are giving to our children I would have done much better, I think.* And with the educational opportunities that are available for our young people now, if we had that, I think I would have excelled, you know, gone high. But my parents, they never really pushed us. They were concerned, but education wasn't stressed as much as it is now. And the opportunity for black people to advance wasn't as good as it is now [emphasis added].

By educational opportunities this informant, like other Burghersiders, means that there are more opportunities for blacks and Mexican-Americans to get jobs and wages more compatible with their education than there were in the past. This development is an important influence in the emerging attitudes of Burghersiders—young and old—toward education.

Until recently, blacks, Mexican-Americans, and some other ethnic minority groups tended to accept the American folk theory that the goal for each ethnic group is to become "assimilated" into the Anglo group, that is, to lose its uniqueness as a separate group and become "just Americans" (see Gordon 1964; Glazer and Moynihan 1963). Thus, over the years blacks have developed elaborate methods for achieving "equality" and "integration" with Anglos; individual blacks who looked white and others who bleached their skins and processed their hair "passed" into Anglo society when they could.

In Stockton there are many Taxpayers who strongly believe that the educational and other problems of blacks and Mexican-Americans will be solved only when these minority groups become totally assimilated or integrated with the dominant Anglo group. However, new developments are taking place that question not only the possibility but also the desirability of these ethnic minorities becoming "assimilated" into the Anglo groups. Blacks and Mexican-Americans now think that, at least for them, the theory that America is a "melting pot" where people lose their ethnic identities may be a myth. They point out that although blacks and Mexican-Americans have been in Stockton since the city was incorporated in 1850 they have not turned into Anglos. The emerging ideology among these people opposes the notion of assimilation and stresses the need to accept and appreciate separate ethnic identities in American society. The new ideology teaches people that "Black is Beautiful"; that is: *If you are black stay black; don't pass as white; don't bleach your skin; don't process your hair, wear it natural.* Among Mexican-Americans there is similar emphasis on accepting themselves as they are and valuing their "cultural heritage." Mexican-Americans use terms like *"La Causa"* and *"La Causa de la Raza,"* to describe these new developments; blacks employ phrases like "Black is Beautiful," and "Black Power." I shall call all these developments among blacks, Mexican-Americans, and similar groups the "Movement," a term that is sometimes employed by the people themselves.

The Movement is certainly one of the strongest sources of influence on the educational aspiration of Burgherside children today. In Stockton, the Movement emphasizes not only pride in ethnic heritage and identity, but also in ethnic progress. It teaches that progress is to be achieved through education and the social and economic development of the black and Mexican-American communities. Some of the spokesmen point out that black and Mexican-American people have failed to achieve high educational and economic status in the past because they followed the criteria established by the dominant Anglo group. The Movement therefore stresses other criteria and techniques to encourage education. This may be illustrated from a discussion of scholarship awards that took place at a MAPA (Mexican-American Political Alliance) meeting in the Fall of 1969. MAPA members had sponsored a "community dance" and raised a $700–$800 scholarship fund. At this meeting the chairman explained that the money would be used to award 15 scholarships. Throughout the discussion school grades were not stressed as the criterion for the scholarship; anyone who applied would be considered since, *There are many reasons why people receive poor grades in school.* Such an attitude assures even the poorest students that they also can gain scholarships to further their education.

In 1967 the Black Unity Council in Stockton organized a school boycott to dramatize what they considered "the evils of the system." This boycott also served to dramatize for young blacks the importance of education. Following the boycott the Council submitted to the school district a list of eight "demands" which "aimed at improving the education of the black child. [SUSD 1969b:4428–4430]." Several months later a similar list was submitted to the same Board by the MAUFA, that is Mexican-Americans United for Action (SUSD 1969b:4586, 4623), and, still later, by the Council of Spanish-Speaking People. Since 1969 some black and Mexican-American teachers have organized the Black Teacher's Alliance and the Mexican-American Educators' Association, respectively, to promote the education of the children of their ethnic groups. Also in 1969, black and Mexican-American students' organizations held conferences and workshops that focused on education. The crisis at Edison High School in the spring of 1969, the yearlong controversy over school integration, and the Board of Education election on October of 1969 all served to dramatize for Burgherside children the need for education.[3]

The Movement also promotes the idea that education is very important through ethnic newspapers, occasional radio and television programs, and conferences and workshops which feature some of the leading spokespersons. Burghersiders' children learn of new developments in black and Mexican-American education through the news media and from visitors from other cities. Ethnic newspapers such as *El Hispano* or *The Black Panther* play a very important role in fostering new ideas about education, teaching Burgherside children that good education is necessary not only for getting good jobs but also for "upgrading" their community. A series of exchanges appearing in *El Hispano* in 1969, and avidly read by some of my informants, will serve to illustrate this point. One of the writers described the situation as follows (Huizar 1969:5):

Many Chicanos, who have lived in the *barrios*, know what it is like to have bad housing, no food, no money, no jobs, and at the same time to have ten kids in the family.

Some of the Chicanos make it through school and become lawyers, businessmen and so on; instead of coming back to the *barrios* which he once knew to help his people, he goes to the Whiteman's world. Now he's going to live like him because he has made it. To me he isn't a Chicano any more. Now he is a coconut, brown on the outside and white on the inside.

In order for a Chicano to stand high in the world, he must have good education and we must help each other, members of *La Raza*, a proud race, to fight the power structure which keeps us down in this so-called "free world." Without these things we are a forgotten race . . . that is why I joined the Brown Berets and believe in *La Causa* for now there is truly a cause.

---

[3]A riot occurred at the predominantly black and Mexican-American Edison Senior High School in the spring of 1969. This was followed by weeks of confrontations between school authorities and various segments of these two ethnic groups.

It is necessary to differentiate between what I have called the "Movement" and the specific organizations through which the Movement is manifested. The former is essentially a social movement as defined by Aberle (1966:315): "an organized effort by a group of human beings to effect a change in the face of resistance by other human beings." Specific organizations have developed within the Movement, but their goals and techniques are not always in accord with its goals. Among blacks in Stockton these organizations include the Black Panthers, the Black Unity Council, the Black Theater Club, the Black Teachers' Alliance, and the Ebony Young Men of Action. Those in the Mexican-American community include the Mexican-American Political Alliance, the Council of Spanish-Speaking People, the Brown Berets, the Dos Centavos, and the Mexican-American Educator's Association.

Many young Mexican-Americans are not members of the Brown Berets and many black youths are not in the Black Panthers. However, the literature of these organizations, including that on education is widely read and their ideas are usually discussed at gatherings of friends, at parties, in barbershops and coffeeshops, on school parking lots, and at formal organization meetings. On such occasions the status of ethnic education and the policies and practices of the local educational system are discussed. Young people are told on such occasions to *Get all the education you can.* One Mexican-American described the influence of the Brown Berets as follows:

> *They encourage us to get good education. They tell us to go to school as far as you can. Get all the education you can. I think they're right too. Yea. I dig the Brown Berets except when they get to being militant, you know. But it's seldom that they are militant.*

Another kind of social movement, which I call the Education Rehabilitation Movement, has also influenced the attitudes of Burghersiders toward education since 1965. This nationwide movement began in 1965 with the discovery that some children who came from what were called culturally, socially, and economically "disadvantaged" areas were not fully benefitting from the education system. The goal of this movement is to provide "equal educational opportunity" to the disadvantaged children by (*1*) searching out the forms and extent of their disadvantages; (*2*) analyzing the nature and extent of "learning disabilities" that these disadvantages have created in the children; and (*3*) providing suitable educational programs to enable disadvantaged children to "catch up" with others in their schoolwork. The Education Rehabilitation Movement is essentially a middle-class or Taxpayers' movement in behalf of "disadvantaged people" like Burghersiders. It is a social movement outside the black and Mexican-American communities, and its aims and methods are not always acceptable to the groups it seeks to "rehabilitate."

The Educational Rehabilitation Movement has also helped to develop new attitudes toward education in Burgherside. The ideology of the (Ethnic Identity) Movement developed partly because the Rehabilitation Movement classified black and Mexican-American children as "culturally deprived" or "culturally disadvantaged." Ethnic minority groups have responded by asserting that their cultures are both different from and equal to the dominant Anglo culture, and that the difficulties black and Mexican-American children experience in the formal education system do not arise from inferior or "deprived" cultural backgrounds. Black and Mexican-American people, especially young people, now emphasize education partly because they want to correct certain misconceptions about their communities. The Rehabilitation Movement has also stimulated the interest of Burgherside children in education because it has increased the number of teachers and other school employees of ethnic minority backgrounds. The increased contact between Burgherside children and black and Mexican-American educators encourages them to aspire to teaching and other professions.

Aspirations for Higher Education and Better Jobs

A few weeks before the high school crisis in 1969 I had interviewed some Burgherside and Southside students about their goals in education. I asked the students (1) how far their parents went in school, (2) how far their parents would like them to go in school, and (3) how far they themselves would like to go in school. Table 4.7 reports their responses. Nearly 50% of the students want to finish four years of college and an additional 27% want to complete two years of college. Furthermore, the educational goals of Burgherside children exceed the goals their parents have for them, which is particularly significant since Burgherside parents tell their children mainly that they want them to "finish school." Thus the children regard their parents' expectation as low; they want to go further.

Burgherside children have relatively high educational goals, but many feel that they will not be able to attain them. The difficulties they frequently mentioned, given in Table 4.8, include "lack of ability" or "the grade problem," need for guidance or for "knowing what to do," lack of money, and racial discrimination. Students from other neighborhoods in South Stockton also worry about these things. For comparative purposes I have included their responses with a breakdown by ethnic group.

Some who want to go to college do not think their "grades are good enough." Some do not know if they are taking "the right courses." Others do

TABLE 4.7

Educational Goals of Burgherside Children Compared with (1) Education of Their Parents and (2) Educational Goals of Their Parents[a][b][c]

Grade level	Mother's educ. (87)	Father's educ. (80)	Parents' goal for child (56)	Child's own educational goals (104)
0–3rd	8.05	27.5	—	—
4–6	25.29	31.25	—	—
Jr. high	28.74	11.25	—	1.92
Jr. high and voc. t.	4.6	6.25	5.36	1.92
H.s.	27.59	21.25	7.14	13.46
H.s. and voc. t.	4.6	2.5	32.14	11.54
H.s. and 2-yr. col.	1.15	—	39.29	25.96
H.s. and 4-yr. col.	—	—	10.71	13.46
H.s. and 4 + yr. col.	—	—	1.79	28.85
Other	—	—	3.57	2.88

[a]Source: Author's interviews with Burgherside students.
[b]Note: Data in column (3), parents' goal for child, came from students rather than from parents and the students were not asked to specify sex of parents.
[c]Values expressed as percentages.

TABLE 4.8

Reasons Junior and Senior High School Burgherside and Southside Students Felt That They Could Not Go on to College or Technical School

Reasons given	Burghersiders (72)	Southsiders by ethnic membership				
		Anglo (52)	Black (90)	Mexican (101)	Filipino (35)	Oriental (49)
"Grade problem" (Ability)	38.89	40.38	41.11	35.64	25.71	46.94
Guidance	13.89	13.46	8.89	11.88	11.43	6.12
Money	22.22	25.00	23.33	32.67	37.14	24.49
Discrimination	1.39	3.85	5.55	—	5.71	2.04
Other, unspecified	23.67	17.31	21.11	19.80	20.00	20.41

[a] Source: Author's interviews with Burgherside parents.
[b] Values expressed as percentages.

not know how to choose a college or "how to make out the application." Still others worry that even if they make the grade and receive adequate guidance they will not have enough money to continue their education. One student said, *If you have no money, you have no future. Most of the students feel that after they complete twelfth grade they cannot further their education because of money problems.* Burgherside students worry little about discrimination in gaining entry into colleges because they have heard that colleges and universities are *now* seeking students of minority backgrounds.

One of the main reasons Burghersiders want education is to "upgrade" themselves, to be able "to get a better job." The words "better" or "good" are used in comparison with the jobs their parents now have. Table 4.9 shows that the occupational goals of Burgherside children are for "clean" jobs (professional, clerical, etc.) whereas most of their parents are doing "dirty" jobs (semiskilled and unskilled labor). Unless they want to become teachers, most children have no intimate knowledge of anyone in the professions of their choice, and most have no specific knowledge of the requirements of such professions. For instance, some students who want an "office job" cannot describe the job they want beyond saying that it is a "clean job."

Parents' influences are stronger than the school's in shaping the occupational interests of Burgherside children. Parents encourage their children to aspire to "good jobs" or "clean jobs," because (*1*) it is for

TABLE 4.9

Types of Jobs Preferred by Burgherside Junior and Senior High School Students Compared to Types of Jobs They Indicated Their Parents Were Doing in 1969 [a] [b]

Types of jobs	Percentage of parents in types of jobs		Percentage of students preferring types of jobs (97)
	Fathers (101)	Mothers (98)	
Professional	—	1.02	41.24
Supervisory	0.99	1.02	—
Clerical	—	4.08	13.40
Sales	0.99	1.02	—
Service	1.98	12.24	7.22
Skilled	14.85	—	15.46
Semiskilled	19.80	3.06	4.12
Unskilled (labor)	37.62	11.22	—
Other, unspecified	23.76	66.33	18.56

[a] Source: Author's interviews with Burgherside parents.
[b] Values expressed as percentages.

their own (the children's) good to do so; (2) it will bring financial reward to them; (3) it will "upgrade" them and their families; (4) it will "upgrade their race"; (5) it will provide them with the opportunity or ability to qualify for the jobs. The influence of peer groups is quite small because friends do not know any more about the job world than the student does himself. Many students in Burgherside have not been influenced by anyone in their choice of occupation, as Table 4.10 indicates.

TABLE 4.10
Persons with Whom Burgherside and Other Southside Students Said They Had Discussed the Types of Work They Would Like to Do When They "Finished School"[a]

Persons with whom discussions were held	Percentage of students holding such discussions in Burgherside by ethnic membership of all Southside students interviewed					
	Burgher-siders (76)	Anglo (38)	Black (66)	Mex.-Amer. (76)	Filipino (22)	Oriental (30)
Teacher or counselor	3.95	2.63	13.64	3.95	—	3.33
Member of own family	15.79	26.32	25.86	23.68	31.82	16.67
Close friend	2.63	2.63	4.55	2.63	—	[10.00
Nobody	77.63	68.42	56.06	69.74	68.18	70.00

[a] Source: Author's interviews with Burgherside and Southside students.

There are strong indications that the educational goals of Burgherside parents and their children are higher than they were some years ago. In the past these people tended to feel that education would not solve their economic and other problems, and therefore they probably did not stress the importance of education as they do today. What has increased their desire for more education is their observation that in recent years new opportunities, good jobs, and better wages appear to be becoming available to blacks and Mexican-Americans with good educations. In addition, the new ideas about ethnic identity and other social events have helped to point to the need for more education. The question that follows from this chapter is: To what extent are Burghersiders achieving their educational goals?

CHAPTER 5

School Performance in Burgherside
as an Adaptation

Introduction

In this chapter I shall show that Burghersiders are *not* achieving their educational goals and that the reason for this is the adaptation they made in the past, when members of subordinate minorities were not allowed to receive social and economic benefits for their education. Although in recent years reports of new social and economic opportunities for blacks and Mexican-Americans with good education have increased Burghersiders' desire for education, these opportunities have not actually been experienced in Burgherside itself. So far neither Burghersiders nor the schools have lost their old ways of coping—which lead to school failures.

Various measurements can be used to show the extent to which Burgherside children are achieving their educational goals; these include: (*1*) the results of state-mandated tests given to the elementary and senior high schools each year, (*2*) classroom accomplishments as indicated by the letter grades children receive, (*3*) the rate of Burgherside school dropouts, and (*4*) the percentage of Burghersiders continuing their education beyond the twelfth grade. Quantitative data for the present study are available only for classroom grades.

In the state-mandated tests Burgherside elementary school usually shows one of the poorest results in the school district; Burgherside senior high school also receives the poorest results among the three senior high schools in the district. I was not able to compile figures for Burghersiders who dropped out of school or who progressed in their education beyond high school, but both informants and my impressionistic observation put the dropout rate relatively high, and the number of those who go on to college relatively low. The only statistical evidence I shall use in assessing how well Burghersiders are accomplishing their educational goals is the record of the children's work in the classroom.

What Classroom Success Means in Burgherside

The majority of Burgherside children at the elementary and junior and senior high schools receive grades of "C" or "D" in classroom work. Very few students receive "A"s; in fact, only four elementary school students and no junior and senior high school students in the neighborhood had an average recorded grade of "A" in 1969. Their grade pattern is shown in Table 5.1, which represents only those Burgherside students for whom complete records were available in 1969.

TABLE 5.1
Average Grades of Burgherside Children [a]

	Percentage of children at each school level receiving average grade				
School level	"A"	"B"	"C"	"D"	"F"
Elementary (194)	2.06	29.38	55.67	12.89	—
Jr. high (74)	—	1.35	45.95	43.24	9.46
Sr. high (46)	—	13.04	60.87	26.09	—
Total Burgherside students (314)	1.27	20.38	54.14	21.97	2.23

[a] Source: Stockton Unified School District.

Differences in parents' education, occupation, and family structure do not account for differences in the children's grades. Some children with a "B" average come from single-parent homes, or have relatively "uneducated parents", or are from families supported by Public Assistance. Some with an average of "C" or "D" have two parents who are relatively well educated and who support their families by their own wages. Children who have language difficulties as well as those who are fluent in English have averages of "C" or "D". There is no appreciable difference in the performance of children of different ethnic backgrounds, although the small number of Filipino children are doing better generally; Table 5.8 on page 88 illustrates this for the elementary school children.

PERFORMANCE IN SUBJECT AREAS

The same subjects are taught to all elementary children. Specialization begins in the eighth grade and the number of subjects offered increases in subsequent grades and through high school. Table 5.2 shows that most Burgherside children average "C" or lower in the various fields of study offered at the junior and senior high schools.

TABLE 5.2
Accomplishments of Burgherside Students by Grade [a]

Grade	Percentage of students receiving grades				
	"A"	"B"	"C"	"D"	"F"
7 (26)	—	—	38.46	50.00	11.54
8 (23)	—	—	47.83	47.83	4.35
9 (27)	—	3.70	55.56	29.63	11.11
10 (14)	—	14.29	50.00	35.71	—
11 (9)	—	22.22	55.56	22.22	—
12 (22)	—	9.09	68.18	22.73	—

[a] Source: Stockton Unified School District.

A study of the actual courses taken by Burgherside junior and senior high school students reveals some important points: First, especially at the senior high school, Burgherside students receive grades above "C" mainly in "applied" courses rather than in "academic" courses. These "applied" courses include music, physical education, homemaking, arts and crafts, industrial education, business education, and work experience. Second, in both "academic" and "applied" fields, Burgherside students tend to take the "low courses" rather than the "advanced" ones; few Burgherside students, for example, take "Advanced English," or "Advanced Math." Thus those who "excel," that is, who receive grades better than "C", "excel" at the "basic" rather than the "college prep" levels. For instance, senior high students are doing well in reading, but it is *Remedial Reading*! Many cannot read. The third point follows from the first two: Most Burgherside students want to go to college but do not take college-preparatory courses. Of the 87 senior high school students, only one has taken a chemistry class; a few have taken biology; and no one has taken physics. Burgherside students, where they have a choice, take what several informants call "dead-end" courses: student service/work experience, stage-crafts, homemaking, and so on. Again, although Table 5.3 shows that many Burgherside students take music, business, and crafts courses, these are also regarded as "dead-end" courses; in their occupational choice the students do not plan to become musicians, businessmen, or craftsmen.

TABLE 5.3

Average Grades Received by Burgherside Junior and Senior High School Students in Various Curriculum Areas [a]

Courses in curriculum areas	Percentage of junior high students receiving average grade			Percentage of senior high students receiving average grade		
	"F"—"C"		"C"+ —Above	"F"—"C"		"C"+ —Above
English	(77)	77.92	22.08	(85)	88.53	16.47
Reading	(66)	90.06	9.94	(57)	49.12	50.88
Social studies	(75)	90.67	9.33	(85)	87.06	12.94
Speech	(3)	—	100.00	(23)	60.87	39.13
For. lang.	(13)	38.46	61.54	(53)	62.26	37.74
Math	(75)	70.67	29.33	(87)	80.46	19.54
Gen. Sci.	(71)	90.14	9.86	(71)	78.87	21.13
Bio. and health sci.				(18)	44.44	55.56
Chem./physics				(1)	100.00	—
Music	(53)	56.60	43.40	(70)	48.57	51.43
P.E.	(68)	73.53	26.47	(83)	36.14	63.86
Homemaking	(24)	33.33	66.67	(46)	26.96	63.04
Arts and crafts	(54)	62.07	37.93	(69)	46.38	53.62
Ind. ed. A				(15)	46.67	53.33
Ind. ed. B	(6)	66.67	33.33	(21)	66.67	33.33
Ind. ed. C	(8)	62.50	37.50	(22)	63.64	36.36
Bus. ed.	(8)	62.50	37.50	(70)	64.29	35.71
Stu. service/ work exp.	(5)	40.00	60.00	(37)	16.22	38.78
Photog.	(19)	77.78	22.22	(7)	14.29	85.71

[a] Source: Stockton Unified School District.

The Concept of "Standard Work"

The majority of Burgherside students are "satisfied" with their school grades in the context of the neighborhood "standard." Even students who have a lower than "C" average say that they are "satisfied" and some are "very satisfied." Table 5.4 gives Burgherside students' feelings about their school achievement. As the table shows, seventh and eighth grade students feel satisfied even though none of them has an average of "B" (see Table 5.3 above).

TABLE 5.4

Burgherside Children's Feelings of Satisfaction toward School Accomplishment [a] [b]

Grade		Very satisfied	Satisfied	Somewhat satisfied	Dissatisfied	Very dissatisfied
7	(12)	—	58.3	16.7	16.7	8.3
8	(18)	5.6	50.0	27.8	16.7	—
9	(16)	17.6	41.2	17.6	5.9	11.8
10	(26)	7.7	65.4	15.4	3.8	7.7
11	(20)	30.0	50.0	15.0	5.0	—
12	(12)	33.3	33.3	16.7	16.7	—
Total	(104)	15.2	51.4	18.1	9.5	4.8

[a] Source: Author's interviews with students.
[b] Values expressed as percentages.

Burgherside students are satisfied with their school accomplishments in the context of what constitutes "satisfactory achievement" within the neighborhood. They are judging their own work by their neighborhood "standard" and not by the general notion of what constitutes good progress in the schools.[1] Therefore a student who has an average grade of "C" or lower considers his progress satisfactory by Burgherside standards although he may consider his work unsatisfactory when he compares it with that of students from other neighborhoods. I shall illustrate this notion with the following excerpt from an interview with a twelfth-grade student, who is failing most of her subjects but still thinks she is doing "standard" or "average" work.

ANTHR.: *I would like to know the reasons why you are going to school.*
STUDENT: *Because I want to go to college.*
ANTHR.: *Why do you want to go to college?*
STUDENT: *To get a good job. Some people go because they have to—otherwise their parents will be mad at them, if they are not yet 18 years old But I plan to go to college because I want to go.*
ANTHR.: *How are you doing in school?*
STUDENT: *I think I am doing well.*
ANTHR.: *What do you mean by doing well?*
STUDENT: *Well, I am not getting "F"s and "D"s. I get mostly "C"s—but*

---

[1] As used here the term, "standard," refers to the evaluations (usually in terms of letter grades) that Burghersiders expect from their teachers. That is, it refers to the "average letter grade" they expect their teachers to give them for their accomplishments in the classroom. It does not necessarily represent what Burghersiders themselves think they deserve for these accomplishments. In Chapter 7 I shall describe how teachers contribute to the idea of "standard" or "average grade" and how this serves to maintain the adaptation of school failure in Burgherside.

sometimes I get "A"s and "B"s—if I like what I am taking, like my
job at school.[2] Otherwise I get mostly "C"s.
ANTHR.:   *Do you consider getting "C"s doing well in school?*
STUDENT: *Yes, it is the standard, the average. Most people in my neighbor-*
      hood get "C"s.

In the fall of 1969 I tried to find out the extent to which the notion of
"standard work" is shared by the students. I asked Burgherside students:
When you think of the schoolwork of other students in your neighborhood,
how would you describe your own schoolwork? Nearly half of them, as
shown in the Table 5.5, considered their schoolwork to be average or
standard.

TABLE 5.5
How Burgherside Students Evaluate Their Classroom Performance in Comparison
with the Performance of Other Children in Their Neighborhood, by Ethnic Groups.
(Only Blacks and Mexican-Americans Were Interviewed.)[a][b]

Evaluation of schoolwork	Blacks (30)	Mexican-Americans (36)
Among the best	13.33	11.11
Above average	30.00	27.78
Just about average	50.00	44.44
Below average	3.33	16.67
Probably among the worst	3.33	—

[a] Source: Author's interviews with students.

[b] Values expressed as percentages.

I also asked the students to explain why they evaluated their schoolwork
as they did. The typical explanation by those who judged themselves to be
"just about average" was that most students in their neighborhood are at
their level. One student in twelfth grade explains: *Because all the students*
in my neighborhood that I know is just about average, so I would say that mine
[my record] *would be no higher or lower than theirs. So it would be just about*
average. An eleventh grader says: *The kids in my neighborhood don't seem*
to be the type of kids who would do better than average. But they are not
dumb either. One informant in the ninth grade said that: *Even though this is*
Burgherside there are still some smart students who live in the area. But a
student does not have to be smart to do "standard work." One student in
eleventh grade states: *I am not smart or dumb. But there is one thing—I try.*
Those who consider themselves better than average reject the Burgherside
standard as "too low" for them. **Students do not try to raise the level of the**
"standard" through competition. In fact, only one girl feels she is "above

---

[2]The informant works for two hours a day as an aide at the neighborhood elementary
school under the High School Work–Experience Program.

average" because of her competitive attitude: *I try hard, and if some students do better than I, I try to catch up or sometimes beat them, if possible.* Students who are doing lower than "standard" work excuse themselves by saying that some are even worse.

"STANDARD WORK" AND ETHNIC AFFILIATION

In Burgherside most of the students are black or Mexican, and Burghersiders tend to see their work as representative of their ethnic group. For instance, one Mexican-American girl said of the Mexican students: *It's rarely you run into a Mexican who doesn't do average work in school. Unless they are the type who just like to fool around like some kids I know at school. We're really not different,* another said, *just because we're not from the same race doesn't mean we're either smarter or dumber. It really depends on the type of work. If we really put our mind to our work we do it.*[3] I asked a young man in the twelfth grade if he would describe himself as above average in comparison with other students of his race, and he corrected me, saying, *You don't explain it right. I think you should put down* [i.e., add] *the same average also because* [in] *my race we're all about the same.*[4] A black student in the twelfth grade agreed: *Because some student is just smarter than the students of their own race. But of the black students most of them are just about average. So I would say my work would be just average.* Table 5.6 shows how students rate themselves within their own race.

TABLE 5.6

Students' Evaluation of Their Classroom Performance in Comparison with the Performance of Other Students of Their Own Race [a][b]

Rating of own performance	Blacks evaluating own performance (30)	Mexican-Americans evaluating own performance (36)
Among the best	16.67	15.00
Above average	26.27	22.50
Just about average	56.67	52.50
Below average	—	10.00
Probably among the worst	—	—

[a]Source: Author's interviews with students.
[b]Values expressed as percentages.

[3]That is, every Mexican-American student is capable of doing an assignment or classwork if it is the type of assignment that interests him. Therefore they are all "average."

[4]"Should put down same average," should include a sixth choice, "same average," meaning "Do you consider your work to be the same as the work of other students of your own race?" Of course, this means the same as "Just about average."

Burgherside parents share the notion of "standard" or "average" work. When you ask parents, *How are your children doing in school?* they often say, *Oh, I guess they are doing all right; just about average.* But Burgherside parents interviewed in the formal survey reported themselves as "satisfied" with the progress of their children, even when their children are receiving the grade of "C" or less. Tables 5.7 and 5.8 show the extent to which the parents of elementary school children are "satisfied" and the nature of their children's school progress. No attempt is made to relate the progress of a particular child and the degree of feeling of satisfaction of his parents. Nor does Table 5.7 represent all the parents. The purpose of the two tables is simply to show the pattern of response in relation to students' progress.[5]

TABLE 5.7
Burgherside Parents' Satisfaction with Their Children's School Progress [a b]

Ethnic group	Very satisfied	Satisfied	Dissatisfied	No opinion
Black (30)	26.64	59.94	6.66	6.66
Mexicans (58)	37.84	49.88	12.04	—
Other (11)	9.00	49.00	39.00	—
Overall (99)	31.31	52.52	13.13	3.03

[a] Source: Author's interviews with Burgherside parents of elementary school children.
[b] Values expressed as percentages.

TABLE 5.8
Average Grades of Burgherside Elementary School Children by Ethnic Groups [a]

| Ethnic group | Percentage of students receiving grade of | | | |
	"A"	"B"	"C"	"D"
Anglo (8)	—	25.00	62.50	12.50
Black (86)	3.49	30.23	50.00	16.28
Filipino (8)	—	37.50	62.50	—
Mexican-American (90)	1.11	28.89	58.89	10.11
Unspecified (2)	—	—	100.00	—

[a] Source: Stockton Unified School District.

[5] I believe that if all the parents were interviewed the result would not be significantly different. I know many parents who said they were *very* satisfied although school records show that their children are receiving grades of "C" or "D." The policy of the school district forbids giving an "F" grade at the elementary school level.

INTERPRETING BURGHERSIDERS' "SATISFACTION"

Do these Burgherside parents really feel satisfied about their children's progress in school? My impression, based on my intensive interviews with parents, is that the way they really feel is just the opposite. These parents have more complaints than praise regarding their children's progress in school.

There are three main reasons why many Burgherside parents indicated that they were satisfied with their children's school progress in the formal survey taken in the spring and summer of 1969. First, parents tended to give "favorable" responses to the question because they *thought it was for the school.* Many felt that if they said they were "satisfied," *they* [the School District] *would do more for the kids.* They wanted to "please" the school authorities by telling them what they wanted to hear in the belief that the authorities would in turn *do a little more* for them. This type of attitude extends to other areas in which Burghersiders see Taxpayers as potential benefactors.

The second reason parents gave favorable responses to such a question is that some Burgherside parents do not know enough about their children's progress in school. For example, the survey included several Mexican nationals who do not understand the grading system used in Stockton schools.

The third and perhaps most important reason is that Burgherside parents, like their children, are "satisfied" on the basis of the "neighborhood standard." They compare their children's progress to this "standard." For Burghersiders, the "standard" is what they think most people in the neighborhood or their "race" get, not necessarily what they can get. Thus one of the paradoxes in Burgherside education is that the people appear to be "satisfied" with accomplishments far below their goals.

The "Standards of Performance" in Stockton's Education System as Seen by Burghersiders

Burghersiders are fully aware that their standard is below that of Northside and of Taxpayers, but they make no noticeable efforts to raise it. They tend to picture the education system in Stockton as divided into three tracks, each representing a different "standard of performance" for different regions and ethnic groups in the city. If these three tracks are represented as shown in Table 5.9, Burghersiders and other Southsiders, as well as most blacks and Mexican-Americans, would be in the middle track, whereas Northsiders, Anglos of Northside, and most Orientals would be in the high or upper track. The low track would be occupied by some Burghersiders,

TABLE 5.9

Regional and Ethnic Placement in the "Track System" of Stockton's Education as Seen by Burghersiders [a]

Track	"Standard"	Region	Ethnic groups
High	"Above average"	Northside	Anglos of Northside, Orientals generally
Middle	"Average"	Burgherside "Southside" neighborhoods	Anglos of Southside, Most blacks and Mexican-Americans
Low	"Below average"	Southside; Burgherside residents "who have not seen the light"	Some Southside Anglos, blacks and Mexican-Americans "who have not seen the light"

[a]Source: Author's interviews with Burgherside students.

some Southsiders, including some blacks, Mexican-Americans and Anglos—all of whom are described as *people who have not seen the light,* that is, people who do not understand the value of education. In terms of standards of performance, the high track is "above average," the middle track is "average," and the low track is "below average."

BLACKS AND MEXICAN-AMERICANS

These two groups are regarded as "just about average" by Burghersiders. Both are said to be doing "the same standard work" and do not try to surpass each other. Table 5.10 shows how students from each ethnic group rank their group's performance in relation to other groups.

The students explain the similarity in their description of black and Mexican-American students by saying that the two groups live in Burgherside and Southside, are minority groups, experience social and economic discrimination, and are poor. As one student put it: *These two races* [blacks and Mexican-Americans] *in our school, I feel, are being treated the same; if we were being compared with the Orientals it would be worse. But the blacks and the Mexicans are the same.*

BURGHERSIDERS THINK "ORIENTALS ARE BORN SMARTER"

Burghersiders consider Oriental students not only the smartest, but born smarter. *Now, don't get me wrong,* a black eleventh grader said, *there are some really smart black students that go to my school. But when it comes to being intelligent the Orientals take the prize. They seem to be much brighter*

TABLE 5.10

Blacks and Mexican-American Students Compare the Schoolwork of Both Groups[a][b]

Evaluation	Black students evaluating themselves in comparison with Mexican-American students (30)	Evaluation	Mexican-American students evaluating themselves in comparison with black students (40)
Very much better than Mex.-Am.	6.67	Very much better than blacks	—
Better than Mex.-Am.	20.00	Better than blacks	10.00
The same as Mex.-Am.	73.33	The same as blacks	77.50
Probably worse than Mex.-Am.	—	Probably worse than blacks	12.50

[a]Source: Author's interviews with students.
[b]Values expressed as percentages.

than the black students. A Mexican-American boy in the ninth grade said, *They are born smarter. They like and want to learn. Mexican-Americans think they already know things, so why work hard?* Many people in Stockton, including Taxpayers, talk of the Orientals as "the smart ones." Teachers use them as examples of "good students." Sometimes they say their own children are not as smart as the Orientals. Black and Mexican-American students constantly talk about the "smart Orientals." Table 5.11 shows the way Black and Mexican-American students compare themselves with the Orientals.

One Burgherside student even complained that she gets very poor grades because there are too many Orientals in her classes; she tried to transfer out of her English class for this reason but the counselor wouldn't let her. Membership in the honor roll in 1968–1969, based on scholastic achievement at the junior high school, also confirms that the Orientals are the "smartest" (see Table 5.12). Furthermore, a study of the average grades received by more than 400 students in the same junior high school in the 1968–1969 school year shows that Orientals do very much better than Burghersiders and better than blacks and Mexican-Americans generally. No Oriental had an average grade of "A," but nearly 50% of them had an average grade of "B"; only 10.26% averaged "D" and none had less than "D." The situation for Burgherside students is the opposite: Only 3.07% averaged "B" whereas nearly 55% (54.61) averaged "D" or less (see Table 5.13).

TABLE 5.11

Black and Mexican-American Students Compare the School Work of Students of Their Groups with That of Orientals[a][b]

Evaluation of schoolwork of own race	By black students (27)	By Mexican-American students (35)
Very much better than Orientals	—	—
Better than Orientals	—	—
The same as Orientals	33.33	20.00
Probably worse than Orientals	59.26	68.57
Much worse than Orientals	7.41	11.43

[a]Source: Author's interviews with students. Some students refused to answer this question.
[b]Values expressed as percentages.

TABLE 5.12

Membership in the Junior High School Honor Roll in 1968–1969 by Ethnic Groups:[a]

Ethnic group	Percentage of school population	Rank order in honor roll
Mexican-American	36	5th
Black	28	4th
Anglo	16	3rd
Oriental (Chinese, Japanese)	9	1st
Filipino	5	2nd

[a]Source: Author's interviews with school officials.

Burghersiders believe that Oriental students are the smartest because some of them are born smart, and also because Oriental parents make their children smart. *Because sometimes, and in this case parents are very strict on Orientals, and since* [because of their] *National Heritage* [culture] *they were always taught and have more thinking in school. Mexican students don't have this* push *very often,* said a girl in the twelfth grade. Another explained *Their parents push them more—so they do best in school. They want to try more and get ahead.* But the evidence that I collected from black, Mexican-American, and Oriental students lends no conclusive support to the notion

TABLE 5.13

Letter Grades Received by Junior High Students from Burgherside and Other Southside Neighborhoods in 1968–1969, by Ethnic Groups[a]

Burgherside/ ethnic group	Percentage of letter grade received				
	"A"	"B"	"C"	"D"	"F"
Burgherside (163)	—	3.07	42.33	46.63	7.98
Anglo (74)	—	9.46	47.30	39.19	4.05
Black (162)	—	4.94	45.68	43.21	6.17
Filipino (17)	—	29.41	52.94	17.65	—
Mex.-Am. (151)	—	4.64	52.98	36.42	5.96
Oriental (39)	—	46.15	43.59	10.26	—

[a]Source: Stockton Unified School District.

that Oriental parents *push* their children more than black and Mexican-American parents do.

One common explanation is the Orientals want to get ahead, so they pay more attention to their lessons, listen to the teacher, and do their school assignments. One student said, *Orientals, I feel, think of the future, not of the present and want to make something of himself.* Another said that: *Because the Oriental students have always been very studious—they do studying first whereas Mexican-American students would rather have fun first. But Mexicans also learn too.* Oriental students are said to be more persevering:

> *The Oriental students are very smart people. I cannot say why but one thing I know—no matter how hard the work is, they try their very best to get it done. [But] my race is the kind that roam around the street and drink, smoke weed, and they hardly do any kind of schoolwork—that's some, but others study hard in school.*

But according to other informants, some Orientals get good grades because they cheat in exams. Most Burghersiders agree, however, that black and Mexican-American pupils do not get as good grades because *Most of them haven't been working up to their capacity.*

"Anglos Are Not Born But Made Smarter"

Burghersiders believe that the Anglo students are smart but not born smart like the Orientals. They are often made smart.

In fact, some Anglos on the Southside are "so dumb" that black and

Mexican-American students are smarter. However, many Burghersiders still consider Anglos to be "a bit smarter" than Blacks or Mexican-Americans (see Table 5.14).

TABLE 5.14

Black and Mexican-American Students Compare the Schoolwork of Their Respective Ethnic Groups with That of the Anglo Students [a][b]

Evaluation of schoolwork of own group	By black students (31)	By Mexican-American students (32)
Very much better than Anglos	3.23	3.12
Better than Anglos	—	9.38
The same as Anglos	45.16	53.13
Probably worse than Anglos	45.16	34.38
Much worse than Anglos	6.45	—

[a]Source: Author's interviews with students.
[b]Values expressed as percentages.

Since, according to Burghersiders, Anglos are not born smarter than blacks and Mexican-Americans, why are they smarter? Burgherside students believe that some Anglos become smarter through hard work. A twelfth-grade student said, *One reason is that an Anglo student would take school more serious than the black student. They* [Anglos] *probably work and study harder in school than black students.* Anglo students are said to have more incentives to work hard than black and Mexican-American students.

> [They] *think a little more of their schoolwork* because they know that they have more opportunities in the society. *Blacks and Mexican-Americans sometimes give up too easy with the Anglo students.* The Anglos try harder because they believe that they are the head of every business in the U.S. Most Anglos don't give minority groups any chances or opportunities [emphasis added].

Another reason given is that Anglo parents "push" their children to do well in school more than do Burgherside parents because they know that there are good opportunities for their children if they get good educations. One girl in tenth grade said, *Well, because the black and Mexican-American students just don't believe in doing the work as much as the Anglo students do. Their parents* [Anglos] *see to it probably that they get their work done first. They study their books harder and better than we do.* Some feel that teachers make Anglo students appear smarter: *Teachers give more attention to white students than black and Mexican-American and their learning experience is more advanced.*

Junior and senior high school students are assigned their classes on the basis of their test scores; and Burgherside students, who generally score low, do not get advanced classes, which are considered "too hard for them." They are assigned "low courses" that are not challenging to them, and they feel bored and refuse to work hard, getting poor grades, which indicate to the counselors that: *These children cannot perform even in low courses.* Some Burgherside children complain that because Anglos get more challenging lessons, they learn more and appear smarter. One ninth-grade girl said: *Some* [black and Mexican-American] *students won't try to learn. They talk and throw things around in class* [because] *some classes are too easy—we know how to do this* [addition in arithmetic]. *We need to be into fractions. Some whites have higher classes.* In Burgherside, students often say that in their classes they are not learning anything serious or new.

Burghersiders believe that the Anglos of Northside are "smarter" than Southside Anglos, blacks, and Mexican-Americans *because they have money.* They think that these Anglos have better schools, better facilities, and better teachers. According to a senior high student, they have: *the teachers that are going to really teach you something and they* [the teachers] *probably don't fool around as much as these teachers do over here on Southside. They just get better learning than the ones on Southside.* Northside Anglos use books described as "harder," but Southside students are *taught the same old work* [books] *over and over. So they don't try to learn, they don't get any work done.* Furthermore, Northside students, according to Burghersiders, come from homes that are: *filled with books, magazines, and newspapers.* [They] *start reading when they are young and continue.* Therefore: *Now that they are in higher grades the work is not so hard for them to understand. The work is hard for most of us* [on Southside] *to understand because we played too much in the elementary* [school].

In the view of Burghersiders, Northside parents have money to "buy" better education for their children. Their school budget is said to be higher than that of Southside schools. They can afford more school trips, paper, better books, "which are lacking in Southside schools." So the Northsiders have better education and smarter Anglos: *The work they give to our grade level on Southside is about two grades lower than that given to students on Northside.*

Some Burgherside parents say that teachers in Northside schools do not give Northside students "C"s or "D"s because they are afraid of the rich Anglo parents, so they give "A"s. The following interview excerpt illustrates this point of view.

ANTHR.:   *... Now, getting back to education, do you think that there is a difference in the way children from South Stockton are doing in school as compared to the children in North Stockton? Are they doing the same kind of work or is one group doing better than the other?*

MOTHER: *Are you asking if I feel that the classes are the same or that the grades are the same?*

ANTHR.:   *That the grades are the same.*

MOTHER: *I feel that the grades are the same. I feel that the smartest black boy, when he gets an "A," the smartest white boy across the town gets an "A" too. But I feel that a black boy gets a "D" over here I think that a white boy over there will not get a "D" grade.*

ANTHR.:   *Why?*

MOTHER: *For the simple reason that a student from that part of town, their parents are usually doctors, lawyers, and teachers, and so forth. And the children in this part of town are not. Their parents come along and donate five or six thousand dollars. The teachers can't afford to give him a "D" when his child actually deserves a "D." These kids over here I feel that their parents are poor and don't give anything. So they* [the teachers] *can afford to give them anything. What you are saying is that the kids on that side of town are smarter than the kids on this side? No. I don't believe that.*

ANTHR.:   *You don't believe that?*

MOTHER: *No.*

ANTHR.:   *But you are telling me why the grades are really different. Well, do the kids, like your kids, do they talk about this?*

MOTHER: *No. They only feel that they are getting a dirty deal because they say, "Oh, they have this and that and that." And like I tell them, I don't care what they put in their classrooms—that do not mean they are going to put them up here* [pointing to her forehead]. *I don't care what kind of materials or what kind of machinery they got, that doesn't mean that they've got more sense than you do. And I have always felt that black students will have to work twice as hard to get an "A" as the white students do. And as I said before it is just because the white students on the Northside of town, their parents can afford it, to come along and donate three or four hundred dollars or five or six thousand dollars a year to get it off their income tax. We might as well face it; you own the school and here I come and give you five or six thousand dollars and I have a child there. Would you give him a "D"?*

One pupil in the eleventh grade believes that pupils from Southside work harder (although they don't necessarily get better grades) than those from Northside. She feels that pupils from Southside are mistaken in thinking that the other side is better just because it has better schools and better teachers: *But that's not true. In fact, more South students try harder than the North—because the North think they don't have to try because they have money anyway.*

Despite some of these theories, the general feeling in Burgherside is that Anglo students in Northside schools get better grades because they work harder. One young man in twelfth grade said: *It is because the Northside kids actually think of homework as something to do. Southside kids think that it is just wasting time.* Another student in the same grade agrees: *To me it seems that, to tell you the truth, Southside is so dumb that they don't even come to school; while the students at Northside just about all go to school and get good jobs.* Still another student says that *It is because the students on the Northside are more of the studying kind of students; but the students on the Southside don't care about the future.*

School Failure Is Due to Lack of Seriousness

The data that I collected from Burghersiders and school personnel through a variety of techniques—participant-observation, intensive interviews, questionnaire surveys—indicate overwhelmingly that Burgherside children lack a serious attitude toward their schoolwork. At the same time Burghersiders appear to have high educational goals, as I have already pointed out. Furthermore, when Burghersiders compare themselves with Anglos and Orientals, they state quite clearly and voluntarily that these two latter groups are doing well in school because they take their school lessons seriously and work hard. Then they say that in contrast blacks and Mexican-Americans (like themselves) do more poorly in school because they do not take their school lessons seriously and do not work hard. Here, then, lies the problem. If Burghersiders have high educational goals, like Anglos and Orientals, and if they know that the latter achieve their goals because they take their work seriously and work hard, why do Burghersiders not do the same? Why do they "give up" rather than persevere as do the Anglo and Oriental students who are faced with similar "educational handicaps" such as poverty, language, lack of books in the home, and the like? I wish to repeat one basic point before I attempt to answer these questions: **Burghersiders do not fail in school because, although they try, they cannot do the work; that is, they do not fail because they do not have the ability. Rather, Burghersiders fail in school because they do not even try to do the work. They are not serious about their schoolwork, and therefore make no serious effort to try to succeed in school.**

An important clue that will help us to understand why Burghersiders behave the way they do in school is their frequent reference to lack of future opportunities—the lack of opportunities for them to get good jobs with good wages when they finish school, because of their racial and ethnic backgrounds. Several people said during interviews that they do not believe that blacks and Mexican-Americans like themselves can "make it" in Stockton or elsewhere in America. They contrast their situation with that of Anglos who, they say, *know that they have more opportunities in the society.* The Anglos therefore: *try harder because they believe that they are the head of every business in the United States* [and they] *don't give minority groups any chances or opportunities.* When junior and senior high school students were asked what makes some people in Stockton successful and others unsuccessful, many indicated that racial background is an important factor in both cases.

Burgherside parents and other adults are equally preoccupied with the problem of lack of equal opportunity with Anglos to participate in the social and economic life of their community. I already mentioned that some Burgherside parents did not continue their educations because they felt that in the end they would not be able to get the jobs and wages commensurate with their educations. In general, Burgherside parents appear to be teaching their children two contradictory attitudes toward education. On the one hand, they emphasize the need for more education: *You are not going to grow up to be like me. Get your education.* On the other hand, they teach their children both verbally and through their own lives that it is not easy for Burghersiders who have "made it" in school to "make it" in society. They believe that for one of them to get a good job he must be "twice as qualified" as a Taxpayer competing for the same job. A Burghersider who merely has the same qualification as a Taxpayer has no chance of success in a competition with a Taxpayer. That is why, Burghersiders say, they become discouraged and give up, saying, *Oh, I know I will never make it.*

On several occasions during my study, spokesmen for Southsiders protested to the city council and the County Board of Supervisors against discriminatory practices in hiring. In 1969 the City Council responded by sponsoring a "workshop on equality" to deal with such problems.

The relationship between education and job opportunity in Southside and Burgherside may be illustrated by what happened to a Mexican-American nonfarm-labor family in 1969. The wife had completed an Associate of Arts degree from San Joaquin Delta Junior College, and, with her husband's encouragement, wanted to work to save up money so she could go back to school to qualify as a teacher. For almost one year she could not get a job, although she had several interviews. Then in the fall of 1969 she was hired by a company based in Texas. The manager of the Stockton office told her she would work for a week on a trial basis. But when the general manager arrived from Texas two days later she was fired, ostensibly because there were too many people working there. The couple argued that the general manager: *did not like to have a Mexican person working for his company.* When she went back to pick up her check two days later, she discovered that an Anglo woman had been hired to take her place. Her husband concluded the story by saying that:

> *White people have always felt that they are superior to all other groups. And when the minority people begin to protest and challenge this superiority complex the white people begin to shout the slogan of "law and order." But the only solution to the problem, you say, is "education." "Education will do it" All right, now you take my wife: She has four years of college* [i.e., junior college] *and yet she can't get a job.* Now education is not the only answer. It is one of the answers but not all the answer [emphasis his].

In spite of all the current publicity on new and sometimes preferential opportunities for minority people, Burghersiders, both parents and children, are still not sure that the only thing necessary to become successful in Stockton is education and hard work. They do not yet find concrete evidence of such opportunities in the lives of those with whom they are most closely associated. One ninth-grader, for instance, told me that her father had been working hard all his life and yet he is still poor. The fact that neither parents nor children see job opportunities as fair or equal certainly affects their attitudes toward school as the following interview excerpt shows:

PARENT: *In other words, you have to show that you are better than the white man. If you are going to take a test or if you are going to interview for a job your test* [result] *has to be far better than the superior's— which is supposed to be the white man. Otherwise they won't even look at you; they won't even hire you.*

ANTHR.: *Do you think that many Mexicans feel this way?*

PARENT: *Yes, most of them do. That is why, mostly that is why, when you have a Mexican going to school, say high school and graduates from high school, he will not look—if he is taking some type of, say, commercial or a higher education if he feels inferior—I mean, you know, say he never had good marks, better marks than the white man—he feels that he is not up to it. Because he has to feel himself that he is* twice as better [than the white] *before* [he will go].

ANTHR.: *Now, how does this reflect on the way Mexican-American children are doing in school? Does it make them try harder or does it make them not try at all?*

PARENT: *Well, the ones, the Mexican as I know him, as I have experienced myself, when you start school you become very interested in school. I had*

the best grades in school from the first to the seventh grade. I had the
best school grades. I had "A"s. I was an "A" student. Once I had learned
as I became more aware of prejudice and, the teachers themselves told
me that I should not take print-shop because print-shop was a white man's
job—I lost interest. They told me that.

ANTHR.:   *Your teacher did?*

PARENT: *Yes. They told me that. They said, "Take auto mechanic." They*
said, "If you want to take workshop you will never get a job as a car-
penter." They said, "Take auto, at least you can fix your own car."

In Southside, including Burgherside, parents are transmitting to their
children two contradictory ideas about education. The emphasis they now
place on the need for good education is neutralized by what they convey
through their own personal experiences and their gossip about friends,
neighbors, and relatives: education does not really pay if one is black, or
Mexican-American. Burgherside children are more sympathetic to their
parents' experiences than Taxpayers realize. By the time a Burgherside
child reaches junior high he will have learned directly or indirectly that
"education is a meaningless way station to nowhere" because of the restricted opportunity structure in the postschool world (Miller 1967).

The belief that to compete successfully with the Anglo, a Burghersider
has to be "twice as good" or "twice as qualified" gives rise to the idea that
blacks and Mexican-Americans cannot and should not compete with
Anglos. Those Burghersiders who believe that blacks and Mexican-Americans cannot compete successfully with Anglos also believe that they themselves should not even try to do so. They think that they are "dumb."
When Burghersiders feel this way they become more and more alienated
from their schoolwork. They no longer worry about doing their homework
or doing well in tests, as one teacher observes: *They don't care anything*
about the tests. I had a child and I say, "Why don't you want to make good,
to make a good grade on the test?" But they are not concerned. The tests
don't bother them at all. For half the time they won't even try. I once showed
the result of the state-mandated tests for the three high schools in Stockton
to a group of Burgherside senior high students. It showed that their school
had the worst performance; the reaction of the students was that it did not
matter.

This attitude toward education and success is much older than the
Burghersiders I studied in Stockton. It is an attitude that Burgherside parents
took over from the older generation of blacks and Mexican-Americans,
and are passing on to their own children. The people feel strongly that they,
as blacks and Mexican-Americans, have been denied reasonable social and
economic benefits from education. They blame their lack of opportunity
to get good jobs and wages on the institutional barriers in Stockton and in

American society in general. They therefore think it is no use trying to "make it" in school since they can't "make it" when they leave school. Thus, Burghersiders have, unconsciously perhaps, withdrawn from trying to compete for school success.

CHAPTER **6**

How School Failure Adaptation Is Maintained:
A Lag in Community Effort

Introduction

School failure in Burgherside, as we have shown, is an adaptation that has developed over a long period of time. In spite of the recent increase in the desire of Burghersiders for more education, the pattern of behavior that underlies their adaptation has not changed. In the last two chapters I have tried to explain what caused the adaptation, *why* it exists; in this chapter and the next two I shall show *how* it is maintained.

Although the original cause of the adaptation—the lack of opportunity to derive social and economic benefits from education—seems to be changing, those mechanisms that have been created to sustain it are still more or less the same. Burgherside children's frequent absence from school and classrooms, their mobility from school to school, their lack of seriousness over their classroom work, and their general lack of good study habits are important factors. Burgherside parents appear to help or "push" their children more than teachers and Taxpayers are willing to acknowledge, although some parents, of course, do not help their children effectively for various reasons. But parents also teach their children that they cannot make it in the white man's world. In Burgherside, peer groups mainly pull the children away from their goals.

102

Children's Efforts to Achieve Their Goals

SCHOOL ATTENDANCE

In spite of their apparent enthusiasm about education, the average daily attendance of Burgherside children is relatively poor. This is borne out in my study of two-year attendance records of all the neighborhood children from kindergarten through twelfth grade. These records show that on any given day many Burgherside children do not go to school and that those who are absent each day range from kindergarten to twelfth grade children. Table 6.1 shows that even in the kindergarten 63% of the children are absent about 12% of the school year. With the exception of grades five, six, and twelve, more than one-third of Burgherside children are absent about 17% of the school year. The records of grades five, six, and eight are not complete. Those in twelfth grade have slightly higher attendance records because they know that excessive absenteeism could prevent them from graduating at the end of the year.

Absence from school is entered in the record as either legal or nonlegal, depending upon the specific reason. A legal absence is one permitted by

TABLE 6.1

School Absenteeism among Burgherside Children by Grade, 1968–1969[a]

Grade of student	Percentage of students absent in given blocks of days (by number of days)					
	31 or more	21–30	11–20	1–10	0	Incomplete records
K (45)	56	7	16	22	—	—
1 (31)	35	10	6	48	—	—
2 (35)	31	9	31	29	—	5
3 (38)	26	5	32	34	3	—
4 (39)	28	10	21	38	3	—
5 (34)	9	3	29	50	9	19
6 (36)	6	11	28	56	—	14
7 (26)	19	31	27	23	—	7
8 (not recorded)						
9 (25)	20	12	36	32	—	7
10 (37)	30	11	30	30	—	8
11 (38)	24	21	11	37	8	3
12 (21)	14	9	45	32	—	—

[a]Source: Attendance record, Washington Elementary School, Marshall Junior High School, and Edison Senior High School.

the school; the school may authorize a child's absence *(1)* if he is ill; *(2)* if he is away on school business, such as a football game. The basic difference between legal and nonlegal absence is that in the former, the school district does not lose its state apportionment for Average Daily Attendance, whereas it does in the latter.

The school handbooks at the junior and senior high school levels tell the students the grounds for legal absence. Most students use these "legal" reasons to obtain permission to be absent from school. When in the spring of 1969 I asked Burgherside students the common reason for their absence from school, most of them (73%) listed "illness," the "legal" reason (see Table 6.2). School officials say that it is not possible to check in every case whether or not the absent child is ill. A child is permitted to be absent on the grounds of illness *(1)* if he procures a doctor's report; or *(2)* if his parents call the school to say he is ill. A school nurse with whom I discussed the situation agreed that illness may sometimes be falsely used as an excuse; the children sometimes forge doctors' reports and parents' notes.

TABLE 6.2
Reasons for School Absenteeism[a]

Reason	Percentage of Pupils (104)
1. Pupil ill	73
2. Family illness	3.8
3. Parents need help	4.8
4. Mother late to prepare student for school	0
5. No wish to be in school for the day	8.7
6. Assignments not done	1.0
7. Other	8.7

[a]Source: Author's interviews with students.

Intensive interviews with both Burgherside children and their parents revealed that children are often absent from school for reasons other than illness, such as because they are bored with school, because they do not see how the type of education they are getting will improve their situation, or because their parents need them at home for various reasons.

I studied a few chronic cases of absenteeism because of "illness" in the fall of 1969. Some of these children were definitely sick, but others, especially the older ones, stayed home because they did not like school and were nevertheless usually able to produce "doctor's statements" to confirm that they were not well.

After making an analysis of Burgherside school attendance over a two-year period (1967–1969) I selected a number of parents and students for more detailed study of the problem. I usually informed the subjects that I had studied the attendance records and that I wanted to know the real reasons for certain patterns of attendance. Confronted with this kind of information, Burghersiders gave reasons for nonattendance that clearly differed from the "official reasons" obtained in an earlier interview; compare Table 6.3 with Table 6.2 from earlier interviews.

TABLE 6.3
Why Students Are Absent from School[a]

Reason	Percentage of students giving reason (64)
Dislike school	29.69
Don't take education seriously	14.06
Influence of friends	12.50
Parents/family situation	12.50
Want to have fun	10.94
"Don't need" classes	9.38
Dislike teachers	7.81
Language problem	1.56
"Sick and shut in" (i.e., "illness")	1.56

[a]Source: Author's interviews with students, fall 1969.

One twelfth-grade girl who missed 25 of the 177 days in 1968–1969 said: *School is really a bore for most students. Students feel if they cut or don't care they can go elsewhere where you can really have fun. And if most students are late they just don't go because three late slips and you get suspended. That is why I have missed so much school.* When a student complains: *There ain't nothing in that class for me,* he means either (*1*) that going to school and attending a particular class will not improve his chances of succeeding, or (*2*) that he is not learning anything new in school or in the class. Most complaints of this sort take on a second meaning. A junior high school student said of his science class: *It is that same old stuff I learned in the grade school.* An eleventh-grade student said of a biology class, *It is the same old stuff I learned in the ninth grade; there ain't nothing new there.* Another high school student said: *The teachers don't teach them nothing they don't know already and why come to school to listen to the same thing over and over again. There probably ain't nothing in school to do and you get tired of just sitting, listening to teachers.* Perhaps the students feel this way because they are placed in "low courses" where there is little challenge and much repetition of earlier work level.

Those who dislike school also include: [those] *who don't take education seriously and all they think of is just getting into mischief and having fun. They think school is just a place to go and meet and mess around with friends.*

Furthermore, children who are not usually permitted to go out on dates or to parties by their parents use truancy from school as "a chance to get away."

When questioned about their frequent absence from school, Burgherside students tend to give "legal reasons" first, that is, illness. But the real reasons evolve gradually with continued probing, as the following case illustrates.

ANTHR.: *Why is it that Mexican-American students are absent from school so much?*

STUDENT: *You know the best thing I think for it is that it has to do with the family.*

ANTHR.: *What do you mean?*

STUDENT: *You know, most of the families from the Southside where Edison is, you know, they say a percentage of the family is poor. I guess they get embarrassed from wearing the same clothes every day, almost every day. Sometimes I myself have done that too.*

ANTHR.: *Because of your clothes?*

STUDENT: *Yea. See if you're wearing the same clothes that they're wearing. And the percentage of them, some of them are sick. A lot of them are sick.*

ANTHR.: *They are sick?*

STUDENT: *Yea.*

ANTHR.: *Do you know what kind of sickness they're sick from?*

STUDENT: *Well, what I think is that—you know, Southside—*

ANTHR.: *What kind of sickness do they have?*

STUDENT: *Mostly they're coming down with cold right now. Right now everyone that I talk to, especially Mexican-American, in my school, they say that they catch cold or fever and all that. Now they say that flu is coming back again. So they say that they catch all these they can't make it. But my point of view is that, you know, their parents have to be poor.*

ANTHR.: *You mean to catch cold?*

STUDENT: *Yea. But the school bus, you know, it goes just so far and sometimes the students have—I guess they sleep late. They're late to get up and catch the bus. I have been late a lot of times but sometimes I call a friend to come pick me up.*

ANTHR.: *About what time do the students go to bed?*

STUDENT: *I say, eight o'clock. Like now at Edison they passed a paper asking you know how much sleep you get, what you get and all that. And many students I have talked to don't get up until nine or ten o'clock.*

ANTHR.: *Oh, really?*

STUDENT: *Nine or ten o'clock, they'll be in bed. Then Saturdays and Sundays, you know, go out.*

ANTHR.: *You mean that they go out on Saturdays and Sundays and then they sleep till nine or ten o'clock the next day?*

STUDENT: *Yea.*

ANTHR.: *O.K. What about during the weekdays? Do they go out during the weekdays?*

STUDENT: *Yes. I would say, yea, because, you know, they throw parties. And then there are a lot of things going on. So I would say that they would go out. They do go out.*

ANTHR.: *Do the students ever think that going out on week nights might hurt their schoolwork?*

STUDENT: *Yea, I think they do. And this is another problem too which I was going to bring up right now. Talking about the Mexican-Americans, you know, the Mexican-Americans at Edison,* you know, some of them isn't interested in school, you know. *They think they are dumb and won't make it. So sometimes some of them don't even care at all* [emphasis added].

As Burgherside children get older and are "pushed" into higher grades their records of failure grow and they increasingly feel that they won't "make it" in school and society. These older children are the ones consistently absent on Mondays and Fridays. One of them explained it as follows: *Well, you know, on Mondays people are absent because they went out too much during the weekend and may be drunk. So on Mondays they are not quite ready for school. And by the time Friday comes people are already feeling tired of school. So they don't go.*

In general, Burgherside parents want their children to attend school more regularly. One parent who grew up in Burgherside used her own experience to show that many parents do not know when their children are absent from school:

> *When she was in high school she developed the habit of forging her mother's signature on notes she sent to school to excuse her absence because she was ill, or needed at home. After delivering the notes she usually returned home to play with friends who were also absent from school under similar pretenses. Her mother found out about this one day when she unexpectedly came home from work in mid-morning. Her mother, the informant said, "found out that I had been doing this all along and she sure gave me a whipping." In 1969 her own daughter was doing almost the same thing and she was very unhappy about it.*

Some parents contribute to school absenteeisms in several ways. Non-English speaking parents sometimes keep their older children home from school to accompany them if they are going shopping or to the hospital.

An eleventh-grade girl, a good student, who missed 29 days of school in 1969, said: *Sometimes students may go with their parents to the doctor and other places to interpret for them. As for cutting classes I don't know because I have never done this.*

Effects of Absenteeism on Burgherside Children's Schoolwork

Each year the principals' Annual Reports emphasize attendance problems: *Poor attendance continues to be a serious problem in our schools. We cannot teach those who are not there.* Or, *With increase in irregular attendance and with the increase of student personnel changes this year, it has been very difficult for the attendance office to keep up.*

It is not only the total number of days a child is absent from school, but also the pattern of absenteeism, that creates a serious learning problem. In the early grades, for instance, school attendance is sporadic. A child may come to school on Monday when a new reading lesson begins, and then may be absent on Tuesday; on Wednesday, if he returns to school, he is one day behind but is forced to join the rest of the class wherever they may be. When this pattern is repeated again and again the child falls farther and farther behind in his lessons, especially since he cannot make up at home what he misses at school.

Burgherside parents do not seem to realize that irregular school attendance has adverse effects on children's schoolwork in the early grades. They claim that at this stage, especially in the kindergarten, children "are not learning anything"; that is, parents feel that the teachers do not really teach them, and that the children only spend this time playing at school.

Attendance and enrollment for all the grades are lowest at the beginning of the school year. At this time, farm work is just beginning to taper off. Some of the migrant families have not returned to enroll their children, and some children enroll late because their fathers, away working, do not come back in time to buy their school clothes and other supplies. The older children sometimes work in the fields until the second or third week of the school year. The rate of absenteesim rises in winter also because some Burgherside children return with their families to Mexico.

INTERSCHOOL MOBILITY

In addition to irregular school attendance, late enrollment, and early withdrawals, some Burgherside children frequently move from one school to another, either within Stockton or from one district to another (see Table 6.4). There are always some difficulties in adjusting to the new curriculum and to the social environment of the new school. It is interesting to compare the Filipino and Mexican-American children. Although both groups are largely made up of farm-labor families, the

TABLE 6.4

Interschool Mobility of Burgherside Children by Ethnic Group and School[a]

Group	Percentage of transfers, by group and school					
	0	1	2	3	4–plus	No record
Elementary						
Anglo (11)	45	18	27	—	9	—
Black (108)	73	15	8	2	2	4
Mex.-Am. (123)	71	19	5	6	—	12
Filipino (8)	88	13	—	—	—	1
Other (4)	50	25	25	—	—	—
Jr. High						
Anglo (16)	69	31	19	—	—	—
Black (39)	92	5	13	—	—	1
Mex.-Am. (27)	74	11	7	4	4	—
Sr. High						
Anglo (7)	86	14	—	—	—	—
Black (41)	73	7	10	7	2	6
Mex.-Am. (39)	94	3	3	—	—	2
Filipino (3)	67	33	—	—	—	—

[a]Source: School records.

Filipinos have more regular school attendance and low interschool mobility.

Transfer from one school to another within the district is associated with a change in household residence. Some Burghersiders have been forced to move by "urban renewal," freeway construction, and so on (SUSD 1967a:2). Between 1965 and 1968 about 130 households were displaced from Burgherside and relocated in other neighborhoods. A few years before, a similar displacement had brought several households into Burgherside.

Children also move from school to school for economic and other reasons. People on public assistance sometimes move into leased or public housing in or outside Burgherside because it is cheaper. For example, one informant with two children was renting an unfurnished one-bedroom apartment at almost half her monthly income. She later moved into a two-bedroom public housing apartment renting for $30 less. Furthermore, when they are employed, which may be more or less seasonally, mothers may send their children to live with relatives or babysitters in Burgherside. A few parents may transfer their children from one school to another, using the addresses of relatives or friends in the neighborhood where their preferred school is located; this happens if parents feel deeply dissatisfied with their neighborhood school. When couples are separated or divorced and move from their common residence, or when grandparents intervene in the case of chronic marital disputes and take the children to live with them the result is usually a change of school for the children. Finally, a few children are sent to live with relatives or in foster homes in Burgherside or other neighborhoods because their parents are in jail or at the State Hospital.

Movement into and out of Stockton schools is associated with labor migration, and labor conditions in Stockton certainly encourage people to move frequently from one school district to another. Burghersiders are not the only ones who move, but they tend to move more frequently and in higher proportion than children of Taxpayers. Table 6.5 compares the interschool mobility of students in Burgherside schools with that of students in other attendance areas.

TABLE 6.5
Stockton Interschool Mobility by School[a]

School	Number affected, by type of mobility			
	Within district transfer	Out of district transfer	In school transfer	Dropout
Jr. High				
Fremont	120	140	304	20
Hamilton	166	148	185	27
*Marshall[b]	155	98	159	105
Stockton	87	111	289	4
Webster	72	123	215	9
Sr. High				
*Edison	199	100	65	197
Franklin	213	94	268	191
Stagg	204	107	131	126
Other				
Gateway	38	9	83	15
Home instruction	40	10	39	2
Continuation	62	12	401	95
Total	1966	958	2149	791

[a]Source: Stockton Unified School District.
[b]*represents Burgherside schools.

WORK HABITS IN THE CLASSROOM

Burgherside children do not try seriously to accomplish very much when they are working in the classroom. I observed this lack of serious effort in several elementary, junior, and senior high school classrooms, and my discussions with students and teachers confirmed this observation.

Teachers tend to divide their students into (*1*) those who can or want to learn and (*2*) those who cannot or do not want to learn. Some junior high school teachers call those in the first category "the regular students." One teacher said: *I call them* [the second group] *the Sunday school pupils. That's what they are.* Elementary school teachers call the two groups the "conscientious workers" and the "restless ones" respectively, and I shall adopt these terms in describing pupils' work habits in the classroom.

Teachers describe the "conscientious workers" as students who attend school regularly, listen to teachers, follow instructions, work quietly, and always complete their work; they play and laugh only when they are supposed to do so. One teacher described Jean, a "conscientious student," as follows: *She takes her schoolwork very seriously. She works hard and is an excellent citizen. She is very good in participation, too.* "Conscientious workers" are often the teacher's favorite students and they get more attention during class lessons.

Burgherside children may be classified as "conscientious" or "restless" students as early as their kindergarten year. Once a teacher assigns a child one label or the other, subsequent teachers use it as a basis to evaluate the child year after year. Sometimes the next teacher will simply write "ditto" in the child's file. In Burgherside, however, the "conscientious workers" do not necessarily excel in their studies. Jean, for example, now in the fourth grade, described as "a conscientious worker" since her kindergarten year, has never received a grade above "C."

To the teacher, the "restless ones" constitute the "behavior problems." They do not listen to the teacher or follow instructions during their lessons. They talk out of turn and do not sit still for long, and sometimes they wander from one part of the classroom to another. Although more boys than girls can be described this way, some of the "restless ones" are girls. They come from all ethnic groups. Some of the "restless ones" are "good students," but teachers believe they could do much better "if they were not that way." Most, however, are very poor students. Teachers believe that they are poor students *because* they are restless, although a few believe that they are restless because they are poor students. The "restless ones," like the "conscientious workers," do not change over the years. A few examples are given below.

Case 1:   Restless but a Good Student

KINDERGARTEN TEACHER: *He does good work. Can make his name. He does not like to do anything very long. Appears nervous.*

FIRST-GRADE TEACHER: *Does good work. Is a noisy chatterbox. He seems to enjoy school activities.*

SECOND-GRADE TEACHER: *Much too noisy. He is an annoyance in the room; but does good work.*

THIRD-GRADE TEACHER: *He is a good student but still talks too much. He doesn't pay attention, then has to ask what he is to do.*

FIFTH-GRADE TEACHER: *He does very good work and tries very hard to be successful. He is a big talker but does quieten down when asked.*

Case 2:   Restless and a Poor Student

FIRST-GRADE TEACHER: *He had no previous school training and much time was lost while we worked on behavior problems. He has shown a great improvement and I believe he is a normal capable boy; often has to be convinced he didn't have to fight for everything.*

SECOND-GRADE TEACHER:[1]   *A behavior problem. Doesn't conform. Works hard.*

SECOND-GRADE TEACHER: *He is still a behavior problem—he has little ability to concentrate or sit still.*

SECOND-GRADE TEACHER: *Behavior improved considerably since his first few days. Also great improvement in his handwriting.*

THIRD-GRADE TEACHER: *He has a behavior problem. Could do better with better habits. Not able to concentrate too long—talks and plays a great deal. No pride in neatness.*

FOURTH-GRADE TEACHER: *He still has behavior problems, but has shown maturity this past year. He rushes through his work and is very messy. He does try hard to do well.*

FIFTH-GRADE TEACHER: *Immature if only bigger. It is necessary to prod him to do his work. Poor work habits.*

SIXTH-GRADE TEACHER: *His potential needs to be tapped more fully.*

Case 3:   Overactive and a Poor Worker

KINDERGARTEN TEACHER: *He has a fair vocabulary. Hard to sit still. Doesn't always follow directions. Poor work coordination with crayon for his age.*

---

[1]This class had at least three different teachers during the year.

FIRST-GRADE TEACHER: *He goes from one activity to another. Seldom completes work begun. Talks out of turn frequently. Likes to do just the opposite of anything asked of him. Wants attention.*

SECOND-GRADE TEACHER: *He knows words but he reads one or two lines and stops and stares into space. Never follows through with a game—gets in the wrong place at the wrong time.*

THIRD-GRADE TEACHER: *He is a word reader. He lacks comprehension. Some days he seems to try. Most days just uncooperative. Behavior problem.*

FOURTH-GRADE TEACHER: *He has shown progress. He strives for correctness. He is very neat and particular about his work. He has spells of pouting and teases a great deal. Improved with new glasses. Slow.*

FIFTH-GRADE TEACHER: *His work is always neat. He teases an awful lot. He has periods of not wanting to do anything. He will work fine with someone, but goes to pieces without constant supervision. He lacks comprehension. He is way below grade level. Usually wants things done his way. Talks out of turn very frequently. A behavior problem constantly.*

Case 4: Restless, Capable of Doing Better

KINDERGARTEN TEACHER: *He talks "eternally"—talks faster than he can think. Has good reasoning. Is very observant.* Cannot *sit still. Does not like to use crayons.*

FIRST-GRADE TEACHER: *A good helper. Mixes well. Tends to promote disturbances. Goes from one activity to another. Difficulty in keeping still.*

SECOND-GRADE TEACHER: *He has difficulty in keeping quiet, but has shown vast improvement. Work in all subjects—writing has improved.*

THIRD-GRADE TEACHER: *Has been a good boy this year—trying hard to behave. Capable of doing good work.*

FOURTH-GRADE TEACHER: *Very poor work habits. Has tendency to waste much time playing. Is capable of being a much better student.*

My study of the school records and interviews with Burghersiders showed no appreciable differences in family background between the "restless ones" and the "conscientious workers." Some come from homes on Public Assistance; others come from families relatively well off economically. Some have only one parent; others have two-parent families. The parents of some "restless ones" are "very interested" in their children's academic progress, cooperative, even involved in school activities, whereas the parents of others establish no contact between the home and the school.

Discipline Problems in the Classroom

The "restless students" at the elementary school are said to become the "Sunday school students" at the junior and senior high schools. They are regarded as "disruptive" or "students with behavior problems." All these labels, of course, merely reinforce the behavior they describe; they shape teachers' attitudes toward the pupils and also influence students' reactions to their teachers. Among Stockton teachers it is rumored that those in Northside schools spend 50% of their time trying to appease parents, that is avoid criticisms, whereas those in Southside schools spend an equal amount of time handling "behavior problems" in their classrooms. A study of teachers' comments on all Burgherside elementary school children shows that teachers regard many of them as "behavior problems." My own observations and discussions with teachers, as well as the conversations and jokes among teachers at lunch and coffee breaks confirm this.

I saw the first serious discipline at the school in the fall of 1968. One sixth-grade boy was refused admission on the grounds that his presence "would be disruptive" and he was recommended for the "continuation school," which also refused him. This boy stayed out of school for almost a year before he was admitted to the junior high school. His mother was extremely upset by this incident. Also in the fall of 1968, a group made up of sixth graders and junior high school boys was suspected of using drugs. A combined effort of the elementary school and the Neighborhood Association succeeded in transforming them into a boys' club known as "The Girl Watchers."

Within the classroom, individual teachers employ various devices to deal with "disruptive children". When a teacher is unable to "control" a particular student she sends him to the principal, who uses a "reasoning technique" in disciplining those children sent to her office; that is, she tries to convince them that they should do what they are asked to do "because it is for their own good." In some cases she contacts the parents.

Teachers at the high schools send the children they cannot "control" to the deans or vice-principals. The teacher first attempts to stop "disruptive behavior" by talking to the student involved. If this fails then he sends the student to the dean with a "blue slip" indicating the date, the student's name, the time and place of the offense committed, and the nature of the offense. Upon receiving the "blue slip" the dean may consider any of the disciplinary actions described in the following examples:

STUDENT A: *Referred to me* [the teacher] *as "Mr. Shit" in class. Case has a book called "Steel Magic" overdue since November 14th. She has refused to do anything about it. This same thing happened last year and she was equally uncooperative.*

ACTION: *The student had a conference with the Dean of Girls and returned the book.*

STUDENT B. *Offense against person and willful disobedience. Threatening to fight ————— in Dean's Office. Causing disturbance in cafeteria. "Very disturbed" but fairly cooperative.*

ACTION: *Two-day suspension.*

STUDENT B. *Blue slip. Writing in book in ink. When told to stop she became impudent, yelled at me, "It won't hurt the old book." No respect for school property or school rules: "I don't have to pay for my book, etc. etc." Still feels she can do as she pleases.*

ACTION: *Conference with dean.*

STUDENT C. *Yellow slip. C came into the room and started running her fingers through (a boy's) hair. (She has done this before, and I have asked her not to do this.) Today I asked her to stop—told her to stop— didn't, kept giving me an argument. Therefore sent her to the office.*

ACTION: *Suspended from class period for two days.*

STUDENT C. *She came into class very loud, had been walking with a friend who was making faces at me. Let her tell you who. When asked to sit down she stood up and said, "Mr. —————, what does F——— mean?" very loudly. When I said I am not going to answer that she said, "See, he don't know." I want her out of my class tomorrow. She needs some real guidance. I'm not listening to her kind of talk and don't think the rest of the class should either.*

ACTION: *Conference with student and parent.*

In the case of a serious offence or a recalcitrant offender, the student may be expelled after consultation with a higher authority. There are many types of slips within each school, and they mean different things. At the junior high a "blue slip" always involves a conference with the dean; a "yellow slip" incurs an automatic suspension. At the senior high a "blue slip" from a teacher or any of the staff means immediate suspension although the dean determines the suspension period.

A very high proportion of Burgherside children at the junior and senior high schools are affected by incidents of "disruptive classroom behavior," which often means that on those days when they are in school a good percentage of their time is not actually spent on learning. Each time a teacher has occasion to label a child as "disruptive," the whole class must wait while the teacher attempts to "control" him, writes a note to the dean, and receives the student back into class after his conference. A student sent to the dean may spend a considerable amount of time waiting for his turn since there are usually many others sent for conferences by other teachers. The conference may end with the student being (*a*) sent back to his class, (*b*) suspended, (*c*) sent to "continuation school," (*d*) excluded from a particular class or school, or (*e*) expelled.

The "Push" of Burgherside Parents

Teachers and Taxpayers say that if only Burgherside parents would take the trouble to ask their children about their school work from time to time, the children would become more interested in their lessons. One teacher said: *One of the things* [they ought to do] *might be talking to the children; well, find out what they did in school.* But most Burgherside parents already do this. One parent said: *I ask my children practically every day, "What did you do in school today? Is your homework done? How come it isn't done?" if it isn't done.* Some parents ask their children about schoolwork once a week; there are, of course, some who rarely ask at all as Table 6.6 shows.

Burgherside parents use various techniques to encourage their children to "finish school." The more educated parents assist their children with their schoolwork, especially elementary school children. One mother

TABLE 6.6
How Often Burgherside and Southside Parents Ask Their Junior and Senior High School Children about Their Schoolwork, According to Students[a,b,c]

How often parents ask about schoolwork	Burgherside and Southside students responding to the question					
	All Burgher- siders (69)	Anglo (49)	Black (94)	Mex.- Amer. (111)	Filipino (27)	Oriental (34)
Almost every day	18.84	28.57	22.34	24.32	37.04	23.53
Once a week	31.88	34.69	28.72	26.13	14.81	23.53
Once a month	17.39	14.29	13.83	16.22	11.11	23.53
Once a quarter	20.29	12.24	15.96	19.82	29.63	23.53
Almost never	11.59	10.20	19.15	13.51	7.41	5.89

[a]Source: Author's interviews with students.
[b]Values expressed as percentages.
[c]Note: Data for students in other Southside neighborhoods have been included to show how Burghersiders compare with them. As the table shows, there are parents in each ethnic group who do not ask their children about school. However, more than 50% of the parents in each group ask about schoolwork at least once a week.

receiving public assistance described how she taught her children to read, complaining that teachers did not teach them and were only interested in their salaries. Of her eight-year-old son, whom she taught to read and count, she said: *Oh, yes. Gave him eight hours and he learned to count. And my little boy said, "Mama, I wish you were my teacher."* She believed that children *should not be promoted if they don't do well.*

When Burgherside children are losing interest in school, their parents are usually concerned if they know; some parents may not find out what is really happening until it is too late. Sometimes parents are afraid to contact their child's teacher or counselor to find out what can be done if he is having difficulties in school. On a number of occasions during my study I undertook to arrange meetings between such parents and teachers. Parents do not always accept their children's version of their problems at school and therefore like to talk with the teacher *to find out the truth.* For example, one girl who often stayed home from school usually told her mother, *Oh, Ma, that teacher just don't like black folks. She don't like colored folks.* But when her mother investigated her stories, she found that her daughter was *"cutting up" in school* [i.e., fooling around] *and cursing the teacher out.* A couple whose son was doing poorly at school went to see his counselor and then had a serious discussion with him: *Consequently we talked to him quite extensively about his grades and his future and everything. He said that he's going to make an effort, to make an effort in the classes he's really failing so badly.*

A survey of Burgherside and other Southside students indicates that if their parents discover that they are losing interest in school and are wanting to drop out, their parents try to encourage them to stay in school (see Table 6.7). But Burgherside parents rarely find this out in time. A Mexican-American father said that once a child drops out of school it is hard for him to get back; therefore it is advisable to encourage children to stay in school by explaining to them the consequences of dropping out.

Burgherside parents are proud of their children's accomplishments. In addition to material rewards for good grades, they display their children's paintings and drawings, their first letters, their first typing, and the like. Good report cards and letters of commendation from school, letters showing that the child is "extra smart," and prizes are proudly displayed to a visitor. The junior high school usually sends letters of commendation to parents whose children have a "B" average or better. Burgherside parents carefully preserve such letters to show to friends, relatives, and other visitors. A Burgherside mother once said as she showed me a letter from the school about her son:

You see this, Mr. ————. I am not bragging. My children are very smart children. Well, I've got a baby; I think this one is the baby.

She got this one [Certificate of Good Citizenship]. *She has really got "A" in all her grades. Every grade she makes she gets one* [award]. *And for well-behaved in school* [Good Citizen] *and getting along with people. And my boy, he got a Certificate of Merit for being such a good boy. I had a letter from school last year, my 17-year-old boy. They just wanted to tell me that they appreciated the way I raised my children. He gets along with everybody. He never causes any trouble. He loves everybody. He tries to keep everybody together. And we just want to take a little time in prayer to thank God for giving us such a wonderful boy. And I have raised my children that way, Mr. ————, to love everybody and most of all God. . . . And I have never had any trouble, not at the schools and not anywhere. I am very proud of them.*

This family is partially on welfare.

Burgherside parents say that they eagerly await their children's report cards, and when they receive them they hold conferences with their children about their grades and their school work in general. If the grades are good, the children are rewarded (see Table 6.8); if the grades are bad they are asked to explain why and may be punished; those receiving bad grades are generally told to work harder and make better grades.

The usual reward for making good grades, "A"s or "B"s, is money. The amount varies but the average is one dollar for an "A," fifty cents

TABLE 6.7

What Burgherside and Southside Parents Do When They Find Out Their Children Are Losing Interest in School, as Reported by the Students[a,b,c]

	Burgher-side (69)	All Southside				
		Anglo (61)	Black (95)	Mex.-Amer. (112)	Filipino (30)	Oriental (36)
What parents do						
Explain why education is important	47.83	42.62	50.53	37.50	46.67	44.44
Just talk it over with child	30.43	32.79	29.47	41.07	40.00	41.67
Talk it over with teacher	7.25	6.58	7.37	7.14	3.33	2.78
Punish the child	8.70	6.58	7.37	7.14	3.33	—
Do not care	5.80	11.48	5.26	7.14	6.67	11.11

[a]Source: Author's interviews with Burgherside and Southside students.
[b]Values expressed as percentages.
[c]Note: The inclusion of data for other Southside students shows how Burghersiders compare with these. Again, note the small percentage of parents who consult with teachers when their children are having problems in school.

TABLE 6.8

Junior and Senior High School Burgherside and Other Southside Students Report What Their Parents Do When They Receive Their Report Cards[a,b]

What parents do	Burgher-side (65)	All other Southside				
		Anglo (48)	Black (81)	Mex.-Amer. (100)	Filipino (25)	Oriental (32)
Reward the child for good grades	24.62	31.25	18.52	26.00	16.00	21.88
Punish the child for bad grades	7.69	6.25	11.11	14.00	8.00	15.63
Discuss why grades are as they are and advise child to do better	44.62	37.50	39.51	34.00	44.00	53.13
Do nothing, "just look at it"	21.54	20.83	29.63	22.00	32.00	9.38
Parents do not get report cards	1.54	4.17	1.23	4.00	—	—

[a]Source: Author's interviews with students.
[b]Values expressed as percentages.

for a "B," and perhaps twenty-five cents for a "C," the "average grade." Parents often punish their children for getting "D." A child who is getting poor grades may be threatened, blamed, and occasionally beaten. I did not actually observe any parent beat his child for receiving poor grades, but both students and their parents say it happens. Children are sometimes promised higher rewards if their schoolwork improves. In the following excerpt, a black couple describe what happens when they receive their children's report cards. Each child gets one dollar for every "A," just as he gets some "straps" (i.e., beating with a belt) for every "D."

ANTHR.: *What do you usually do when the children bring home their report cards? You know, when they bring home their grades?*

FATHER: [Father, mother, oldest daughter all laughing; I laughed too.] *Well, we have a system. Usually I punish them. See! And I make them get* [hold onto] *this chair and I strap them up a little.* [Everybody laughed.]

MOTHER: *So many licks for each grade lower than a "C".*

ANTHR.: *Oh, really?*

FATHER: *Yes. Warm them up a bit.* [everybody still laughing] *And, of course, we have a—and we also give them so much money as an encouragement for the good grades that they get. See! So, just an effort to try to encourage them, you know. And, of course, when we feel that they could do better, no doubt they could do better. And we feel that, well, now if I say, "Now if you come home with a "D" you're going to get so many lashes" you see, oh, maybe he won't get no "D." You see! But this happens quite often. . . .*

ANTHR.:   *That they get "D"s?*

FATHER: *Yeah.* [laughing]

ANTHR.:   *What do you give them when they get "A"s?*

MOTHER: *We give a dollar for every "A" and fifty cents for a "B."* [Everybody laughed.] *And our second son, he gets strapped when he gets "C"s, because we know he has more ability than the others to get better grades. But "C" sometimes we feel it can't be helped. And we know that he can, so he gets swatted more than the rest of them for allowing that.*

ANTHR.:   *Then does he usually get above "C"s after that?*

MOTHER: *Usually he gets "A"s and "B"s. Most of his grades are "A"s and "B"s.*

FATHER: *Yeah. Of course, if he falls short then he disciplines himself. See! Studying more, making special effort in order to bring his grades up because he is very grade conscious himself. He wants to become a doctor and he is working toward that. And at this age he is very much enthused about it. You know, he's talked much about it and we have high hopes that he'll keep this interest. And he went out to the University and took special tests out there and the professor out there said that he certainly have the ability. Then every summer he gone to a special school over at Webster, for extra-bright children, you know, extra-smart, as they call it. So he gone over there and he is pretty sharp. He is coming along, he's coming along and we are really proud of him.*

ANTHR.:   *That's really good. Now, I'm still on these lashes. How many lashes does a person get if he received a grade of "D"?*

FATHER: [To his wife] *How many was it?*

DAUGHTER: *About five.*

MOTHER: [Everybody laughing] *Yes.* [looking at daughter] *She only had to get some once and after that her grades have gone up.*

ANTHR.:   *Good for her.*

FATHER: *Ten?* [Everybody laughed.]

ANTHR.:   *Ten? Well, I wouldn't want to get that.*

MOTHER: *You have to come around when they happen to get bad grades and see how they get ten with a switch.* [everybody laughing] *They think their Daddy is trying to kill them.*

ANTHR.:   *Do they recognize why you do it?*

FATHER: *Well, we're concerned and, you know, we would hate for them to feel, "Well, look at Daddy, he don't care. I can get any type of grade." See! That's not good. I mean that's not so with us because we are concerned.*

In the following interview with a Mexican parent, the price of an "A" is also a dollar. But instead of "swatting with switches" the parents "kid" their children for getting "D"s. The mother confessed that her son is too big for her to "swat" and their father leaves school affairs very much to the wife.

ANTHR.: *Do you talk with them when they bring home their report cards?*
MOTHER: *Yeah.*
ANTHR.: *What kinds of things do you tell them?*
MOTHER: *Well, if they get "A"s I tell them that I am really proud of them. If they get "C"s or "D"s I kind of kid them about it. I talk to them in a kidding way, you know. Right now we give them a dollar for every "A."* [We both laughed.]
ANTHR.: *I wish I were your child.* [We continued laughing.]
MOTHER: *So we have to find things that will keep their interest in their schoolwork so they don't get "C"s.*

Some Burgherside children do not receive enough "push" from their parents partly because their parents do not know that they have problems in school, and partly because they are not capable of helping them. This is particularly true of children who live with their grandparents. One customer in a barber shop said that he was visiting his 11-year-old daughter living with her grandmother when he discovered that his daughter was getting "C"s and "D"s in school. The child's grandmother explained that the girl did not want to take her advice to take studying seriously. So the man told his daughter: *Well, I can't take you with me on my vacation unless your schoolwork improves. And I will give you one dollar for every "A" you get on your next report card.* When the next report came, the informant said, *That child had only "A"s and "B"s. The teacher wrote a lot of comments saying she just did not know what happened to her.* Other black men in the barber shop agreed that many parents do not know how their children are doing in school if the children live with grandparents or if they lie to their parents, even signing their parents' names on their report cards and then sending them back to school.

Lisa's case is another example of how children deceive their parents or grandparents, whomever they happen to live with. The story is told by her 65-year-old grandmother who has been taking care of her since she was a baby. Lisa, a tenth-grader, has been absent from school frequently in the last couple of years. She rarely does her school work and has been suspended a number of times. When the school sends a message to her grandmother, Lisa makes sure she does not get it by taking it out of the mailbox and destroying it. At other times she asks the school to send messages to her mother, who apparently is lenient with

her. Then one day in 1969 she was suspended for three days and the grandmother was finally invited for a conference with the dean of girls. The
grandmother reacted with fury to discovering what Lisa had been doing,
playing off her mother and grandmother:

> *I goes over there, I calls on the, the dean of girls. And I went there and
> talked with her. And so she tells me that my granddaughter wasn't doing
> her lessons and she was standing in the hall talking. And then she go on
> to tell me that this wasn't her first time. I say, "You mean to tell me
> this wasn't her first time?" She says her [Lisa's] mother came over. I
> say, "You mean to tell me her mother came over? And Lisa live with
> me? And she don't live with her mother? And I'm taking care of her?
> I will call her mother and question her." And I told Lisa's mother,
> "Now if she was goin' 'ficiate with her that way and I'm working and
> supporting her ever since she was a baby," I say, "Now, you take her
> back because I ain't goin' stan' it." I says, "Anything goes wrong with
> her," I say, "it's your place to tell me." And I went to her mother and
> told her what the consequence was. And her mother said she was abso-
> lutely wrong. Said, "She sure would have told you."*
>
> *So, well, I whipped my granddaughter. I whipped her with a rod like
> that. And I haven't had any more trouble. I haven't had any more trouble.*

The junior high school discovered in 1968 that many parents were
probably not getting their children's report cards:

> In February we mailed out the semester report card. The reaction from the parents
> confirmed our suspicion that in many cases it was the first report card the parents
> had seen in quite a while. This, I think, illustrates how wide is the communication
> gap between the school and the parents, probably in all disadvantaged areas. We
> shall again mail the report cards during the week following the close of school
> [SUSD 1968a].

Some Burgherside parents do not "push" their children by helping them
with lessons or homework because they either lack the formal education
background or do not know English well. One senior high school girl
attributed her reading difficulties partly to the fact that her parents, though
very interested in her education, could not help her. She said:

> *Yes, my mother is interested that I should learn in school. But you see,
> that's not enough. She can't speak English. Like if she knew how to
> speak when we were small we used to go and ask her for help, she didn't
> know the answers. And like this one (pointing to her little sister in the
> first grade), we tell them, "Go and study and don't mess up like we did.
> If you need help come to us and we will help you." You see, there was*

*no one we could go to and ask for help when we were small. And the
teachers will not do it because the teacher hasn't got time for it. And
when you go and ask him he will tell you, "Go and sit down; I am tired
of your not doing your work." And in my family there was no one to
go and ask for help.*

The "uneducated" parents, then, do not "push" their children adequately although they want them to get a good education. Burghersiders
recognize that the "uneducated" parents do not "push" their children
because they do not know how to "push" them. One senior high school
student said, [*these*] *parents don't understand. They can't tell you what they
don't know. They just say "Go!"*

Another problem of the "uneducated" parent is further explained in
the following excerpt from an interview with a parent:

PARENT: *And I don't really think that parents is not really concerned. But
if you are not educated you just don't know.*
ANTHR.: *You think they don't know?*
PARENT: *I feel they don't. Truly so. I feel, I feel they just—all right, say
it is this way. If you see this book you might want to read this book
but if you never went to school you can't read it at all.*
ANTHR.: *That is true.*
PARENT: *But you might want to. So this is what I am saying. I don't feel
that they just turn the children away but they just don't know what to do.*
ANTHR.: *They don't know what to do?*
PARENT: *Yeah. They just don't know and it is too late for them to learn.*

Burghersiders insist that "lack of know-how" on the part of the parent
must not be equated with "lack of interest."

A few "uneducated" parents do not "push" their children because
they themselves do not see much value in formal education, but parents
who think this way are very few in Burgherside. Such parents include
some Mexican nationals who are in Burgherside temporarily to work to
save some money and then return to Mexico. Also included are those
parents who think that even if their children "finished school" they would
not be able to get good jobs because of various forms of discrimination
against people of minority-group background. Furthermore, some Mexican
parents do not feel that girls should be encouraged to continue their
educations beyond high school, although they emphasize the need for
boys to go farther in school. One of the best students in Burgherside was
told by her father that she should not plan for college because he, as a
parent, would not benefit from her education. In an interview she said:

I agree that some parents don't care. Like my Dad, for instance: he wanted me to stop going to school. He said I wasn't going to become anything. My mother is sort of interested. I would like to go to college, but like I said my father isn't interested in my going to college. He said he wouldn't get any benefit if I went to college and then got married. He said my going to college would just have been a waste of time. That's why for now I really don't plan on going to college; maybe during my senior year I'll decide otherwise.

Most Burgherside students feel that their parents care about their education. The following statements from interviews will serve as examples of how students evaluate their parents' attitude and interest toward their education:

1. *I disagree* [that parents don't care]. *I can only speak for myself. My parents do take school seriously. My dad is always lecturing, stay in school because you will only get one chance and learn all you can.*

2. *My parents didn't have an education but because they saw how much they suffered without one they don't want me to grow up like they did. I feel that's how other parents feel. They want me to have the things they didn't have.*

    The parents who do not care about their children are the ones who don't care about themselves. But their kids can still make the best of it if they really want to.

3. *I could only say that there are only a few parents who are willing to help their children and who care at all about education. They say, "Since I didn't make it, I expect you to make it."*

4. *My parents agree all the way that you should complete school and get a good education. But I still do poorly in school this year.*

5. *My mom really cares about what I want to become* [a teacher]. *She told some of the teachers she works with and they let me help them on a field trip one time. I got a group of my own.*

6. *In my home my mom and dad are both very interested in my education. In some cases parents don't care because they have too many other children and other worries; and if the student doesn't care neither will the parents.*

7. *Well, I feel if my parents don't care how or what I'm doing in school, I wouldn't either. But mine care.*

8. *My parents care. But they didn't have a good education. It is only up to me to further my education. They only encourage me to do my work.*

9. *Maybe there are some parents that don't care if their children get a*

good education or not. But I know of no parent that doesn't care if their child didn't get an education.

10. *My parents wish they could go back to school.*

11. *Mother gets angry if I don't do my homework. I'm glad. She helps me to do better in school. She's pleased with my grades at report card time.*

12. *If your parents don't care you won't care. But Oriental students do good anyway. My folks care—if I was in trouble they were upset; but my Dad didn't care if I was in a fight—he felt I needed to stand up for my rights. I get five dollars for every "A" I get.*

    Maybe they [parents who don't care] *didn't have anyone to care about them so they don't know how to care about their own kids' grades.*

13. *They do care. It's just that they want these kids to have education they did not, so they could get a good job they did not get.*

14. *I think most parents care. But if the kids want to learn they could. The parents can't stop you from learning. If you want to learn you will. If you don't want to, it is not your parents' fault.*

15. *Parents do care a lot about their children's education, more than anything.*

16. *My parents care. They tell me how hard it is and was for them without an education. And I need one more than they do or did. And because they were black.*

Interviews with Burgherside parents and children show that parents begin to point out the need for hard work and success almost from the first day the children begin school. This is illustrated by the answers that the children gave to the following question: *Do you remember what happened the first day you went to school? What kind of advice your parents gave you?* The students' responses are shown in Table 6.9. Many students do not remember what their parents told them the first day of school, and some parents told their children "nothing."

In addition to the long-range goal of "finishing school," parents want their children to do well in their various courses, "to make good grades." Some parents, especially those from Mexico, do not understand the grading system of "A" "B" "C" "D" "F". But they expect their children to do well, to study hard and *learn all you can.* Students interpret this to mean, *You should get good grades.* Table 6.10 shows that most parents expect their children to receive the grade of "B" or better. For comparative purposes I have included responses by children from other neighborhoods broken down by ethnic group.

Even those who are very poor students admit that their parents "push" them, and want them to "finish school." Sometimes they try very hard

TABLE 6.9

Parents' Advice to Children Entering School [a,b]

Advice	All Burgherside (41)	Anglo (33)	Black (43)	Brown (54)	Filip. (19)	Oriental (20)
A. Mind the teacher	19.51	33.33	15.22	18.52	15.79	15.00
B. Stay out of trouble, don't fight, etc.	17.07	30.30	34.78	35.19	21.05	45.00
C. Work hard, succeed	24.39	24.24	23.91	18.52	21.05	30.00
A and C	12.20	3.03	8.70	7.41	10.53	—
B and C	26.83	9.09	17.39	20.37	31.58	10.00

[a] Source: Author's interviews with Burgherside students.
[b] Values expressed as percentages.

TABLE 6.10

Letter Grades Expected by Burgherside and Other Southside Parents [a,b]

Expected grade	Burghersiders (73)	Southsiders, by ethnic group				
		Anglo (51)	Black (95)	Brown (109)	Filipino (27)	Oriental (34)
"B"–"A"	69.86	74.51	69.47	67.89	74.07	94.12
"C"–"B"	24.66	25.53	25.26	28.44	11.11	5.88
"D"–"C"	4.11	1.96	3.16	2.75	14.81	—
"F"–"D"	—	—	—	—	—	—
Do not care	1.37	—	2.11	0.92	—	—

[a] Source: Author's interviews with students.
[b] Values expressed as percentages.

not to let their parents down, as this twelfth-grade Mexican-American student said:

> *My parents' goal for me is to see me graduate from school; they get very worry when I get bad report card, yes, they talk to me; they try to make me understand that education is Number One in the world. Without it I wouldn't be anything, so that what my Mom wants me to do is to finish school and she will be very happy and I am going to make her happy and finish school.*

Such students may still get poor grades in spite of parents' interest and assistance. Students do not blame their parents for their failure. As one ninth-grade student explained:

> *My mother and father tell me to go to school but I come once in a while.*

They get mad and talk to me. They try to bring me up right (coming to school regularly, doing right things, etc.) but I guess they are not doing so well. I've been a lot of trouble. It is my fault for not listening.

From the children's point of view, then, Burgherside parents "push" them in many ways to get a good education: (*1*) advising about the importance of good education, (*2*) helping with homework and lessons generally, (*3*) supervising schoolwork and attendance, (*4*) rewarding for good grades and punishing for failures, (*5*) providing financial assistance to them while they are in school, and (*6*) making and enforcing certain rules of behavior to help them succeed in school. No one parent does all these things; some parents emphasize some things more than others. Burgherside parents use both reward and punishment "to keep children interested in school." A high school senior reported:

My parents show me [their concern] *by giving me advice and building up my spirits and hopes in being somebody. They help me in every* [way] *possible they know. They tell me to study hard and sometimes they "punish" me for not doing well and "award" me* [prizes] *when I do well. They didn't finish school all the way; so they expect me to do better.*

With the exception of "uneducated" parents, Burgherside parents do "push" their children, but their children still fail in school.

The "Pull" of Peer Groups

If Burgherside parents "push" their children to achieve their goals in education, their friends pull them away from these goals. The children enjoy having many friends, but they recognize that these friends often have a bad influence on their schoolwork. I put the following questions to a number of junior and senior high students who were selected for intensive individual interviews in the fall of 1969: (*1*) *Some people have told me that black and Mexican-American students are not doing well in school because of the influence of their friends. Do you agree?* (*2*) *If your friends are responsible for the kind of schoolwork you are doing, could you explain* why *and* how?

Most of the students interviewed agreed with the first question. A few who disagreed said only that students should not allow friends to influence them: *It is up to the individual to resist bad influences,* one high school girl said. *Friends don't and can't force you to do anything you don't want to do.* Another student said: *I feel, no one can make you do anything if you don't really want to.* When they were asked what advice they would give to a cousin from a small town in Arkansas or Mexico who transferred to their school in Stockton, students said they would advise the new student (*1*) to have fewer friends: *Don't make a lot of friends; study hard in school and try to do your best;* (*2*) to avoid listening to the wrong people: *I would just say—don't listen to the wrong people—and think you're going to get good grades;* (*3*) to choose his friends carefully: *He should try to pick his friends well, to learn all he can, to pay attention to his schoolwork, and not to get into trouble;* and (*4*) to avoid "having fun" with friends: *Don't get involved with social affairs and the kind of kids who always go out on weekends.*

A few students consider that their work is superior to that of their friends because their friends are less serious about their work. One student said:

> *Because most of my friends don't really try ... most of my friends don't really care non-whatsoever about their schoolwork.* Another said: *Most of my friends don't really try to get good grades and perhaps don't really care. ... 'Cause most of my friends would rather fool around than pay attention to their work. They think it's a lot easier for now but they will regret it later in life.*

Peer groups do not stress making good grades at school. No one is penalized for doing poorly; almost everyone tries to be average. A junior high school student reported: *They keep up with me, and we don't try to get higher than each other.* A senior high school student said: *We do basically the same type of school work; we normally be at the same kind of outing together and in some cases have the same classes.* Sometimes a group of friends in one particular class may decide to work hard: *One or two of my friends that I have in Math all got "A"s and "B"s like I did,* a student reported. *But in English we got "C"s, which made the rest of our report card look bad. Her* [i.e., the teacher's] *way of teaching is what we dislike.* Occasionally a student who has an "average brain" but "smart friends" works extra hard to keep up. A junior high school student said: *My friends are pretty smart but I tried on tests a little harder.* And a senior high school student also reported: *Many of my friends I have in my classes are* [smart] *and if I see they get a better grade then me on one test I try harder on the next one and try to get just as good a grade as them. So far I don't feel behind.*

THE PRESSURE AWAY FROM SCHOOL STUDY[2]

Students are pressured by their friends to be "average," through diversion from studies. For example, a junior high school student reported:

---

[2]The reader is reminded that among Taxpayers' children, peer groups do not necessarily encourage their members to do well in school either. Coleman (1965) studied adolescent subcultures in 10 high schools and concluded that "In almost every case, the leading crowd

Some friends always want you to run the streets with them when you could be studying a test. "Aw man, you don't have to do no homework, come and go with me." Some will say that. Friends often encourage you to do wrong and have fun, a twelfth-grade student said. *They encourage you to forget about your education and study "because it ain't worth it." They influence you a lot and you go along because they're your friends.* Another senior high school student agreed: *This is true, friends have a lot to do with it. They will influence you to cut classes and school or to go drink and other things.*

Sometimes friends who dislike school deliberately *try to mess you up.* One girl in high school said: *Some of the friends don't like school and just because they don't like school they try to mess up friends' grades. I think if a friend is like these he is not a friend and he should let his friends educate himself.*

Friends who are poor students are jealous and may: *try to mess you up. Because if certain people are trying to do well,* said a twelfth-grade student, *then the others put them down and criticize them.* These friends tell the students that school "is not worth it," that they can make it more easily outside school. A junior high school student said: *Friends are responsible because they tell Mexican students not to speak English—"It's not worth it—in all the stores uptown you can get help if you speak only Spanish." They talk them out of going to class or doing the work—to make the teacher mad. Some could do the work if they were by themselves—others feel school is for kicks, just to have fun,* another junior high school student said. Students who already feel they are "dumb" or "stupid" are also told that the school cannot help them, as several students reported:

> *Friends can encourage a person or try and brainwash a person that school is for the birds. And if you're dumb, you're dumb, and school won't help. Or, they may tell you that there are better things to do than go to school.*
>
> *Yes. Tell you school is no good, you won't learn anything. That's why a lot of them cut. Or they can give the teacher a bad time—she in turn gives you a bad time.*
>
> *Yes, some do. If it's a good friend you would want to do what he wants. They'll say, "That teacher's stupid—he can't teach" and give the teacher a bad time.*

---

tends in the direction of the athletic, in all cases *away* from the academic ideals of the brilliant student. . . . The relative unimportance of academic achievement, together with the effect shown earlier, suggest that these adolescent subcultures are generally deterrent to academic achievement [pp. 111, 117]." What at first appear to be peculiar to Burghersiders may actually be a part of adolescent subcultures in Burgherside *and* Taxpayers' neighborhoods.

There are two main reasons why students yield to peer pressure away from their studies. First, some students feel about school as their friends do, and so leave their school work to join friends even before they are asked: *Yes, they see that their friends are doing nothing and they say, "Why should I?"* If a student dislikes school or believes that school "isn't worth it" he then prefers to be "with the crowd." This is illustrated by the following interview with a twelfth-grade student.

ANTHR.: *So you think that the influence of your friends affected your schoolwork?*

STUDENT: *Yes. Because, you see, a friend, well, a lot of kids say, "If he is not going to do this I am not going to do my work. If this kid goes to that thing I want to go too," you know. "If he doesn't want to go to school I won't go. I want to go and have nice time too." Because that is the way I used to do.*

ANTHR.: *And when you said you would go to have nice time did you think about how this would affect your schoolwork?*

STUDENT: *No. Like I said I didn't like school. So any time I could get out of going to school I would be happy.*

Second, students yield to peer pressures to avoid unpleasant consesequences such as fights, ridicule, exclusion, and the like. Namecalling is the most frequent form of peer pressure. *They always call you names because you do your work,* said one student. *Sometimes your friends will call you a square if you do your homework. And after a while you start believing them and do not do so good in school,* another reported. As reported by a junior high school student, teasing is another effective technique:

> *Some groups of friends will make fun of someone that does well in school because they can't do the work or don't want to. I've known friends to do poorly in their schoolwork on purpose so they wouldn't be teased. Or, they would bother them* [call them, talk] *while they are doing their work.*

A senior high school student reported the same techniques: *In some cases friends are the causes of poor schoolwork. The reason why is because some students are afraid of what their friends might say if they get good grades or attend all their classes without cutting.* At the junior high school, students may be physically compelled to do as their peers: *Your friends will try to get you to do what they want you to do (e.g., talk in the class and you have to talk back to them). If you go against them they'll fight you.*

Some Burgherside students know the academic consequences of complying with peer-group expectations. A student who *hangs around school haters* soon begins to say: *I hate school, I don't want to go to school, I don't want to learn anything. School isn't worth it.* His grades get poorer and poorer. He and his friends may begin to *pick fights and act crazy* (e.g., stealing, smoking, etc.) and *take speed* (i.e., amphetamines). When a student has reached this stage the school has no positive meaning for him. But many students begin to worry about the consequences of their behavior only when it is too late. Take, for example, the issue of tardiness:

ANTHR.: *Why are students late to school and to their classes?*
STUDENT: *Well, lateness is higher, right now, you know, because students are going to see one friend and they stop walking and talk with her. And when they are going back to the class they meet another person or sometimes, they just fooling around in the hall, you know.*
ANTHR.: *Doesn't the student know he should go to his class in time and talk with his friends during break?*
STUDENT: *Yes, they know, but I guess they don't believe it.*
ANTHR.: *The students don't believe it?*
STUDENT: *No. You know, later on they feel sorry when they get the suspension slip. They think it over and say, "I should really, shouldn't really got the suspension."*

Because of their friends, some students get suspensions; others are sent to Peterson Juvenile Hall, expelled, or "pushed out." One student was "pushed out" because: [he was] *running around with a group of wrong boys and all that jazz. They didn't feel any good about school or anything.* Another informant who was also "pushed out" joined *a group of pimps, hustlers, and drug-pushers.* He left the group when the older members advised him to go back to graduate from school. They told him they make money fast but also lose it fast and often end up in jail or doing field labor. But in 1969, a year after leaving the gang, this informant had not gone back to school. A brother of another school dropout said: *They got their chance and lost it.*

Some Burgherside students do not know the consequences of dropping out:

STUDENT: *One thing that I would say right now, is that I don't think they know or think of what would happen in the future, when they drop out of school.*
ANTHR.: *They didn't know?*
STUDENT: *They don't know. The only time they know is when they are in trouble. When they go for jobs, you know, as secretary or as policeman.*

They go and whoever they talk to say—"Have you got your high school diploma?" and the students say "No." And they tell him, "Well, we can't use you. You have to be a high school graduate; you get your diploma." And that's when they go back to thinking why they did not work, you know, to graduate.

Although some Burgherside children report that they study with friends occasionally, most report that playing, riding about, watching movies, and "going out" are their major activities. Other activities commonly mentioned are taking pills, cutting classes, drinking, and weekend night parties. Thus the "push" which Burghersiders give to their children is for the most part neutralized by the "pull" of peer groups.

CHAPTER 7

How School Failure Adaptation Is Maintained: Teachers and the Expression of Clientage

Introduction

Taxpayers say that the purpose of educating Burgherside children is to enable them to become Taxpayers when they grow up. Good educations will enable Burghersiders to get good jobs and good wages, move into good neighborhoods, and become Taxpayers, as was explained to Burghersiders by an incumbent candidate for the board of education in the 1969 election.

Teachers are the professional people hired to achieve this goal for Taxpayers and Burghersiders. However, it would be a mistake to see them only in their professional role. They are also Taxpayers whose attitudes and approach to Burghersiders are often determined more by their status as Taxpayers than by their status as teachers. On their part, too, Burghersiders see teachers first of all as Taxpayers. Their experiences in dealing with teachers shape in many respects their attitudes toward school, education, and the wider community. The relationship between teachers and Burghersiders therefore contributes in many ways to maintain an adaptation to school failure in the neighborhood.

Burgherside "Problems": Two Conflicting Definitions

Imagine that you have walked into one of the occasional Burgherside Target Area Meetings at the Neighborhood Center. Some Taxpayers (including teachers) are present to find out what to do about "Burgherside problems" and to explain the role of their agencies in solving these "problems." Others are present out of curiosity. You notice, however, that the Taxpayers are doing most of the talking, telling Burghersiders what is being done or planned for them. Each representative concludes by saying: *I will be glad to answer your questions, if you have any.* A few self-appointed spokesmen for the poor and ethnic minorities respond in worn out clichés about the conditions in Burgherside, while most Burghersiders do not express their real views on the issues. Taxpayers often go away thinking that they have succeeded either in discovering what Burghersiders need or in winning their cooperation in making Taxpayer-sponsored programs work. However, separate interviews with Taxpayers and Burghersiders show that the two groups hold very different views on the causes and remedies of "Burgherside problems." Consider, for example, the typical views expressed in such interviews on the following issues:

ISSUE: The transfer of a Burgherside elementary school principal.

A TAXPAYER: *Yes, that principal was here last year. He was here, oh, for four years, I think, and did a fine job. Before that time this used to be a tough area. Now the real tough area in the district is over there. We figure that he can handle the situation so we sent him there.*

A BURGHERSIDER: *Like I say, that's what they always do. They don't want us to get ahead. When someone like this man there is trying to know the community and help our children they send him away.*

ISSUE: Why Johnny has "problems" at school.

A TAXPAYER: *We don't know what to do about kids like Johnny. We don't know what is wrong with him. He can't do anything. He can't sit still in the class. He can't behave even when the teacher tries so hard to be nice to him. His work is so bad. And his mother won't come for conference.[1] We don't think that his family is interested in his education. A lot of these families aren't. They don't care. I guess the trouble is their background.*

A BURGHERSIDER: *These teachers? What do they care, you know? They are just coming over here because of the money, you know. They don't care nothing if our children don't learn nothing. Whenever I pass by the school*

---

[1]That is, parent–teacher conference.

over there the children are always playing. And the teachers are always driving away at three o'clock. It's not like that back home.[2]

ISSUE: New school program.

A TAXPAYER: *Well, we know the situation is pretty bad and we are trying to do all we can to help these children. I think we've now developed a fine program. We just have to see if this won't do it. It should help the kids to do better in their schoolwork.*

A BURGHERSIDER: *Yea, you know how they treat us. You know how they use rats for science experiments. That's what they do with our children. When they get new programs they try it on our children first to see if it works.*

ISSUE: Youth unemployment.

A TAXPAYER: *You see, this is a land of opportunity. Anyone who wants can succeed. But nowadays some people just want you to do things for them for nothing. Now you see my [own] son, he is out there pulling grass this summer to make some money. Why can't these people do the same thing and help themselves? That's nothing to be ashamed of.*

A BURGHERSIDER: *Well, like I say, last year my son there he applied for a job there at the County Building, you know, he applied for a job two weeks before school was out and he didn't get it. They said he was late to make application. This year he applied two months before school was out but they still didn't give him no job. They told him to come back in two weeks and they told those other white boys to come back in two days. Now my other son there in Vietnam he finished school* [high school] *and he didn't get no job. And he said, "Mama, there's no job. I'm going into the army." Then they say, "Why don't you go and work in the field?" But what's the use to go to school, you know, if after you finish school the only thing is to go back and work in the field? Like I used to tell my kids, "See, I didn't have no education," because I reach second grade, "that is why I work in the field." Now they say, "How come you don't work in the fields?" when you finish school.*

Some Taxpayers recognize that they hold different views from Burghersiders but they argue that this is because there is inadequate communication between Burghersiders and themselves. They therefore emphasize communication between the schools and the homes. What Taxpayers usually mean by "communication," however, is "sending information" to the homes—by writing, phoning, or through personal visits—to tell Burghersiders what the teachers and the schools are doing for them and what is expected of them. It is believed that if parents know these things

---

[2]"Back home" means rural Southern United States or rural Mexico.

they will cooperate and become more interested in their children's education. But Burgherside parents who receive such information do not necessarily behave as Taxpayers expect. For example, a new teacher at Burgherside elementary school decided in the fall of 1969 to meet with parents of her students to tell them what she planned to do, and learn about their own ideas. A week before the meeting she sent a written message in English and Spanish to these parents. Several parents were also contacted by phone and encouraged to attend, and a written reminder in English and Spanish was sent to the parents through their children on the day of the meeting. Yet few parents came to the meeting.

The "communication gap" between Taxpayers (teachers) and Burghersiders is not merely a function of "inadequate information," as school officials argue, but reflects the fundamental differences in their conceptions of the problems of educating Burgherside children. Taxpayers hold certain beliefs about Burghersiders that determine the way they define the Burghersiders' problems and the kinds of remedies they propose to solve these problems. Similarly the way Taxpayers see themselves differs from the way Burghersiders view them. It is these differences that are partly responsible for the "communication gap" between the two groups.

Social Distance: Origins of Teacher–Parent Stereotyping

With one exception all the people who control the education of Burgherside children—teachers, counselors, administrators, secretaries, aides, and janitors—live outside Burgherside. There is both physical and social separation of Burghersiders and their educators. The two groups have few opportunities to meet during the working hours; teachers driving into the neighborhood each morning pass Burgherside parents driving out to work as maids and laborers in Taxpayer neighborhoods and elsewhere. After work, each group returns to its own neighborhood. Even teachers at Burgherside elementary school see little of residential Burgherside, except for a small area called "Vietnam Cabins," occupied mostly by winos and transient male laborers who belong to the "no class" category in Burgherside's social stratification.[3] The junior and senior high school teachers rarely visit Burgherside. School representatives or personnel from the central office visit the neighborhood only for occasional meetings dealing with some school crisis affecting neighborhood children. Only one incident during

---

[3]This portion of Burgherside is called "Vietnam Cabins" by Burghersiders because of frequent fights in the area (see Map 1, Chapter 2). Burghersiders also say that their neighborhood is made up of upper class, middle class, lower class, and "no class" people. Winos and transient male laborers belong to the "no class" and they are the ones who live in "Vietnam Cabins."

my study brought representatives from the junior high school into the community. This was a neighborhood meeting, called by the Neighborhood Improvement Association in connection with school buses. The principal of the junior high school, the director of the school district transportation, and a representative from the Inter-Group Relations office came to the meeting. The residents who attended were 12 blacks (6 men and 6 women), 12 Mexican-Americans (1 man and 11 women), and 1 Anglo woman.

Others who visit the neighborhood include home instructors for pregnant students, and a child, welfare, and attendance counselor. School specialists, especially those from the central office, periodically visit the neighborhood elementary school to supervise "remedial programs," to show these programs to visitors, to evaluate them, to meet with the programs staff, or "just to see how things are going."

Teachers' Identity as Outsiders

Burghersiders regard the teachers as "outsiders" who identify more with the schools in their own neighborhoods, attended by their own children than with Burgherside schools where they teach. Burghersiders speak of this situation in contrast to the situation "back home," that is, in the rural South and Mexico (see Chapter 4).

Formal Contacts

Contacts between teachers and parents at Burgherside elementary school take place either at the Parent–Teacher Association (PTA) or the parent–teacher conferences. Parents also visit the school when children put on special programs such as Halloween and Christmas parties, talent shows, fashion shows, and the May Day Parade.

Many Burgherside parents do not belong to the PTA, and those who are members do not attend its meetings regularly. One teacher described the local PTA as very weak: *The PTA out there, of course, is very weak. One night we went and outside the teachers I think there were about four people there. Sometimes, of course, they have meetings in Burgherside Community Center, you know, and more people go. But outside that I would say it is a weak PTA.* My own observations at the PTA meetings during my study support this view. Table 7.1 shows that nearly 50% of the parents interviewed did not attend any PTA meetings. To attract more parents, PTA Meetings are sometimes combined with other school programs to which many parents do go, because their children are taking part. The PTA may sell "soul food" or Mexican food there to raise money for its activities. More parents attended such programs in 1969, which provided a few opportunities for teachers and parents to meet informally.

TABLE 7.1

Burgherside Parents' Attendance of Elementary School PTA Meetings in the 1968–1969 School Year [a,b]

	Blacks		Mexican-American	
Attendance	Male (11)	Female (24)	Male (24)	Female (33)
Most meetings	9.09	16.67	—	6.06
Some meetings	36.36	41.67	45.83	45.45
Member, attended no meetings	18.18	8.33	20.83	12.12
Not a member, attended no meetings	36.36	33.33	33.33	36.36

[a]Source: Author's interviews with Burgherside parents.
[b]Values expressed as percentages.

PARENT–TEACHER CONFERENCES

Parent–teacher conferences provide another opportunity for contacts between teachers and parents of elementary school children. At the end of each quarter the teacher schedules conferences with parents to discuss their children's academic progress.

Many parents do not go to these conferences, and most who do go are women. Table 7.2 shows that nearly 40% did not attend any conferences in the 1968-1969 school year.

TABLE 7.2

Attendance of Parent–Teacher Conferences at Elementary School during 1968–1969 School Year [a,b]

	Black		Mexican-American		
Attendance	Male (11)	Female (21)	Male (24)	Female (33)	Other (12)
Three times or more	—	33.33	16.67	30.30	58.33
Twice	18.18	38.10	12.50	12.12	8.33
Once	9.09	4.76	8.33	12.12	16.67
Never	72.73	23.81	62.50	45.45	16.67

[a]Source: Author's interviews with Burgherside parents.
[b]Values expressed as percentages.

Parents usually say that they have "no time" for the conferences that are scheduled in the afternoons, when most employed parents are at work.

Burghersiders say they cannot easily get permission to attend the conferences during working hours.

Only 21 parents interviewed said they visited the school more often in 1969 than in 1968. Others, however, visited the school less often in 1969. Teachers' records indicate a similar proportion of contacts to noncontacts with parents in two years, 1967–1969 (see Table 7.3).

TABLE 7.3
Percentage of Elementary School Students Whose Parents Had Contact with Their Teachers in 1968–1969 and 1967–1968[a]

Parent group		1967–1968			1968–1969	
		Contact	Noncontact		Contact	Noncontact
Mexican-Amer.	(102)	49.02	50.98	(125)	47.20	52.80
Others	(106)	81.13	18.87	(132)	82.58	17.42
Total	(208)	65.38	34.62	(257)	65.37	34.63

[a]Source: Stockton Unified School District.

At the junior and senior high schools there are no parent–teacher conferences, nor is the PTA an effective means of parent–teacher contact there. At the end of the 1968–1969 school year, one school report stated:

> For reasons which I would be hard put to define precisely, PTA seems to have a bad name. A reorganization and reorientation is in order. . . [The president] concurs with me that, while continuing to operate under the PTA "umbrella" we should eliminate the formal PTA business meetings, observance of Founders' Day, and similar folderol [SUSD 1969c:7].

The other school made a similar report: "The PTA is not strong—there are many reasons for this. The entire burden in the behalf of the school is being carried by seven or eight very dedicated individuals [SUSD 1969e:21]."

FORMAL CONTACTS THROUGH THE CHILDREN

Usually, each elementary school teacher has the same students all day and all the school year. Thus, in time she comes to know them fairly well, and the teachers and parents may come to know one another through the children.

Each teacher in the junior and senior high schools holds classes for six or seven different groups of children every day. As a specialist he is mainly concerned with teaching his subjects and leaves contact with parents to other specialists. The deans or vice-principals contact parents if disciplinary problems require parents' conferences. When problems occur between a student and his teacher, the dean or the vice-principal first attempts to mediate between them by holding a conference either with the student or with both the student and his teacher. If the problem is serious or persistent, the dean sends a note home requiring the parent to phone or appear with the student for a conference within a specified time. One student who was in trouble with teachers several times had the following note sent home to his parents.

I would like to quote a blue slip sent in by ———— with your son this morning. "A leader, in the wrong direction. He is always starting something, then says, 'Not me,' when corrected. Refused to accept any correction, a poor attitude. Writes on lab materials, also on his desk top. Thinks that he can say anything any time. He refused to do assigned work, opened sliding door to the next classroom, would not sit down, talking out loud, writing 'Soul Brothers of the World' on the blackboard after being told not to, disturbing others constantly."

I hope that you will be able to reason with the boy—evidently I haven't been as successful as I should have been. I have talked with him on several occasions about what is expected of him.

At the elementary school notes sent to parents are more in the form of a command than a request for a conference. The following are examples:

Type One

Dear ———— ,

Because of the behavior of your child——you are requested to have a conference appointment with me. Until the conference has been completed and I have been assured of future satisfactory conduct your child is not to attend school.

Please come to my office at this school with your child at ——.

Sincerely,

————————

Principal

Type Two

To the parent of ————

———— has been in some serious difficulty at school.

The nature of this difficulty is:————————————————————

If this behavior persists, other actions will have to be taken. I think that a serious talk to your child concerning this matter would prove most helpful in providing good behavior.

Sincerely,

————————

Principal

I have read the above note.

————————

Parent signature

In the case of truancy or excessive absence from school, the child welfare and attendance counselor contacts parents, sometimes preceded by the following note:

Dear ——— ,

Because of a seemingly regular pattern of absence of your child from school, I am sending the following information to you. It is an extraction from the Educational Code of California, Section 17114, and I quote:

"The parent, guardian, or person having charge of any minor required to attend school must compel his attendance. Any parent or person having control or charge of a child subject to these provisions, who fails to perform any duties of school attendance, is guilty of a misdemeanor and liable to the following penalties:

For the 1st offence, a fine of not less than $10.00 nor more than $50.00, or imprisonment for not less than five days nor more than twenty-five days, or both fine and imprisonment."

It is my duty to enforce this section of the Code and I ask your cooperation in helping me to do so by establishing a more regular pattern of attendance by your children at school.

Sincerely,

———————

Principal

In 1968–1969 the Intergroup Relations Office acted as a "go-between" for teachers and parents. Junior and senior high school teachers pass on academic problems to counselors.

Teachers and parents may meet during school crises. A large number of teachers and parents attended the junior high school PTA meeting on November 20, 1968. The meeting was called at the request of MAUFA because of conflicts between black and Mexican-American students at the school. Teachers and school administrators acted as mediators between two groups. A crisis at Edison High School in the spring of 1969 triggered a series of meetings between the various interested parties in the school— pupils, faculty, parents, and the Board of Education. In one of these meetings, in April, 1969, parents, pupils and teachers discussed necessary changes in the school.

How Teachers and Parents Learn about One Another

Given the nature of their contacts, teachers and Burgherside parents have very little opportunity to learn anything substantial at first hand about one another. However, parents learn more about teachers from their children and from gossip with friends, neighbors, and relatives. The children are the most important source of parents' knowledge about teachers and about what goes on in the schools in general. Parents often learn about new "remedial" programs from their children rather than from the publicity put out by the schools. An illustration of this is the way in which information reaches parents regarding the bilingual education program introduced into Burgherside elementary school at the beginning of the 1968-1969 school year. Of 105 parents interviewed at the end of the year, 22 had not heard about the program; 46 heard about it from their children; 10 from teachers;

14 through the PTA; 13 from friends, neighbors, and relatives. Yet the school employed various techniques to publicize the program during the year: A PTA meeting was held in September of 1968 to explain the program; articles about the program appeared periodically throughout the year in the *Stockton Record,* a local newspaper; children put on several bilingual shows at the school.

Teachers, too, have ways of learning about the Burgherside parents and community other than personal contact with parents. They read about Burghersiders and "their problems" in the newspapers, in agency reports, and indirectly through books and articles written about the poor, "disadvantaged," and minority groups and through "in-service training." They learn from gossip with friends, neighbors, and relatives who employ Burghersiders in their homes or businesses. Teachers also learn through gossip with their colleagues, especially in the lunchroom. For example, during a lunch break one day some teachers were roaring with laughter as they talked about Burgherside students and families. One teacher not amused by the jokes said to me: *You know, the attitudes of some of these teachers are hardly such as to encourage achievement in the students.*

I have described here the general pattern of teacher–parent contact and the scanty knowledge the two groups have about each other. There are some exceptions. Some teachers really know the community and are known and liked by Burghersiders. As will be seen in Chapter 8 the principal of the elementary school and some of the teachers, to a lesser extent, participate in the programs of the Neighborhood Association and the neighborhood center. Another school principal occasionally attends church services in Southside in order to visit informally with his students and their parents. He is active in a voluntary association dealing with some problems of Southside people. These teachers, however, are a minority. In general, physical and social distances between teachers and Burghersiders are great, and this lends itself to stereotyping, which, in turn, strengthens the patron–client relationship that teachers initiate with Burghersiders. The job of teaching and learning in the neighborhood is complicated by this type of relationship.

Problems of Communication between Teachers and Parents

A symmetrical patron–client relationship between teachers and Burghersiders makes "meaningful communication" between the two groups difficult. Teachers claim to be *doing something about the problems of Burghersiders,* specifically by teaching their children. They believe they are helping to raise the status of Burghersiders to Taxpayers, and they expect Burghersiders to reciprocate by demonstrating, according to teachers' criteria, their gratitude, interest, and cooperation. Burghersiders acknowledge the importance of teachers' services but maintain that teachers are already rewarded in salary, fringe benefits, and the like. Hence they do not generally accept the obligations which teachers expect of them.

Another aspect of the patron–client relationship involves the power relation of the two groups. Burghersiders are "target area" residents, and members of minority groups; they are Nontaxpayers and powerless. Teachers, as representatives of Taxpayers and of the dominant ethnic group, represent the power structure. Teachers decide when, where, why, and how they will interact with parents. Many regard themselves as service-oriented patrons and expect Burghersiders to reciprocate with manifest interest and cooperation if their "problems" are to be solved. Burghersiders do not accept the situation as defined by teachers; but, since they need what teachers have to offer, and since they have relatively little power to insist otherwise, they comply with teachers' expectations.

Their very desire to meet the teachers' expectations blocks communication. The teachers' image of Burghersiders differs from the Burghersiders' image of themselves and is often distorted. Teachers frequently interpret the "problems" or needs of Burghersiders as psychological and clinical. Burgherside parents do not define their "problems" in these terms, but when teachers invite them for conferences they tend to behave in ways that conform to the teachers' definition, chiefly for two reasons. First, they know that teachers, as Taxpayers, will not interact with them according to their own definition, as colleagues; indeed, a parent who insists on so interacting with a teacher may be called "uncooperative." Parents comply because they are afraid of compromising their children's chances to succeed at school. Second, Burgherside parents usually go to see teachers because of "trouble," for which they imagine teachers hold them partially responsible—particularly since teachers often explain students' difficulties in terms of their "home background," that is, their family, their parents, and their neighborhood. If a mother behaves in accordance with the teacher's definition, she is excused from personal responsibility for her child's problems since she shares her apparent failure with other parents in her neighborhood. Her behavior confirms the teacher's beliefs about Burghersiders, and this, of course, reinforces the patron–client relationship, and prevents any real dialogue about the educational problems of Burgherside children.

Difficulties arise, however, when a parent who has learned to conform to the patron–client role expectation goes to a teacher who defines teacher–parent relationships differently. This rarely happens, but when it does, communication is still difficult, as one teachers reports:

And I have some who come and who just want to talk about their own problems. And if I start to talk about their child then right away they are back to their own problems. You know, they want to talk about what is bothering them, rather than the child's problems.

A parent plays the role of a client with problems to escape being blamed for what she sees as the teacher's reponsibility. Burghersiders say that the teacher sends for parents *after* the child has already failed his lessons. Why, they ask, does the teacher not send for them at the initial stage of the child's difficulties? A mother who learns in time that her child is having some difficulty in school is in a better position to help him, but teachers usually wait until the child has actually failed in his studies to send for the parent and to blame the "home environment" for the child's failure. Among friends, relatives, and neighbors, parents criticize teachers for failing to do their jobs well, but they almost never express this opinion openly to teachers. On the contrary, when a Burgherside mother goes to a conference she tries to reinforce the teacher's belief that the "home environment" is responsible for the child's problems.

PARENTS' ANALYSIS OF TEACHERS' ANALYSIS OF PARENTS' PROBLEMS

When Burgherside parents are playing "the teachers' game" they do not necessarily believe either what they tell the teachers or what the teachers tell them. The following discussion at a parents' meeting in a Southside neighborhood shows that although parents do not openly reject teachers' views, they do not necessarily accept them either. The discussion began when I asked the parents what reasons teachers give them for their children's failure in school.

FIRST MOTHER: *The environment* [the group burst out laughing]. *The environment, they say.*

SECOND MOTHER: *The environment is the reason I come across mostly— the fact that these kids are raised in this environment of low income and the fact that they don't have rugs on their floors. And they don't have the encyclopedia in their homes, you know. That these are the reasons that these kids can't achieve.*

ANTHR.: *It couldn't be the encyclopedia because I came across several homes where there were sets of encyclopedias and other reading materials.*

FIRST MOTHER: *We don't feel that this is the true reason for it to be an explanation to be offered that our children cannot learn, that our children do not want to learn. And that their parents have amounted to nothing. So the kids can't amount to anything either. Now, this is the attitude they have.*

THIRD MOTHER: *I was told too that the basic education should come from the home, and where there is illiteracy in the home, you know, the kids find it hard to learn, you see, you know.*

FOURTH MOTHER: *In other words, I think too many of our educators don't believe in the fact that any child can learn and that children should not be pre-judged, you know. They have a certain kind of attitude. And this is some of the excuses—and because they're transient and migrant workers, you know.*

FATHER: *You know, they classify this as a second-class area and consequently they do not expect our kids to do better.*

ANTHR.: *Now, I know last fall a program was initiated in certain schools and teachers were being asked to go to the home. Some of the principals have said that they are implementing the program. Now, do the reasons they give to you come as a result of the observation of the teachers visiting your homes? I mean, when they give you these reasons, such as that it is the environment, is it based on the observations they made in visiting your homes and finding out that this is in fact the way things are?*

FIRST MOTHER: *They decided on these things before they ever went to the homes.*

SECOND MOTHER: *I had a teacher to tell me—I guess due to the fact that this lady had never been in a low-income home—and I had this teacher to tell me just a couple of weeks ago that she had gone on a home visit in some of the homes over here—and she said, "Man! They were fabulously furnished." These were her words. She said she was surprised. So I don't know really—I'm sure there are people like us who don't keep on their floors thick carpets and things like that. But she said that she observed in most of the homes that she went into over there—they, you know, they were really marvelous!*

FIRST MOTHER: *She said she was just really surprised that we live like human beings.* [Laughter]

SECOND MOTHER: *You know before they did start the home visit they have a real negative attitude like, you know, we live like—with boxes for tables and these kinds of things. And then when they did start making home visit they turned around and used the other tone that we are all on Welfare and yet—"You should see how beautiful their furniture is. It is better than mine," you know. This is the kind of attitude. So, you know, you're lost, you know.*

Burghersiders and other Southside parents have developed a set of guiding beliefs in their "communication" with teachers. The first is that "teachers think we're dumb," that is, teachers do not think that parents "amount to anything." It is said that some teachers refuse to assign homework to children because they don't believe parents are capable of helping or supervising them. These teachers, parents say, believe that *teaching should be done by professional people who know what they're doing.*

Furthermore, some teachers do not believe that parents are capable of understanding even the grading system used in their children's education. One man reported during the preceding discussion:

> *We have some people, I don't know if they are here tonight, but we have people that have told us that they come into their homes—the teachers have come into them with no preparation whatsoever as far as explaining to the parent to be able to get across the idea of how their children is achieving for the simple reason that they didn't believe that their parents could understand what they were explaining. They put themselves at an educational level with the attitude that this person with his low income, illiteracy attitude, there is no way they could understand what I am trying to tell them or show them by chart or whatever how their child is doing in school. So they come in with one of two ways: Your child is doing good, she's really doing fine, she's improving or whatever; or, your child needs* help. *You know the kind of help I'm talking about—a doctor, a psychologist or psychiatrist or something like this. And were it not for these two attitudes they will not relate. They will not come into the community and actually relate and explain to the people what is going on in the classroom and how the program operates. They don't feel that the average parent in this area can understand this.*

Second, Burgherside parents believe that teachers will not accept their opinions about their own children. Therefore parents go to teachers expecting to listen to the teacher's "diagnosis and prescriptions" or to behave in ways that will confirm teachers' beliefs about "the home environment." I will illustrate this point with two incidents, the first of which occurred during my study.

Case 1.   "The Dean Didn't Get Her Seat Being Dumb"

This incident occurred between a Burgherside mother and a dean who suspended her daughter from school for tardiness. The mother went with her daughter to a conference called by the dean where she pointed out that her daughter's basic problem was: *She always says the first thing that comes to her mind.* That is, she gets into trouble because she appears rude to teachers and to the dean. Then the mother turned to her daughter and said: *If you have to talk to the dean and if you think that you can't conduct yourself like a lady and treat her as an adult—keep your mouth closed.* What next took place between the dean and the mother is described in the following interview excerpt:

MOTHER: *The dean was trying to tell me that this was wrong, that my daughter should be able to open her mouth and express herself. And she says,*

"And if I can't reason with her after she has 'blowed her top'[4] *I will suspend her."*

ANTHR.:   *She will suspend her?*

MOTHER: *Yea. And she says, "And I haven't had a child in this office yet that has blowed their top and I couldn't reason with her." I says, "Well, I know my daughter. She is mine." And I says, "I'd rather for my daughter to keep her mouth closed if she has to come over here and be rude and insult you as a lady, keep her mouth closed. If you says something to my daughter which she doesn't like she should keep her mouth closed. Call me up and let me come and rave because you don't have no school to put me out of. You don't have no school to suspend me from, because I don't go to school." And she says, "Well, I am old fashioned and this is my theory." And I says, "Your theory is fine if it works for you. If it works for you, if it works for some of the students, fine. But I am telling you about my daughter. No one's else but mine. And I would rather my daughter keep her mouth closed." She says, "Well, this theory has worked real good for me. And I didn't get this seat being dumb." I says, "You said that, I didn't." As if you raised your child but you don't know anything about your own child.*

ANTHR :   *She said she didn't get that being dumb?*

MOTHER: *Yea. Like though my daughter is mine but I am dumb* [laughing loudly].

This mother went on to explain that what the dean was really telling her was: *She was smarter than I was. And that I should not question her way, of the way she dealt, you know—that I should not have questioned her for her decision—because that was* her decision . . . *this was my understanding.*

Case 2.   "An Academic Death at an Early Age" Because Teachers Rejected Parents' Diagnosis of Their Child's Academic Problems

Teachers' rejections of parents' diagnoses of their children's academic difficulties often lead to serious consequences for the children. The following is one of the cases I collected, the consequence of which was "academic death at an early age." In the case described here, as in a number of others, the parents say the child was "smart" but: *bored to death because there was nothing challenging to him in school.*

I was invited to dinner by the family. Actually, they bought the groceries and I prepared the meal; we had planned an African dinner. After dinner I talked with the parents for several hours about each of the five children, ranging from fourth- to twelfth-graders, and they were very concerned

---

[4]"Blow her top," that is, act rude or disrespectful.

about their children's education. They described in detail the school career of each child, his aptitude, aspirations, classroom work, school attendance, study habits, and extracurricular interests. They rewarded the children financially when they got good grades on their report cards; they also punished them when their grades were bad.

These parents described their oldest child in the senior high school as doing "less than average work." He received "D"s and "F"s on his report card most of the time. In 1969 his counselor told the parents that their son's aptitude test scores were "quite high," but in his classwork he "simply doesn't try." He was chronically late to school, usually missing his first-period class. Two weeks before my visit the parents had changed the family's morning schedule in order to ensure that he got to school in time. The new schedule required everybody to meet for prayers at 6:30.

The parents repeatedly said: *He's just lost interest.* At one point his mother said:

> *Yea, he's just lost interest. I felt that. Now, he has high IQ. When they take those tests and things over there at school, he places real high. His counselor has told him that he doesn't see why he gets such high scores in those tests—his vocabulary is good and everything, you know—and then when it comes to actual working he don't do anything.*

The father emphasized: *He just doesn't put forth the effort. That is the main thing.*

These parents felt that teachers were responsible for their son's loss of interest in schoolwork. The father described him as "very bright" in the early grades: *Oh, he was doing real well, wasn't he?* But by the time he was in the sixth grade: *everything just left off.* His mother explained what happened as follows:

> *I felt it was because he didn't have the things to interest him—the things that were on his level. He was studying with children that weren't doing very well. And it was no challenge to him. It was, as I said, just too easy. So he just got lazy, you know. He just—well, I felt that the subject ought to be a challenge to him, you know—something new and different. He learned to read very early. And all his numbers and things like this he learned all this quite early. But after he got in the sixth grade he just went blank.*

The parents had diagnosed his problem to be the lack of challenge—*what the teacher was giving him was too easy.* They then went to the school to explain to the teachers, to ask if they could give him something that was more advanced. The boy was losing interest and they didn't want this to happen. But the teachers did not believe them.

The third aspect of Burgherside parents' belief about their interaction with teachers is: "If you think you're dumb, stay home." A parent may not know whether or not teachers actually think he is "dumb"; what is important is that he thinks that the teachers think he is "dumb." One parent said:

When they [teachers and other school officials] *feel that this is your ignorance you don't notice it and so no one can tell. But just because you don't notice it that makes you more afraid. Well, you might not think that I am ignorant but you can't stop me from thinking. You can't stop me from thinking that you think of me as ignorant.*

Another informant said that the "uneducated parent," in particular, will usually not want much interaction with teachers because he will say to himself: *Well, this teacher might laugh at me because I don't reach his standard,* or *I don't know how to talk,* or *I don't dress right.* Some Burgherside parents deliberately avoid teachers; they will not attend parent–teacher conferences or PTA meetings, and they do not want teachers visiting them at home. One teacher reported that she scheduled a home visit with one such mother who left home as soon as she knew that the teacher was driving to her house. Some parents do not attend school meetings and conferences "for lack of time," but others do not go for "other reasons," one of which is that they do not want to *go there looking like a dummy.* A parent is said to "look like a dummy" at meetings or conferences with teachers if: (*1*) she does not understand English *real well*; (*2*) she *don't know what they are talking* and is likely to *get lost,* (*3*) she *thinks* that teachers will not listen to her but will *preach* to her *about their theory*; (*4*) she thinks that teachers think she is dumb.

I attended a number of meetings that teachers called to explain to parents some of their school programs and "ask parents for their cooperation." In these meetings, however, the questions that parents asked were rarely satisfactorily answered because teachers talked most of the time "about their theories." Parents who attend such meetings often leave "looking like a dummy." Since teachers do not answer all their questions, parents think that it is because they are "dumb" and have asked stupid questions.

Teachers and Burgherside parents also have conflicting views of homework assignments. Burghersiders complain that their children are always playing at school instead of studying. As a proof that children are not learning anything at school, they often point out that many children do not get homework assignments. For many parents, homework is significant evidence that children are studying at school.

Some teachers believe that Burgherside parents use homework to punish their children or *just keep them busy at home.* One teacher made a long speech to a group of Burgherside parents on this point. She told them, among other things, that parents use homework to turn learning into a "negative thing." She said: *Take for instance, the child doesn't know something, and the parent continues pushing him and scolds him because he doesn't know it. Then this becomes a punishment. As I have always said, I never give homework simply to be used in keeping the child busy. This is the tendency.* Burgherside parents do not want homework in order to punish their children or to keep them busy. Their children do not usually take their school work home and when parents pass by the school what they observe are children playing in the yard. From this they tend to feel that their children are not learning anything, that teachers do not teach but *just let the children run around all over the place.* If their children are given homework parents are more likely to feel that their children are learning something in school. Yet, when this is explained to teachers, some still insist that parents are not really interested in their children's learning, but just want something to punish them with or to keep them busy.

Teachers who give homework regularly are well regarded in the community as people who "really teach." One elementary school teacher, often described as *really concerned* because he *really teaches them something,* gives homework almost three times a week. Parents feel that if every teacher used the same approach their children would develop good work habits; they would learn to enjoy their school work as they go into the junior and senior high schools.

Trying to learn what Burgherside parents think about their children's teachers—how the teachers are doing their jobs—is difficult, especially if this inquiry is carried out through questionnaires. Parents will usually respond with what they think the interviewer wants to hear rather than what they really think about teachers. Table 7.4 represents the attitudes of Burgherside parents toward their elementary school teachers in a questionnaire interview conducted in the spring and summer of 1969.

TABLE 7.4

How Burgherside Parents Feel about Their Elementary School Teachers and Principal[a,b]

How parents feel	About teachers (90)	About principal (103)
Very satisfied	32.22	49.51
Satisfied	46.67	31.07
Dissatisfied	11.11	9.71
No opinion	10.00	9.71

[a]Source: Author's interviews with Burgherside parents.
[b]Values expressed as percentages.

The majority of parents are "satisfied" or "very satisfied" with the teachers, and nearly 50% are "very satisfied" with the school principal. However, the term "satisfied" should read "I guess they're o.k.," because either they had no personal knowledge of the teachers in general or they gave favorable responses because they thought that the survey was for the use of school officials. Some parents said they had "no opinion" because they were afraid that their children would be penalized if they said they were not satisfied.

The Process of Education: Theories of Teachers and Parents in Conflict

Teachers and Burgherside parents hold conflicting views about the teaching and learning methods suitable for Burgherside children. Parents often feel that the way teachers carry on teaching prevents their children from succeeding in school. I will use the preschool/headstart program to illustrate how parents and teachers differ in their conception of education and the difficulties this causes.

The preschool class (which most of the residents call Headstart) was introduced under the Pre-School Act (State A.B.1331) in 1966. The purpose is to provide "pre-school education" experiences for children certified by the Department of Public Assistance. The class meets for three hours a day from 9 A.M. to 12 noon, Monday through Friday, and is held for 165 of the 177 days of the school year. The staff consists of a head teacher, and an assistant teacher/teacher's aide.

In 1969, when Burghersiders wanted to talk about what they disliked about teachers and their teaching, they often began with the preschool programs. When the preschool class began at the local elementary school in 1966, Burghersiders believed that this kind of program would prepare their children to do well in school. By 1969 many were disillusioned about the effectiveness of the program.

THE VIEWS AND METHODS OF TEACHERS (BURGHERSIDE)

The preschool program was initially based on the notion that Burgherside children were "culturally deprived" and therefore could not learn. The purpose of the program was to remove the "learning handicaps" that the children bring to school from their "home environment." Teachers no longer describe Burgherside children as "culturally deprived"; they now call them "culturally disadvantaged." However, the basic assumptions behind the program remain the same, as does the method of operation.

The teachers' notion that the children do not learn because of their home environment is based partly on local stereotypes about the type of homes from which these children come. The state bill that provides funds for the program specifies that a certain percentage of the children must come from families receiving Aid for Families with Dependent Children (AFDC) and the local Department of Public Assistance is the main channel for recruiting children who participate in the program.

Thus the majority of the children come from a particular type of single-parent family. Taxpayers, including teachers, make a careful distinction between (*1*) single-parent families resulting from the death of one parent and (*2*) single-parent families resulting from "other causes," such as separation, divorce, unwed motherhood, and so on. They speak of these two types of single-parent families as if they possessed two different types of environments. Taxpayers also distinguish between (*3*) single-parent families in Taxpayers' neighborhoods and (*4*) single-parent families in Nontaxpayers neighborhoods such as Burgherside. The "disabling effects of the environment" are considered greatest in types (*2*) and (*4*) and these categories supply the highest proportion of the children in the program.

When teachers speak about the "environment" they mean, among other things, books in the home, material possessions of the families, but more especially the types of adults with whom the child associates in the home—his parents. The image that these parents present in the minds of teachers greatly influences teachers' definition of themselves as service-oriented patrons. And their conception of their client is brought out clearly in the following interview excerpt.

ANTHR.: *Why do you have mostly single-parent families in your program?*
TEACHER: *You know, very often these are really unwed mothers, you see. Very often they're divorced or the father has abdicated and does not work. You know, he does not support the family. He hasn't, in some cases—I don't know specifically, but in general terms—we know that some of the men haven't learned to face their responsibility as the head of the family. In many cases, you know, this is not in their thinking; this is not part of their bringing up. This is beginning to change little by little. We see really some change now over many of the low-income marriages—which is a little more toward stability. But this is going to take a long time, you know, for that part [i.e., Southside, Burgherside] of the low-income community to change. And emphasis is now being placed on that, you know, on the two-parent home.*
ANTHR.: *Why didn't the men learn to face their responsibility as the head of the family?*
TEACHER: *Well, I might know a little bit—it's a special thing. You know most of these families here are Negro families or Mexican-American families. And their family pattern isn't in the same form and functioning as some of the other cultures that we deal with in our program. The Oriental culture has a very stable family cohesiveness. And, the Negro*

family doesn't have this cohesiveness, particularly if they are the core poor black family. And very often the man is not in a good position to manage the family because he has not been given equal job opportunity. And he is probably a dropout from school at his younger age. And the Mexican-American—well, it's a little bit the same story, you see. However, we have more two-parent families among the Mexican-Americans than we have among the blacks. It's kind of interesting, at least in this county. This may not be true throughout the state, you know.

ANTHR.: *And the parents?*

TEACHER: *From the professional point of view we are quite anxious that parents begin to see possibilities, you know, and find their strengths in themselves to resolve some of their own basic problems such as better housing, better consumer practices so that they can know how to buy more economically. So this year part of our thrust is to get the community more doing things for themselves. And it sounds kind of funny but we are trying to get them to learn to draw so that the parent really practices and feels that she can do some of these things herself. So that when Headstart does not exist she is not left again in her previous existence because [now] she has herself. It is a slow road; it does not happen overnight. We are making some pretty good inroads, you know, but it is slow. And we have, you know, a new set of parents to work with each year because they move across town and around town. They are not stable.*

Teachers sometimes describe their relationship with these parents in terms of "partnership:"

You see, the parent sometimes is a good advisor to us. She is a specialist when it comes to her child. She knows more about her than anyone else. And so it has to be a partnership approach in the life of the child. The parent and teacher working together and understanding one another.

But the "partnership" is essentially in terms of patron–client relationship because of teachers' conception of parents:

And it's very important just for the teacher to realize that the parent is there and wearing a dress of size fourteen doesn't mean that she has some bigness and know-how in skills, you know. She needs help and she needs patience and she needs understanding. She needs just as much love as the child does, you know. And when we get these combinations within a teacher things can really begin to happen.

ANTHR.: *Do most of the teachers feel this way?*

TEACHER: *Yes, they do.*

The Preschool Program is divided into three main areas or "domains":

1. *The affective domain:* "activities that build up self-image."
2. *The cognitive domain:* "how the child sees his world; helping him to name things; helping him to internalize facts that are basic for all of us to know. And this has to be done in everyday situations."
3. *The psychomotor domain:* "activities for development of muscle coordination, body rhythm, and general motor skills."

Teachers utilize play extensively in attempting to accomplish their objectives in these three domains. The emphasis on play is borne out in the large amount of play equipment purchased for the preschool, described below.

GP 1: Equipment that should develop large muscles, coordination, encourage creative play, and provide opportunities for building positive image in each child.

GP 2: For muscle coordination and creative expression.

GP 3: For self-expression in music and rhythm development

GP 4: For developing curiosity and interest in science.

GP 5: Transportation toys for stimulating block play, sand play, cooperation and conversation.

GP 6: For developing manipulation, coordination, and perception skills.

GP 7: For dramatic play and language development.

GP 8: For language development.

GP 9: For therapy and dramatic play.

THE VIEWS AND METHODS OF BURGHERSIDE PARENTS

Burgherside parents do not share the teachers' theory that their children cannot learn because they are "culturally deprived" or "culturally disadvantaged." As I will try to show in Chapter 10 Burghersiders mean by "deprivation" something very different from what Taxpayers mean by it. It follows then that Burghersiders reject the basic assumption of preschool program.

Burgherside parents think that the preschool program ought to emphasize the Three "R"s, not play. They say that their children attend preschool to be taught their numbers, their alphabets, and how to write their names. In this way, they argue, their children will develop good learning habits early and carry such habits into their regular grades in subsequent years. One parent expressed this attitude as follows:

> *I feel that to upgrade a person is to teach him at Headstart. At Head-start I think they should be learning them to write their name. I think*

they should teach them to say their numbers, a little bit of their "ABC".
. . . At Headstart I think that they should learn these children something
better than going there and eating some food and laying about on the
floor and rolling over and playing with balls and all that crap. Because
they got a ball at home because your parents is too poor to buy you any-
thing but a ball. They can't buy you no tricycle, can't buy you no bicycle,
so she's got to buy you a little 99-cent ball. But your parents at home is
not educated and so are not going to teach you how to write your name,
or your numbers, or your "ABC." This is where the schoolteacher play his
part. But if you can't get somebody in the school to teach you because
they think they're going to learn you the things you can learn at home
then you're lost.

It is said that on the Northside, Stockton children at day-care centers
learn "their numbers" and "their ABC." The parent quoted above concluded by saying: *I went to day-care center there and those kids at day-*
care centers—they weren't laying on the ground playing—they were sitting
up there saying ABCDEFG, this is what they were doing.

Some parents are surprised that one of the things that children are learning
in school is "to get along together." One mother asked: *Tell me, who can*
get along better than children? A grandmother got very upset while discussing this with me; she said that these children will experience confusion
if teachers teach them to behave one way and their parents teach them
another way.

Burgherside parents also criticize teachers in the kindergarten and the
primary grades, which, according to Burghersiders, are the crucial years
in children's education. If a child is taught properly during these early
years he will have a solid foundation in his education, as he would if taught
properly during the preschool years. Their view is that teachers should
emphasize the Three "R"s at this stage. Several parents reported that, until
a year or two before, children were not taught their "ABC"s until the third
grade. Most Burghersiders consider this to be too late to help the children
to read. One mother asked me:

Do you know, you're in the third grade before you even say "ABC"?
And you can't tell me that you can learn to read without learning your
"ABC." Children should start learning their "ABC" and much of their
numbers and to write their names in kindergarten. And by the time
you're in first grade you should be able to read two or three books while
you are in first grade.

Burghersiders believe that Taxpayers' children in Northside learn to read in the first grade. It is said that Northside children *finish two or three books* by the time they complete first grade *because they learned their "ABC" in the kindergarten.* But, according to some parents, in Burgherside teachers do not think that they should teach children to learn to read; instead, they are "baby-sitting."

According to some teachers, Burgherside parents do not really know what is going on in the classroom. However, much of what the parents say is confirmed by some teachers I interviewed. A former first-grade teacher reported that kindergarten teachers began to teach children the alphabet and counting only in the 1968–69 school year:

> *Now I know this was the case because in previous years I would get children in my first-grade class who had no knowledge of the alphabet unless their parents had introduced to them their alphabet and counting a little bit ahead; but usually I had to try to teach them. But this year they seem like they're trying to do a beautiful job. They're working with the children on their alphabets and numbers and making short stories. This is what I think they should have been doing all along.*

A few teachers agree that in a place like Burgherside it makes a difference to the child's progress if he learns his alphabet before entering the first grade: *Oh, yes, I did notice this—that children that came in, that started the first grade who already had knowledge of the alphabet, they made better readers. It helped.*

Teachers and Burghersiders disagree about the educational needs of Burgherside children, and it is the view of the teachers that is made explicit and that usually prevails. Teachers construct "models" of what children are like, "models" based for the most part on income level, education, percentage of children on Public Assistance, and ethnic composition—the "independent variables" that influence children's achievement in school. They check their models not against real life in Burgherside, but against reports of public agencies and against similar models constructed in other school districts, and inventories of assumed characteristics of "deprived children" or "disadvantaged children" provided by social scientists. All these form the basis on which new remedial programs are created to solve the educational problems in Burgherside. Burghersiders themselves play hardly any role in the formulation of the programs.

One aspect of the bilingual program illustrates the divergent views of parents and experts on how the neighborhood children should be educated. Parents say they want their children to start learning the alphabet in pre-school, to know the alphabet in kindergarten, and by the time they finish the first grade, to have completed two or three books. When the bilingual program was introduced the "experts" recommended that the first-grade pupils should not be introduced to their reader until March, a few months before the school year was over. This led some parents to oppose the program. As one informant pointed out: *Well, now, if they put them off to start on the reader in March how long would they be on the reader from March until June?*

Inability to read is one of the most serious educational handicaps of Burgherside children at all school levels. Parents' explanation of this is that teachers did not teach their children basic reading skills "at the first stage." Some informants pointed out that children usually want to learn to read as soon as they go to school: *Even the first day when the children start school you know they come to school and they want a little book.* Teachers, on the other hand, feel that a child must reach a certain "readiness" before he begins to learn to read from the book.

Some of the things which I have described for the elementary school also apply at the junior and senior high schools. I have described the situation at the preschool and primary grades because this is the level where Burghersiders know most about their teachers. It is also the level they consider very crucial in their children's education. Parents know very little of classroom teaching in the junior and senior high schools; they say that their children are not learning anything—but will not discuss this in detail.

"Some Teachers Don't Belong Here"

Burgherside parents believe that some teachers should never have been sent to teach their children because: *They do not have the right kind of attitude.* These parents base their objections on actual experiences they have had with specific teachers. There were probably about three or four such teachers in 1969. Burghersiders objected to these teachers because (*1*) they did not believe Burgherside children could learn as fast as other children and (*2*) they did not have the right attitude toward the community in general. The following excerpt concerns the encounter of parents with a teacher who believes that Burgherside children are slow.

MOTHER: *Well, there are really two teachers who don't belong here. You know who I'm taking about, but there is two there. There is one teacher we went down there to her class because Lena Mendoza and I wanted to talk to this teacher about Lena's little girl. And Lena told this teacher, "Well, Ann does not like to sit apart from the other twin. They like to sit together, but I think they will learn more if they sit separately." And the teacher said, "Mrs. Mendoza, it is good for them to sit together because they don't like to talk." But Mrs. Mendoza, she knows her daughter but this lady doesn't think so. Mrs. Mendoza told the teacher, "No, I rather they don't sit together." The teacher said, "Oh, I don't know; I don't think it matters. Kids here in Burgherside is a little slow anyway. But I just came here from Texas."* And I asked her, *"How do you know they are slow?"* And she said, *"That's what I heard."*

ANTHR.: *She said that the children in Burgherside are slow anyway?*

MOTHER: *Anyway. And I said, "You came into this school with the wrong attitude."*

SON: *She really did.*

MOTHER: *You came here with the attitude that they are slow anyway. But who told you that?" She said, "This was at the school, you know the Unified School here." And you know, she got it from the administration that they are slow.*

ANTHR.: *Oh, no!*

MOTHER: *And I said, "You haven't got the right attitude to teach here." And she said, "Do you have any children in this school?" And I said, "No. Thank God that I don't." And she said, "Well, I don't know too much about it because I just came from Texas." And I said, "If you just came from Texas you should keep your mouth closed." I feel that they shouldn't let in that kind of teachers. If a teacher came into a classroom with that kind of attitude she is not going to teach because in her attitude she feels that they are slow anyway.*

SON: *Because she is going to teach slow. She is not going to come with all the ways she learned to teach where she came from.*

MOTHER: *She is going to come with the attitude, "They're slow, so I'm not going to work hard today." That's how she is coming in.*

ANTHR.: *Well, I think that is not a good attitude.*

MOTHER: *And this is the kind of attitudes that they have in this part of town. Like, "This kid isn't learning and I'm not going to put much effort into it because they were below reading average last year."*

The second illustration of teachers who "do not belong" in Burgherside is an incident that took place in November 1968. Two elementary school teachers are involved. One of the two teachers had given her class some homework, asking them to find out what happened on November 23, 1963.[5] One Mexican-American girl who did not hear the instructions properly went home and told her parents that their teacher wanted them to find out what was going to happen on November 23, 1968. Her mother had a Mexican-American friend who had an Anglo friend who said she had received a threatening note reading, "You Whities are going to be killed." This mother immediately connected the teacher's supposed assignment and the threatening letter written to her friend's friend. So next morning she went

---

[5] The date of the assassination of President Kennedy.

with her daughter to the school to find out if it was true that "whities" were really to be killed on November 23. The school secretary explained to this mother what the assignment really was.

The rumor continued to spread about the plot to kill "whities." The teacher who gave the assignment was among the most frightened teachers. Three days later the rumor spread to some agency offices downtown. One agency released an employee from Burgherside to investigate the rumored plot to kill "whities." This man and I spent the day investigating the "plot" in Burgherside and elsewhere in Southside. Some Burghersiders, when questioned, commented: *You people at school are always trying to start something. I didn't hear nothing.* One man told me: *Yea. And when they start something like riot they blame it on poor colored folks and Mexicans. You just wait and see.*

At lunch period on November 22nd I reported to the teachers that there was no substance to the rumor and explained how the rumor started, beginning with the teacher's assignment. However, the next morning when I got to school about 8:25 A.M. I found that someone from the central administration office had been "stationed" at the school at the request of two teachers who still believed that "whities" were going to be killed. These teachers, including the woman who gave the assignment, insisted that unless someone came down from the central office to protect them they would not report for work.

November 23, 1968, passed without incident in Burgherside. A few days later, while talking with another teacher, I learned that the two teachers who had asked for protection from the central office came to school on November 23 armed with knives and other weapons. My informant asked: *Can you imagine teachers bringing knives to protect themselves from grade-school students?* Then a new rumor spread in the community about these teachers.

Teachers frequently explain the school failures of Burgherside children as due to their background, "their home environment." Burghersiders say that their children's failures are due partly to "the bad attitudes of teachers." Parents and teachers blame each other, but the children who are caught in the middle believe their parents more than their teachers, thus reducing the possible influence of teachers in classroom learning situations.

Teachers, Pupils, and Learning in Burgherside

A close study of teacher–pupil relationship in Burgherside shows that while quantitatively different from teacher–parent relationship, both are characterized by social distance, mutual stereotyping, and lack of effective communication. The mutual attitudes of teachers and parents just discussed therefore extend to teacher–pupil relationship. I have already indicated that teachers think that Burgherside children cannot learn because they are "culturally deprived" or "culturally disadvantaged." In the last chapter I pointed out some other problems that exist in the relationship between teachers and Burgherside children. For example, many children exhibit what teachers regard as "disruptive behavior," that is, classroom behavior that does not permit them to carry on their teaching. Teachers feel that in order to teach they must "control" such behavior and this often leads the class away from the planned lessons. To simplify their relationship with the children teachers tend to classify them as to whether they are "restless" or "conscientious" students, whether they are "Sunday school" (i.e., non-serious) or "regular" (i.e., serious) students. Such classifications form the basis of mutual stereotyping and interaction between teachers and students. In this section I want to indicate further how the relationship between teachers and students contributes to maintain the school-failure adaptation in Burgherside.

The Regular, the Substitute, the Novice, and the "Battle Fatigued"

During the high school crisis in the spring of 1969, one teacher went so far as to suggest that it was because: *only 5% of the students (were) teachable.* The rest, according to him, were *disruptive and not interested in learning.* But teachers also contribute to the disruptive behavior in the classrooms, especially by the way they manage their classes and teach their lessons.

Many teachers are trying to find new ways of making their teaching more effective. During the same crisis at the high school, I picked up a "list of classroom techniques that are being used" from a waste-paper basket in one school. It was apparently compiled for and addressed to a higher authority in the school administration; it was accompanied by a note, "I am sure you'll find many creative and interesting ideas." Each teacher described his or her approach to classroom organization, management, and teaching. Here are a few examples.

TEACHER 1: *I have broken the classroom down into four groups of activities at one time. Each group is self-contained with leader and materials needed. If a student finishes a project he or she may contact another student to trade places.*

A minimum of two projects is required during a three week period. The students may pick up projects which they wish to do. I have found the students work better under this type [of] atmosphere. They seem to be more responsive, work better, and produce more. So far most of the students have done three or more projects in the allotted time. They also seem to take more pride in their work.

TEACHER 2: *With a student population make-up such as ours, I find the greatest obstacle is in reading ability. Therefore, in order to overcome this deficiency, I stressed conceptual instruction which is based on two methods: (a) Use as much visual aid as possible and summarize when necessary, which not only serves as reading materials but helps students to recall concepts; and (b) physical contact with apparatus and experiments. For students that are incapable to follow directions, demonstrations are performed and explained in which they are taught to do a simple write-up which helps them to express themselves, and, for capable students, they do experiments themselves and have to follow up with an exact write-up. The objective for this type of instruction is to teach students to express visual concepts in their own words.*

TEACHER 3: *I am not trying anything new—except I find myself more tolerant of situations. Whether this is a measurement of the proper way to teach or not I have not as yet come to a conclusion.*

At the elementary school, most teachers break up their classes into ability groups in certain subjects, especially reading. The range of proficiency in some subjects is such that some pupils from one grade usually join with pupils in another grade above or below them. In a third-grade class, for example, the teacher "discovered by use of a reading diagnostic" that the reading levels of her pupils were as shown in Table 7.5.

TABLE 7.5
Third-Grade Reading Levels

Number of children	Reading level
14	3rd grade
7	2nd grade
7	1st grade

[a]Source: Author's observation at a Parent–Teacher meeting, fall, 1969.

Teachers believe that pupils placed in "ability groups" will learn more. The teachers consider this arrangement particularly helpful to "slow" pupils or those who have language difficulties; slower children can start at their own levels while faster children can begin at a higher level. Dividing the children into "ability" groups also allows more individual participation. Teacher aides and/or student teachers (Teachers' Corps) can help the teacher supervise the groups. Some children who need special attention are taken out of the classroom and given additional help. Volunteer tutors sometimes work with individual pupils.

Various types of classroom arrangements under a mature and able teacher can lead to effective teaching and learning. But under new, inexperienced, or substitute teachers the classroom often becomes chaotic so that the children do not learn most of the time. For instance, one new and inexperienced teacher arranged his class in a circular formation with himself sitting at the center. This teacher was never able to teach his whole class at a time; when he faced one section the students behind him would start fighting and throwing things at one another, and when he turned around to quiet them, the group now behind him would start fighting and throwing things. As he tried to quiet one group after another the pupils laughed, left their places, and ran around the room, pushing chairs and tables and throwing books and pencils. My own observation was confirmed by a number of informants.

With substitute teachers (and they are many in Burgherside schools) the problem of classroom management is compounded by pupils' expectations. Most pupils regard class periods with substitute teachers as free periods when no serious teaching or learning will take place.

Another type of "teacher problem" in Burgherside schools is "battle fatigue." One school report describes this problem as follows:

> It seems to me that it is time to examine the possibility of rotation of teachers. Many people—and I am one of them— tend to become "stale" after a given number of years on the same job. Additionally, in terms of the teaching staff of a school such as this, there are cases of "battle fatigue." I therefore suggest that any teacher who has worked in the same setting for ten or more years should be re-assigned into a different type of situation, unless both the teacher and the principal request a waiver of re-assignment. I can think of at least five teachers in my school, all good teachers, but potentially better ones, who would fit this category and profit by the experience suggested above.

One dean commented:

> It is felt that more work can be done in this area [counseling faculty] during the coming year, with a very small percentage of the faculty since the great percentage of office referrals came from a very small percentage of the group. 14% of the teachers made 45% (just under 1000) of the total referrals for the year. [SUSD 1969c.]

Another dean added in this same report:

> This was a particularly busy and frustrating year. . . . Part of this was a reflection of the troubled times in which we live. . . . Part was the result of a few weak teachers and their inability to understand and/or control the students [SUSD 1969c].

The following year in the same school 14% of the teachers wrote nearly 50% of the referrals.

Teachers as a whole are divided on the issue of classroom controls for effective teaching and learning. Some believe that better control can be achieved through "in-service" training that will help them understand the "disadvantaged youth in general, and black and Chicano youth in particular." Others argue that effective classroom management can be achieved by insisting on "law and order" through "clamping down" on students who do not obey rules in the classroom. Following the school crisis of 1969, the "law and order" group of teachers increased in number and persistence. Subsequently many students were being sent to the dean's office for "defiance of authority." The Annual Report of one school comments:

> This is the point at which feelings of "law and order" began filtering through the faculty, and people who were at one time claiming understanding of the students that generally make up our student body began taking stands that the administration was falling down in dealing severely with those students involved in the protests. Some of these people had become even permissive (following in-service training) in handling their own classes. Communication began to disintegrate, and faculty room gossip began to take over, and a divided faculty was the result.

The report concluded by asking:

> Are we going to continue letting some teachers conduct their classes in a "slip-shod" manner, taking for granted those that are doing a fine, conscientious job?

"BUDDY-BUDDY" RELATIONSHIP

One type of faculty-student relationship that affects students' behavior is what some informants call "buddy-buddy"; it can be expressed in three ways. (1) A teacher may "buddy-buddy" with the students through excessive permissiveness. Such a teacher usually makes no attempt to enforce school rules of conduct. He often does not understand when students need real guidance. This type of "buddy-buddy" relationship frequently occurs after some "in-service training." (2) An Anglo teacher may "buddy-buddy" with minority students to demonstrate publicly to his potential critics that he is not "prejudiced," that he really likes the students. One informant described a female teacher who, whenever she saw an untidily dressed minority student, would put her arm around him and say to someone: *Isn't he beautiful?* Minority students generally think of such a teacher as "phony." (3) A teacher may "buddy-buddy" with the students because he wants to be accepted by them. The teacher tries to behave in a way which he thinks the students will approve—he "tries to be at their level." This is done by a teacher who has experienced some difficulty in managing his classes. He believes that if he is "at their level" they will cooperate. It usually does not work.

"Buddy-buddy" relationships have some negative consequences. They prevent teachers from detecting when students need guidance. Students come to regard the "buddy-buddy" teachers as "good guys" and others as the "bad guys." Also, students take advantage of "buddy-buddy" relationships to do things they should not, and this creates more "behavior problems" both inside and outside the classroom.

How Teachers Contribute to the Notion of "Average Grade"

In Chapter 5 I indicated that Burghersiders are content to make what they call the "average grade" or Burgherside "standard grade," that is, a "C" or "D" grade. Teachers contribute to the existence of this notion among Burghersiders. It appears that at least at the elementary level, teachers tend to give the same kind of grade to a student year after year whether or not he worked for it. The result is that children tend not to work hard because they know they will get the same grade whether they work or not. Furthermore, by the time the children leave the elementary school they have not learned to associate a certain amount of work with a certain type of grade.

Some Taxpayers and some Burghersiders believe that the second grade is the turning point in the academic career of many Burgherside children. Taxpayers claim that future dropouts can be distinguished at the second grade and Burghersiders claim that after the second grade their children's school achievement declines.

The Taxpayers' view came to light one day when I was attending a meeting with some of them and someone announced that teachers now believe they can predict a future school dropout in the second grade. Some people at the meeting responded to it as good news: If dropouts can be predicted at that stage then it is possible to provide "remedial treatment" to prevent it. One person even suggested that such children should be removed from "regular" classes and given "remedial treatment." Nobody knew for certain the basis of the prediction but the discussion ended with Taxpayers agreeing that the determining factor is the "background of the children."

The belief that the school achievement of their children begins to decline after second grade was expressed to me by several Burghersiders, who maintained that a child attains his best performance during the second grade, after which his schoolwork progressively deteriorates for the remainder of his school career. Using this theory the Neighborhood Association insisted in 1967 that children should be chosen for the Upward Bound Program on the basis of their achievement in second grade, rather than their junior and senior high school records.

The views expressed by both Taxpayers and Burghersiders about children in second grade are myths. Burghersiders who judge children's progress on the basis of letter grades claim that their children's academic progress begins to decline *after* second grade, whereas their children's records show that their grades tend to remain remarkably constant from the first letter grade they receive. Some Burgherside children are not assigned letter grades during first grade. They are rated as "slow" (S) or "making normal progress" (N). When they receive their first letter grades at the end of their second grade most of them receive either "C" or "D."

Teachers are highly consistent in how they reward Burgherside children for their classroom performance. The letter grade a child receives from his first teacher is repeatedly given to him by subsequent teachers with little or no allowance for any improvement the child may have made in a particular year. The sixth-grade class of 1968–1969 will illustrate this consistency. In 1964–1965, when these children received their first letter grades, 17 of them averaged "C." By 1968–1969 only one of the 17 had improved, receiving a "C" to "B —" one year. That is, 94.12% of these students, in a period of four years and under at least four successive teachers, had shown no academic improvement according to letter grades in their school records.

The tendency for teachers to evaluate Burgherside children as previous teachers have is due in part to the fact that when a teacher gets a new class, she reads the children's past records and forms an opinion about them even before she meets them in the classroom. It is not surprising, perhaps, that throughout their school careers Burgherside children's grades do not improve appreciably. When their grades change it is often from "C" to "D" and vice versa; and the "average grade" in Burgherside lies somewhere between "C" and "D" which constitutes the "Burgherside standard." A record of Burgherside students in junior and senior high schools will further illustrate this point (see Table 7.6). If the average letter grades received by each group of students—seventh through twelfth grade—are examined for each year to the 12th year most students receive between "C" and "D." Burgherside children enter the junior high school with poor grades on their records, and as they progress through senior high school, their grades get poorer and poorer, though the majority tend to remain within the "average grade."

TEACHERS AND THE NOTION OF THE AVERAGE STUDENT

Teachers in Burgherside elementary school, like the children and parents in the neighborhood, subscribe to the notion of "standard work." They describe most of the children as "average" and consistently give them the grades of "C" or "D," which the people regard as "average." Parents report that when they go to Parent–Teacher conferences, a teacher may tell the anxious parent: *Don't worry. Your child is doing all right. He is an average student.*

Teachers distinguish various types of "average students": the "slow average," "poor average," "bright average," and "dull average." The following are typical descriptions of these categories. The "slow average" student is described as "very shy and quiet. Seems to enjoy schoolwork, but

TABLE 7.6

Average Grades Received Each Year by Burgherside Children in Seventh through Twelfth Grade [a]

Present grade of students		Number of students receiving letter grades in subsequent years/grades					
		1964	1965	1966	1967	1968	1969
Seventh	"A"	na	na	na	na	na	—
	"B"	na	na	na	na	na	—
	"C"	na	na	na	na	na	10
	"D"	na	na	na	na	na	13
	"F"	na	na	na	na	na	3
Eighth	"A"	na	na	na	na	—	—
	"B"	na	na	na	na	—	—
	"C"	na	na	na	na	4	11
	"D"	na	na	na	na	18	11
	"F"	na	na	na	na	1	1
Ninth	"A"	na	na	na	—	—	—
	"B"	na	na	na	—	2	1
	"C"	na	na	na	13	12	15
	"D"	na	na	na	10	8	8
	"F"	na	na	na	2	3	3
Tenth	"A"	na	na	—	—	—	—
	"B"	na	na	1	2	3	2
	"C"	na	na	14	14	17	7
	"D"	na	na	15	12	10	5
	"F"	na	na	1	2	3	—
Eleventh	"A"	na	—	—	—	—	—
	"B"	na	1	2	2	6	2
	"C"	na	14	16	18	19	5
	"D"	na	16	14	12	6	2
	"F"	na	—	—	1	—	—
Twelfth	"A"	—	—	—	—	—	—
	"B"	—	1	2	3	3	2
	"C"	10	9	12	11	12	15
	"D"	8	9	6	6	5	5
	"F"	—	—	—	—	—	—

[a]Source: Stockton Unified School District.

is behind in some of his work." The "bright average" "seems bright but doesn't do his work carefully." The "good average" student is a "dependable, hard worker who gets along with his peers. His work is neat—he writes well." Or, "He's a good worker, quiet and willing to do anything." The "poor average" student is "very disruptive in the class. Is very moody and does not work as hard as he could. He has no patience with what others do."

Teachers say that they give letter grades on the basis of students' school-work and test results, but from a description of two children in the same class, it is difficult to see why both should have received the same grades, or why two others received different grades. A study of the teachers' comments on individual children reveals that often the teacher is merely repeating what the previous teacher had said, perhaps changing one word or two. Here are two examples:

Student X

KINDERGARTEN-TEACHER: *X does normal work. Tries very hard and is a likeable boy.* (No grade)

FIRST-GRADE TEACHER: *X is doing good, average work. Is willing to try.* ("C")

SECOND-GRADE TEACHER: *X tries hard, though it takes him somewhat longer to finish his work than others. Stuttering has not improved.* ("C")

THIRD-GRADE TEACHER: *X is very friendly. Tries hard, but is very slow. Stutters very badly at times, then some days he speaks much better.* ("C")

FOURTH-GRADE TEACHER: *Tries very hard. Conscientious about completing all assignments. Very likeable child. Stuttering has improved. Eager to please.* ("C")

The five teachers hardly see any change in X in five years! The second pupil, described below, began with language difficulties. Year after year the teachers note his improvement—but this is not reflected in the grade he receives.

Student Y

KINDERGARTEN TEACHER: *Y likes to color. Does not know names of colors due to the lack of English understanding. Listens well, follows directions.* (No grade)

FIRST-GRADE TEACHER: *Y is doing good average work. He seems to enjoy school.* ("C")

SECOND-GRADE TEACHER: *Y is doing good average work. He seems to enjoy school.* ("C")

THIRD-GRADE TEACHER: *Y's progress has been a delight to witness and encourage. He has made good studies in all areas.* ("C")

FOURTH-GRADE TEACHER: *Conscientious worker. Sometimes has difficulty in reading, seemingly due to Spanish background.* ("C")

Teachers play a very important part in developing the notion of "standard" work in Burgherside. "What everybody gets" is what every teacher gives, which is for the most part "C" or "D." Since this pattern does not really change, in subsequent years the children and their parents come to expect the same grade each time. Also, since during his elementary school years a child never gets below "D," whether or not he tries, some of the children develop the idea that they do not have to work hard to be average.

Burgherside parents sometimes say that their children actually do better in school than the grades on report cards indicate. The suggestion is made, too, that teachers deliberately give Burgherside children lower grades than they would give to Taxpayers' children for the same amount of work. This is illustrated by the attitude of a Mexican-American couple whose son received the following grades in his music class in junior high school in 1969: first quarter grade, "C"; second quarter, "B"; third quarter, "B"; final grade, "C." The couple said that their son's final grade should not have been "C" but "B" or "B −," saying that he did all his assignments and practiced his music at home. They concluded by saying that the teacher was punishing their son with a lower grade because his mother had taken him out of class 15 minutes early one day to keep a doctor's appointment. Another parent suggested that Burgherside children get lower grades because their parents do not have money to donate to the schools.

According to some informants, Burgherside children do poorly in tests because they do not know how to take these tests, nor do they appreciate their importance to their own educational goals. It seems that Burgherside elementary school teachers, for instance, do not explain to the children how to mark their answers in the appropriate spaces on the "bubbles" (IBM) cards before they take the state and other tests requiring the use of such cards. So they fail.

Teachers, like counselors (see next chapter), tend to go strictly by test scores in placing children in courses, without adequate analysis of why individual children performed the way they did on the tests. For example, a child may fail a test because he did not listen to or understand a teacher's instructions. This may be ignored by the teacher who places him only according to the test result. A story told by a mother in another Southside neighborhood about her fifth-grade son will illustrate this. The boy took a math placement test in the fifth grade and scored for a second-grade placement mainly because he was not listening when the teacher explained to the class what to do. Using the result of the test, the teacher decided to place him in second-grade math, although he was to be in fifth-grade level in other subjects. At the parent–teacher conference, the teacher argued: [I] *put him in there because that's where he placed on the test and it wouldn't be fair to the other children to put him where he belonged* [i.e., fifth grade] *because he didn't place there on the test, you know.* His mother, herself a teacher, objected, telling the teacher she should have given him the test again to find out where he really placed. A year later this boy was sent to a private school where he started on tenth-grade arithmetic. His mother concluded: *So this is kind of what happens, you know, on the other end of the scale—if you don't take the time—and there are proofs of these kinds of situations where people don't take care—kids suffer.* A Burgherside child in such a situation would have remained in second-grade arithmetic because most Burgherside parents cannot speak out to the teacher.

It is said that Taxpayers tell their children why the tests are important and that they should do well. Neither Burgherside children nor their parents understand the significance of the state tests, and thus, Burgherside parents do not explain their importance to their children. Some informants pointed out that teachers in Southside, including Burgherside, follow the test instructions too rigidly, refusing to explain the nature of the tests to their students "to avoid making them anxious," and therefore many students do poorly because they do not take these tests seriously. One informant told of a Southside boy who scored 115 on an IQ group test. The school district decided to give him a special test: *hopefully for exceptional class—and he is exceptional,* the informant said. But on the individual verbal test the boy did so poorly that the person who tested him could not understand why he had been sent to take the test at all. The informant argued that the boy did not do well on the individual test: *because the consequences of that test didn't matter a hell of a lot to that kid, you know. He didn't know the importance of the one-to-one testing and he didn't show his ability at all.* Some informants, including teachers, said that the performance of Burgherside children on various test does not represent their true ability; similarly the rewards they receive for their performance in the classwork are often not commensurate with their true ability or accomplishment.

CHAPTER **8**

How School Failure Adaptation Is Maintained:
The Clinical Definition of Academic Problems

Introduction

At the beginning of the last chapter I referred to a Taxpayer who said that the function of the school system is to make Burghersiders into Taxpayers. This is the common view among Taxpayers—especially those associated with the school system—and sometimes among Burghersiders too. This view assumes that Burghersiders differ from Taxpayers because they do not have good jobs, earn good wages, or live in good neighborhoods. Those holding this view assume that Burghersiders **as individuals** have the potential to change their status legitimately within the local system of social stratification, especially through education. They do not seem to consider the fact that Burghersiders, as **subordinate minorities**, have fewer opportunities to achieve the status of Taxpayers than whites do.

Although both Taxpayers and Burghersiders recognize that in theory good education leads to a good job and good wages, and all these combine to make one into a Taxpayer, this is not necessarily the route for Burghersiders, who do not become Taxpayers just because they have good educations. This, then, raises an important question about the real function of the school system for the Burghersiders. Contrary to the goal expressed by the schools of transforming Burghersiders into Taxpayers, they may actually be functioning as a control mechanism over the upward mobility of Burgher-siders, and in this chapter I shall describe some of the ways in which the school system supports the school-failure adaptation in Burgherside, and thus controls their passage into Taxpayer status.

Three "Functional" Myths

The relationship between the schools and Burgherside, like that between teachers and Burgherside parents, is assymetrical, and in both cases does not promote school success. The relationship continues to exist because it is sustained by three myths: (1) the belief that community or parent involvement in the schools promotes academic success, (2) the belief that Burgherside households have no fathers, and (3) the belief that Burgher-siders are caught in "the welfare cycle." Each of these beliefs shapes the attitudes of the school toward Burgherside and Burghersiders, and each is detrimental to the progress of Burgherside children in school.

The Myth of Parent and Community Involvement

The need for Burgherside parents and community to become more in-volved in the education of their children is repeatedly stressed by the schools and by Taxpayers. What the school district means by involvement does not include the participation of parents and Burgherside leaders in making decisions concerning the school curriculum or new programs needed by their children, nor does it include participation in the hiring, evaluating, transferral, or dismissal of teachers, or in the expenditure of the school fund. By involvement, the district simply means that Burghersiders should participate in the noncurriculum programs such as PTA, open house, and other social entertainment planned by the school staff. It is believed that such "involvement" will (1) show that Burgherside parents and community have changed their "negative attitudes" toward school and education; (2) show that they have become "more interested" in their children's education; (3) help them learn better attitudes toward life and society, and thereby become better models for their children at home and in the neighborhood and (4) help them learn the techniques with which to assist their children to succeed in school. The idea that the involvement of low-income and ethnic-minority parents in the schools would promote their children's school success is not new (see Rempson 1967; Thompson 1920), but it has become more pervasive among educators and social scientists since the beginning of the compensatory education program, a program born and nurtured in the idea that children in neighborhoods like Burgher-side fail in school because of their home and neighborhood environments (see Gordon 1968; Coleman 1969). But the evidence from Burgherside suggests that parent and community involvement in the context of a patron–client relationship with the schools does not necessarily lead to improved academic success of children.

How Burghersiders Are Involved

Parent and community involvement are considered desirable at the elementary, junior, and senior high schools attended by Burgherside children. Each school provides some mechanisms for "communicating" with Burghersiders.

There is more communication between Burgherside elementary school and the community, in part because the school is located in the neighborhood. The formation of Burgherside Fire District and its Volunteer Fire Brigade in the late 1950s and of Burgherside Community Council, and later Burgherside Neighborhood Improvement Association in the 1960s, all fostered a closer relationship between Burgherside and its elementary school.

Both the Community Council and its successor, the Neighborhood Improvement Association, have been very concerned about education in Burgherside, especially problems of dropout and "push-out." In the early 1960s the council obtained the use of the elementary school to provide a study hall two evenings a week for neighborhood students at seventh-grade through college levels. (The study hall was supervised by volunteers recruited from the Newman Club at the local university and from a Northside Catholic high school, and by professional teachers recruited from the Central Methodist Church.) The council also used some rooms for adult education classes for teaching English to non-English-speaking residents.

The War on Poverty, when it began in 1965, further strengthened the relationship between the school and the neighborhood in three ways: by increased use of school facilities, new educational programs, and closer association with the school staff. The Neighborhood Association was partly responsible for the introduction of a pre-school program at the school in 1966, and since 1967 it has sponsored and funded a tiny tots program at the school during the summer.

In 1966, one year after the War on Poverty began in Burgherside, the elementary school report to the central administration stated the following reasons for the lack of "parents' involvement" in the school: (1) low level of adult education, (2) personal problems and [negative] attitudes, (3) transiency, (4) self-interest, (5) factionalism, (6) housing shortage and poor housing, (7) threat of possible relocation to make way for new freeway and railroad, (8) inability and ignorance of the school staff "to solve all the basic needs of these people."

Since Burgherside Community Center was not completed until 1967, the Neighborhood Association used the school for most of its activities.

These included talent shows, dances and dance lessons, films, parties, dinners, and public meetings, recreational activities for children during school vacation periods, educational activities such as study halls, adult education, and so on. But Burghersiders also did something for the school, as the following report indicates:

> The Neighborhood Association, Women's Club, teen clubs, P.T.A. have reciprocated by establishing better control and better behavior around the school. They have joined in some mutual assistance of each others' programs and have made large gains for our area. These groups have, in addition, interpreted school programs and attitudes to the community for the betterment of the school. School programs have also been well supported by the Neighborhood groups with both supervisional and financial help [SUSD 1967a: 23].

The activities sponsored by the Neighborhood Association brought the community into the school. The school staff responded. Some joined the Neighborhood Association; some assisted the leaders of the Neighborhood Association in writing programs for the Neighborhood Center, and in planning and building the Neighborhood Center and Burgherside Park. Some teachers assisted in planning and implementing the association's educational programs. Since the beginning of this type of cooperation the principal of the elementary school has always been appointed the chairman of the Education Committee of the association. He has also become the go-between in transactions between the association and the Board of Education or the central administration of the school system.

How did this involvement affect the mutual definitions of the school and the community? It has not altered the basic attitudes of the two sides toward each other. A school report written for the central administration in 1967 stated that:

> These groups (Negroes from the South, Mexicans from Mexico, Texas and New Mexico) have preserved their basic attitudes and the children and adults consequently have a low aspirational level with many personal prejudices. The attitudes of the parents and children have and are undergoing a very dynamic change. This is due largely to the work of the community organizations and the school as a whole [SUSD 1967a:1].

The same theme is repeated year after year, in 1969 stressing that: "the groups [blacks and Mexican-Americans] have preserved much of their basic attitudes . . . " toward school and education.

The school views its involvement in these community programs as a service aimed at changing the supposed negative attitudes of Burghersiders. It hopes to encourage parents to become more interested in their children's education. The school report in 1967 states: "By participating in community programs the school sought to counsel with community leaders and call in other community agencies to help broaden the outlook of the natural leaders in the area [SUSD 1967a :28]." In exchange the school hopes to gain greater cooperation from the community. Burghersiders also gain greater cooperation from the school, which allows them increased use of the facilities and staff.

An action taken by the school district in the summer of 1968 clearly indicated the patron–client relationship between the district and the Burghersiders. The school district, without consultation with Burghersiders (even though the organizational framework existed in the Neighborhood Association) replaced more than 90% of the school staff, including teachers, principal, and secretary, with a new group to implement a bilingual-education program, also introduced without prior knowledge of Burghersiders (see Chapter 9).

Many of the new teachers came from outside Stockton and it was not easy for the school and Burghersiders to re-establish the ties that were ruptured by the wholesale transfer of the old staff. Some new teachers joined the Neighborhood Association, and the new principal became the chairman of the Education Committee. But things were not the same as before; the new teachers were compared to the old ones and the new principal to the former principal. At least one active member of the association left to join the Neighborhood Association in the district to which the former Burgherside elementary school principal was transferred. Some Burghersiders commented about how the new principal dressed, especially after her picture appeared in a Sunday edition of the *Stockton Record*, a local newspaper, as "one of the best-dressed women in town."

One group that gained from the change was the local PTA. The association had overshadowed the PTA between 1965 and 1968, and had partly absorbed its functions. At the beginning of the 1968 school year the new principal began to build up the PTA with the help of the "hard-core members" and the two Burgherside mothers who worked as aides at the school. However, participation in the PTA and its influence remained small throughout my study.

Reports of the junior and senior high schools usually list the following channels for communicating with Burgherside and other neighborhoods they serve: (*1*) social clubs in the neighborhood, (*2*) children to parents, (*3*) PTA and other parent organizations, (*4*) significant community programs, and (*5*) merchants and residents. The social club usually means the Kiwanis and similar clubs, which have no relevance for Burgherside. The schools frequently use the children as channels of communication with parents by (*1*) sending report cards to parents at the end of each quarter, (*2*) sending notices (called "provisionals") to parents whose children's work is "below standard" (i.e., "D" or "F")—parents are supposed to respond by phoning the school, (*3*) inviting parents to confer with counse-

lors on educational planning for their children at the high school, and
(4) sending for parents to hold conferences with the deans if their children
attend school irregularly or have discipline problems. Sometimes these
messages are sent directly to parents by mail or telephone.[1]

The PTA, as indicated earlier, is a very ineffective means of communicating with Burghersiders, even at the elementary school level. Communication through merchants does not apply to the junior and senior high
schools because these schools are located outside Burgherside. On the whole,
Burghersiders are not much involved in the schools.

Why Burghersiders Are Not More Involved in the Schools

The usual explanations the schools give for why Burghersiders are not
more involved are "their apathy" and "their lack of interest in education,"
but these explanations are not entirely accurate. For example, the nature of
the relationship between Taxpayers and Burghersiders partly accounts for
the latter's lack of involvement in the PTA. It is said that the purpose of the
PTA is to promote cooperation between teachers and parents, but cooperation in Taxpayers' schools is different from cooperation in Burgherside
schools. Let us suppose that in Taxpayers' schools teachers favor an "open
classroom" approach to education whereas parents favor the traditional
classroom organization. Both sides may meet to work out a compromise;
if teachers insist on their ideas against the will of the parents they may be
compelled to leave the school.

Cooperation between teachers and parents in Burgherside is of a different
character; it is one between patrons and clients, between unequals. Teachers
almost always assume that their ideas are right whereas parents' ideas are
wrong, and the cooperation they ask of parents is to be allowed to correct
the parents' way of thinking or to have their ideas and programs endorsed
by parents. The PTA constitution explicitly forbids its members to take a
stand on any issue against the official position of the school; that is, the PTA
is required always to support the school administration. But this rule is more
rigidly enforced in neighborhoods like Burgherside.

Because they feel powerless to change what they do not like about the
schools, Burghersiders do not participate in PTA and other school affairs,
and parents do not go to the teachers, the principals, the superintendent,
or the school board to ask for a change. Burghersiders speak of instances

---

[1]The information that parents are invited to confer with counselors on educational planning
for their children is contained in the high school student handbook. In Burgherside parents
either do not know about this invitation or do not understand it because they rarely go to
see the counselors for this purpose.

where "the whole community" made recommendations to the authorities but were completely ignored. One man tells of a situation where 90% of the people went to the authorities (though not the school, in this case), and the authorities did just the opposite of what the people wanted. A similar situation developed in the school district some time after my fieldwork. A group of parents in one Southside neighborhood had some disagreement with a school principal, and the PTA supported the principal. The dissident parents took their case to the Board of Education with supporting signatures of some 450 residents of their neighborhood. According to them, the Board of Education refused to judge their case on its merits and supported the principal.

Parents who feel powerless to bring about the changes they want see no reason they should be involved in the PTA. The schools sometimes erroneously interpret lack of overt protest as a sign of support for their policies. For instance, during the high school crisis of 1969 I interviewed a number of black and Mexican-American parents and found many of them sympathetic with the students. They did not consider confrontation the best way to change things in the schools, but they said that it was the only way that seemed to work.

Some Burghersider parents value education but genuinely believe that their personal involvement in the schools is not necessary for their children to learn. Those from Mexico, in particular, point out that when they themselves went to school, the schools did not demand that their parents be involved—and yet they learned more than their own children are learning in Burgherside. They say that a child who goes only as far as sixth grade in Mexico knows more than their children who are in twelfth grade in Burgherside, and they blame the schools for their childrens' failure. The parents of a fifth-grade Mexican boy complained that he had not yet learned to write letters whereas, *In Mexico,* they said, *the school makes them learn to do this before the fifth grade.* I was told that some people prefer to send their children to school in Mexico because of their belief that the schools there are better and the children learn more. Some of these parents insist that a child should be promoted to the next grade only if he has "passed," and because they think in terms of "pass/fail" they regard all grades from "A" through "D" to be of equal value, since they all mean "pass." Finally, as I indicated in the last chapter, Burghersiders believe that the schools do not send for parents to discuss their children's work until after the report cards are issued because the schools want to blame parents for their children's failures.

Does Parents' Involvement Reduce School Failures in Burgherside?

The school's argument for parental involvement seems to go as follows. Some parents have "negative attitudes" about education, but no overt hostility, and that is why they avoid the schools. They pass on these "negative attitudes" to their children, and that is why the children do poorly in school. The school can prove this by the records of the children's work in school; those whose parents are involved (i.e., have "good attitudes") usually do well, whereas those whose parents are not involved (i.e., have "negative attitudes") usually do poorly. When a mother becomes involved in the school it means that her attitude has changed in the right direction. Her child will notice the change and so change his own attitude and begin to do well in his lessons.

A study of the letter grades that teachers gave to children in Burgherside elementary school in 1967–1968 and 1968–1969 actually supports the contention that children whose parents are "involved" do better ("involvement" is simply defined here as "contact" between the school and the parents). Table 8.1 shows that children whose parents contacted the school in the two-year period received more "B" grades than did children whose parents made no contacts; only the contacts recorded in the child's records have been counted.

An alternative explanation to the school's for this grade differential is possible. When a parent contacts a teacher she interprets the parent's attitude in terms of "interest" and "cooperation." For example, in the 1968–1969 school year, the elementary school teachers described 111 of the 174 parents with whom they had contacts as either "cooperative," "interested," or both. Fifteen other parents were described as "seems concerned" or "seems improving in her attitude." Typical teacher's comments are: *She* [the parent] *is interested in progress* and *She is cooperative.* Since teachers assume that parents who contact them are "interested" and "cooperative," they probably assume that parents who do not contact them are "uninterested," "uncooperative," or both. Consequently these

TABLE 8.1

Percentage of Students Whose Parents Had Contact with Teachers and the Types of Grades Received by the Students [a]

Grades received	1967–68		1968–1969	
	Contact (118)	No contact (66)	Contact (125)	No contact (68)
"A"	2.54	—	1.60	—
"B"	42.37	7.58	28.80	8.82
"C"	44.07	68.18	57.60	63.24
"D"	11.02	21.21	12.00	26.47
N/S[b]	—	3.03	—	1.47

[a] Source: Washington Elementary School Records.
[b] N/S, i.e. normal or slow progress.

teachers may be unconsciously rewarding children whose parents are "interested" and "cooperative" with better grades while punishing those whose parents are "uninterested" and "uncooperative" with poorer grades. This alternative interpretation is suggested by data from interviews with Burgherside parents. Some of them said that they withdrew from active involvement in the PTA and other school activities when they discovered that teachers were giving their children better grades than they deserved. One informant, the mother of an eleventh-grade girl, a potential dropout, is more educated than most Burghersiders. She lives with her husband, and both have good jobs. She said that when her oldest daugher was in the elementary school she used to be intensely involved in the school. Her daughter always got good grades in school, and the teachers were nice to her and told her that they were happy she was involved. Then she discovered that her daughter could not read or write; she realized that her daughter got good grades because of her "involvement." Had she known the child was not doing well, she would have kept her back to repeat grades: *But they always told me how nice my daughter was and all that when she was not doing nothing. So when I found out what was happening I stopped going to PTA meetings and all that.*

BURGHERSIDE FATHERS: THE "MISSING PARENTS"

Burgherside men participate less actively than women in school affairs. In my survey, only 25 men attended any PTA meeting and only 14 went to parent–teacher conferences in the 1968–1969 school year, whereas 45 and 42 women participated respectively.[2]

The schools regard this lower participation by men as understandable; the father is absent in many households. Burgherside is a women's world. School records show that 29.4% of the junior and senior high and 31.5% of the elementary school students are without fathers. The schools also believe that women dominate families even when the man is present as a husband-father. In one school the annual report explained why girls were "more militant" than boys by saying: "It probably reflects the matriarchal character of Negro society. Probably militancy is a necessary first step toward identity which in turn is a necessary step toward achievement . . . [SUSD 1968a:23]." I indicated in the last chapter that school officials think that the types of home environmental influences that prevent children from learning in school are greatest in single-parent (mother-headed) homes in neighborhoods like Burgherside. They also believe that such

---

[2]It is probably equally true that in Taxpayers' neighborhood as in Burgherside more women than men participate in the PTA.

families exist as a matter of tradition because for generations men in these families have "abdicated their responsibility" of working to support their families. As one informant said: *In many cases this* [the assumption of responsibility] *is not in their thinking; this is not part of their bringing up.* The schools, therefore, usually direct their communication with Burghersiders to the women; and this happens even when the husband-father is present. Some school officials must have been surprised early in 1969 when Burgherside fathers took the initiative in arranging a meeting with them because their children were having trouble with a school bus driver (see Chapter 7, p. 137).

Burgherside Men in Education

Although fathers do not go to school functions they are as interested as mothers in their children's education. They learn about school progress and activities from their children and wives, and from community gossip. Burgherside fathers also express strong views about teachers, teaching, the system, and educational goals, as I have described in the previous chapters; but when children live with grandparents by the consent of the father, or with their mother if parents are separated, Burgherside fathers have no direct contact with the schools because the schools channel their communications to the adults with whom the children live.

Burghersiders' Explanation

Burghersiders themselves explain that men are not as involved as women in school affairs for the following reasons: (*1*) Mexican-American men are less fluent in English than are women; (*2*) Burgherside's division of labor allots women responsibility for education; and (*3*) the work done by the men is such that they are always tired when they come home.

Many Mexican and Filipino men who do not speak or understand English well require interpreters to communicate with the school personnel. In such families, the woman is given the responsibility for dealing with the schools, especially if she is a native speaker of English.

Burghersiders, both men and women, strongly believe that the formal education of their children is primarily the responsibility of the mother, whether or not there is a father in the family. They see the wife as a deputy of her husband with responsibility for the children. The man may reward or punish the children for their performance when necessary, and in a period of crisis the man may completely take over from his wife, but the day-to-day activities and involvement with the school are delegated to the woman. This is illustrated in the following interview excerpt.

ANTHR.: *I really wonder why there seems to be little interest on the part of the black men, judging from what I have seen here. Are the black men ever feeling concerned about how their children are doing in school?*

MOTHER: *I guess they are concerned but they feel that the woman is supposed to make sure that everything is done. I hope that they feel concerned.*

ANTHR.: *Are they aware of the problems? Do they ask kids about their schoolwork?*

MOTHER: *When report cards come they do. But all the in-between* [read: minute details] *I don't believe that most men take interest in them. When report card time comes they notice it.*

ANTHR.: *When they notice it* [the report card] *what kind of things do they do or say? I mean, does the report card excite them to feel that they ought to be more concerned or . . . ?*

MOTHER: *If it is good; if it is bad the wife takes care of them.* [Laughing] *He's got the husband's job or the husband feels that whatever he is doing is more important and he's got to go out and do this and that, the things that he has to do. He can't take time to go out and do things like this. And with me if I am working—they didn't always give parent–teacher conferences in the evenings like they are doing now, and when I was notified I had to take time off from work to come and work with the teacher. And I always did this. But a man won't take time off from his job to do a thing like this or, I don't know of any who do.*

ANTHR.: *If they had the time, do you think they would go?*

MOTHER: *I don't think in most cases they would because like I said—this is more or less usually considered something that the woman does.*

Exhaustion from heavy labor, frustrations because of racial discrimination, and loss of faith in the education system discourage many men from becoming involved in the schools; and, further, most home–school contacts occur during the day when the men are at work. Burghersiders explain that men are not able to attend meetings at night because they are too tired from doing heavy work during the day, and my experience in visiting many families in the evening supports this. I found it difficult to interview Burgherside men in the evenings because they sometimes fell asleep in their chairs during our interviews or even before I got there at the agreed time. The following excerpt from an interview with a mother describes the situation:

ANTHR.: *Well, let us talk about black men. . . . Could you tell me more about the attitude of black men toward education?*

MOTHER: *Well, a black man that has a family is not educated—we're talking about poor people, aren't we?*

ANTHR.: *Yes.*

MOTHER: *He is not educated and the job he does, he has to work twice as hard as the white man to hold it. And he is really tired by the time he*

> *goes to this white man's job and works enough for two all day. He is too tired to come along and go to PTA at night time. And that is the whole story. He is just too tired.*
>
> ANTHR.: *Not that he is not interested?*
>
> MOTHER: *It is not that he is not interested. It is just that he is just too tired, you know.*
>
> ANTHR.: *But in the family, in the home, does he talk to the children about their schoolwork?*
>
> MOTHER: *I feel the man talks more; but because the black man usually makes the living he leaves the rest to his wife.*
>
> ANTHR.: *When the children bring home their report cards does he show interest in them?*
>
> MOTHER: *No.*
>
> ANTHR.: *He doesn't? The wife handles it?*
>
> MOTHER: *There's a lot of time that the wife—if the kids need a spanking— there's a lot of time that the wife handles that too. When the man comes home and you tell him, say, "Honey, do you know he went out and did this and that?" And he says "Oh, he di-i-i-id?" because he is too tired to listen.*
>
> ANTHR.: *Really?*
>
> MOTHER: *True. Now I am not going to say that the young black men of today may be different* [i.e., are this way] *but we are talking about black men of my age or older. He is just too tired.*

Burgherside men thus participate less actively in school affairs, but not because they lack interest in their children's education; nor because Burgherside children come from fatherless homes. Most Burgherside fathers I talked to were as interested in their children's doing well in school as Burgherside mothers. However, Burgherside fathers do not express their interest in the forms observable to the Taxpayers partly because of their work conditions, partly because Burghersiders assign the responsibility of formal education to mothers, and partly because the patron–client relationship between Taxpayers and Burghersiders discourages Burgherside men from interacting with Taxpayers unless they are required to do so.

The belief that Burgherside is dominated by women has some negative consequences for education in Burgherside. First, it leads the schools to blame learning problems of the children on "their home environment" and the "home conditions" are often interpreted in psychological and clinical terms. Attention is thus diverted from teaching the children their regular lessons to stressing their need for therapy, teaching them "positive self-concept," and so on. The second consequence is that this belief reinforces the patron–client relationship, which, as I have indicated, does not promote learning in Burgherside.

THE WELFARE RECIPIENTS AND THE "WELFARE CYCLE"

A widespread belief among Burghersiders and Taxpayers is that "some people don't care" about improving their conditions in life through education and work. In Burgherside, every informant claims to know at least one person who does not care. When you interview such a person, however, he will assure you that he cares, but in turn claims to know someone "who doesn't care." Burghersiders speak of three kinds of people who do not care: (1) women on welfare, (2) boyfriends of women on welfare, and (3) children of women on welfare.

Taxpayers make no such distinctions. They believe that most Burghersiders do not care because they are either (1) welfare recipients, who are said to form the majority of those "who don't care;" (2) hard-core unemployed; or (3) the working poor, sometimes called the "hard-core poor." Burghersiders often reinforce the Taxpayers' classification by referring to themselves as "we poor people" in contrast to "those rich people over there," that is, Taxpayers.

I first learned about the "welfare cycle" early in my fieldwork, and began to keep careful notes about it. By welfare cycle, Stocktonians mean that the people on welfare do not encourage their children to do well in school; so their children grow up to become recipients and so on. I ended up collecting several stories about people on welfare and the welfare cycle. For example, I once attended a party at which there were several socially mobile Nontaxpayers, including some former Burghersiders. Everyone at the party expressed interest in Southside educational problems. Our conversation soon shifted to the effects of the welfare program on education. One woman said that adoption laws in California were being amended to allow single women, but not single men, to adopt children—a change that would facilitate adoption of black children even by nonblack people. The informant said that it is difficult to curb illegitimate births among black women because they usually

> want to have babies so they can get money from the welfare. But Taxpayers don't like it because it is costing a good deal of money. The welfare mothers are lazy and don't want to work. They sit while others work and pay taxes to support them.

The speaker was majoring in social science and hoped to become a social worker, when she got "tired of teaching."

Other speakers did not like the welfare program for various reasons: (1) Some women choose to go on welfare because of the money. Someone commented: Why marry or work when you can receive so much money for having babies? They, too, described the "welfare cycle." (2) The children of welfare parents become welfare recipients because they never learn to work to support themselves. (3) Welfare puts unfair financial responsibilities on Taxpayers since many recipients just want to "sit back and suck up" those who are trying to make it. (4) Welfare money does not benefit the children for whom it is intended. Cases were cited of women who used welfare money for clothes, shoes, and boyfriends, while leaving their children without food, clothes, and shoes. I was told that before I came to Stockton there was a dance band at the Civic Auditorium each weekend following welfare payments: *And you should see how those welfare mothers were adorned in beautiful clothes which they have just bought with the welfare money while their children starved at home. Their mothers simply wanted to have a good time.* I heard it said that welfare mothers support their boyfriends. An example was given of a married man in Southside who had many "welfare girlfriends": *He works and makes good money. But at the end of the month he would hand his paycheck to his wife to put into their bank account. Then he would go from one girlfriend to another to collect welfare money from them.* Even former recipients do not hesitate to point out that welfare mothers support their "boyfriends" financially, although they themselves never did it. It is always "the others" who are doing it.

Ambivalence about the Welfare Program

Burghersiders ridicule, gossip, and joke about welfare recipients, but they identify with them when they speak of themselves as poor, unemployed minority people.

At other times they view the program as "very damaging to the families," to values, and to the self-esteem of black and Mexican-American people. Burghersiders oppose the program because (1) It encourages marital instability. Some men say that four-fifths of black marriages end in divorce because the women know they can always get welfare money. (2) The program creates a community of people "who don't care for self-advancement." But neither Burghersiders nor other Southsiders ever publicly speak out against the program: *Anyone who has the ambition of getting somewhere will not speak out against it because it will cost him his future*, according to informants.

The Prevalence of Welfare

I have no accurate information on the number of Burghersiders receiving welfare in 1969, but 45 out of 94 women and 15 out of 41 men interviewed said that they received some form of public assistance, including social security. School records of Burgherside children contained no accurate information on welfare, but Table 8.2 indicates indirectly, in the "unemployed," "on relief," and "unknown" columns, the proportion of children that are from families receiving some aid. Most mothers in the "unem-

TABLE 8.2

Employment and Relief Status of Parents of Burgherside Students as Indicated in School Records [a,b]

Parent	Employed	Unemployed	On relief	Unknown
Father (413)	61.02	1.69	—	37.29
Mother (417)	17.03	41.97	4.08	36.93

[a]Source: School records.
[b]Values expressed as percentages.

ployed" column are housewives, but many women in the "unknown" column are probably on welfare—the children of parents in this column are not necessarily living with their fathers. The school district's information compiled in the 1964–1965 school year indicates that 40 % of the elementary school population, and 19 % of the junior high school, and 24 % of the senior high school attended by Burgherside children were from families on AFDC (Aid to Families of Dependent Children). These figures are high compared to figures for other schools, especially in Taxpayers' neighborhoods.

In Stockton, criticism against the welfare program is normally directed at the Aid to Families with Dependent Children, which is the single most expensive of the eight welfare programs in the county. However, in 1967 the director of the County Public Assistance noted in a departmental memorandum: "The bulk of the money goes for the Adult Program—Aged (33.8 %), Blind (2.2 %), Disabled (14.5 %), and not the much maligned children's program, AFDC."

Life of Recipient Families

I did not investigate every story I recorded about welfare recipients, but I interviewed and observed several families on the program. For mothers on welfare, life is not the "glamor and waste" described by their critics, nor are they happy to be on welfare. Although the older women feel that they are beyond school age, many young women want to go back to school for vocational training. Both the younger and older women know, however, that they cannot easily get jobs with adequate pay even if they have more education. Furthermore, as Arthur D. Little and Associates (1965:133) point out in their study:

> Monetary and non-monetary payments of Welfare payments to the unemployed have been criticized because they discourage persons with low earning power from rejoining the labor force once they become recipients of Welfare. . . .
> An individual earning up to $200 per month who is in receipt of Welfare in Stockton will have his welfare cash payments reduced in proportion to his earning. That is to say, an individual earning $50 in a month will receive $150 in Welfare and an individual earning $75 only $125. At $200 a month earned income, Welfare payment

ceases and disposable income (i.e., gross income less tax) increases with the earned income. The earned and disposable income of a person earning up to $200 per month may be illustrated by the following diagram [Figure 8.1] where the ABL shows how a person's spending power changes at the low end of the income scale.

The study makes it clear that the present system of welfare does not offer a work incentive to recipients:

The persons now earning less than $200/month in S.J. County have no financial incentive to find employment providing a lower average monthly wage level than this figure. Each dollar earned results in a dollar reduction in Welfare payments. In fairness to the employed members of the labor force Welfare payments should taper off as earnings increase. By allowing Welfare payments to decline less rapidly than wages increase, a positive financial incentive to work would exist at all times [Little and Associates 1965].

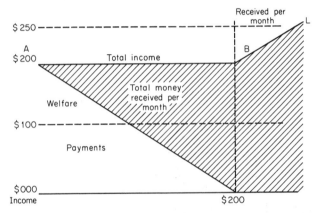

Figure 8.1 Earned income versus disposable income of a welfare recipient earning $200 per month in San Joaquin County. [Source: Stockton Renewal Policies and Practice (Little 1965: 134).]

The women on welfare, like other women, have a social life that includes going to parties, night clubs, membership in various social clubs, and so on. But such socializing is not necessarily paid for with welfare money. In 1969 I visited some night clubs "frequented by welfare mothers and their boyfriends." I did not meet any Burgherside woman, but in general I observed that it was the women's boyfriends who paid for the gate fees, for the drinks, and the like.

In the fall of 1968 I interviewed a long-time welfare recipient about her club activities. One of her clubs is: *for all people to have a good time*, but the same club raises money to award scholarships and for: *social services in the community*. When I interviewed her this club was planning a trip to Lake Tahoe to raise money to remodel its building. This woman also belongs to the Unified Women's Club which at that time was planning a "Black and White Ball" to raise money for an orphan home. My informant was active in these fund-raising activities.

In Burgherside, welfare recipients are also active members of the Neighborhood Improvement Association, the Women's Club (when it existed), and other neighborhood and religious organizations.

I was not able to make a systematic study of the economic life of these welfare families, their needs, spending habits, economic and social values, income, and so on. However, my information on such matters, from quite a few families, suggests that their critics are stereotyping.

Welfare families have difficulty supporting themselves with welfare payments only. In 1969, I recorded over a period of several months the monthly budget of a family of three whose welfare payment was $172 per month. The typical monthly budget was as shown in Table 8.3.

TABLE 8.3
A Budget for the Period of One Month for a Family of Three on Welfare[a]

Income allowance	Expenses	
$172.00		
	Rent (1 bedroom unfurnished)	$85.00
	Food, etc.	50.00
	Utilities	11.00
	Laundry	2.60
	Transportation (bus)	6.00
	Hair, etc.	7.00
	Total	$163.00
	Misc.	9.90

[a]Source: Author's interview.

The family received its monthly payments in two installments of $86.00 each. The landlord initially insisted that the entire rent of $85.50 for an unfurnished apartment with one bedroom be paid with the first installment, but he later agreed to two equal payments on the first and sixteenth of the month. No accurate record was kept, and when the family moved into public housing a few months later the landlord insisted the family still owed him $42.75. Groceries were purchased from a small neighborhood store where prices were very high and quality poor. I took this family one day to buy groceries in a Taxpayers' neighborhood store where the woman discovered that groceries cost much less. Utility bills were never paid on time and she constantly feared that her phone or gas would be cut off. She had no money at Christmas to buy clothes or gifts for her children, although she eventually got some money from her "boyfriends." She did not like to "shack up" with any of the men, though she would have liked to get a "rich white boyfriend" as her girlfriend has done.

This woman looked for a job unsuccessfully for over a year. In the fall of 1969 she went to school to train as a licensed vocational nurse, a field in which jobs are scarce in Stockton area.

In 1969 informants said that a few years earlier the Department of Public Assistance sometimes conducted night checks to make sure that the mothers' "boyfriends" did not live with them. In Burgherside, "boyfriends" lived with two welfare families where they also had children. These men worked and helped to support the families. In one case, over a 15-month period, each welfare payment to the family varied according to the income of the "boyfriend." In each family the children called their mother's "boyfriend" "father" and he referred to them as his children.

Recruitment of Welfare Recipients

Many welfare recipients in Burgherside are not products of the "welfare cycle," although a few families do have two generations of recipients, mother and daughter.

How did the first generation become recipients? In Burgherside the case history of each recipient is unique, but the following general pattern can be noted: (*1*) inability to find jobs; (*2*) fluctuations in farm-labor income; (*3*) conflicts in arranged marriages; (*4*) widowhood, disability, and so on.

Some Burghersiders become welfare recipients because they cannot find employment. In the fall of 1968 the staff at the Neighborhood Center spent a considerable time trying unsuccessfully to get residents jobs. In the later part of my study a center staff member reported: *We are going to give up this kind of service because the center just can't handle it. We don't have the resources and facilities to do it.* Unemployment among black and Mexican-American women is high, as noted previously, and the number of unemployed fathers on welfare has been reported to increase proportionately with the unemployment rate in Stockton (South Stockton Parish 1967).

This tightness of employment conflicts with the aims of Burghersiders, most of whom came originally from the rural southern United States and Mexico "to upgrade themselves" in Stockton through better jobs and wages. One woman, for instance, arrived in Stockton in 1969 with her children, leaving her husband in Arkansas because, *He has no ambition to better himself.* But although she trained as a nurse in Arkansas she could not find a nurse's job in Stockton.

For some Burgherside families, welfare is the only possible supplement to the minimal wage for seasonal labor to which they are subject. One mother described her family situation as follows:

Well, my husband works, but his income varies because we're farm labor. Sometimes he makes $250. And, of course, in the summer time he makes a little bit over $300, or $318. That's farm labor, you know. When he doesn't work they will help me. The welfare will help me when he doesn't make enough. . . . Now, you see, like last month, he made $268, and then they gave me $220, the welfare gave me. You know they deduct from these wages his travelling expenses—how many days he travelled back and forth—from work. And they charge him both. And when he goes for lunch it is so far he can't come home for lunch; and because he has to eat with the rest of the people they charge everybody. We have to pay for it whether he eat it or not because he is a diabetes. That's farm labor.

Migratory farm labor contributes to the welfare rolls in some other ways. Many migratory labor camps do not have schools that can deal with children of different ages and special needs. Arguments about whether or not to settle down in a place like Stockton with better schools leads to the breakup of marriages. The men usually move on and the women with their children settle down to become welfare recipients.

Teenage welfare recipients come from both welfare and nonwelfare families, and they usually become welfare recipients for different reasons from those of the parent generation.

Burgherside women on welfare say that they do not encourage their teenage daughters to become welfare recipients. They tell their daughters that they would be happier in life than they themselves are if they finish school, get good jobs, and get married before they start having babies. Often there is hostility between these women and their daughters if the latter become unwed mothers and welfare recipients. The young mother may be told that she has disappointed the family and also that she must assume the responsibility associated with motherhood.

I also interviewed a number of mothers who were not on welfare, although their teenage daughters were. These women did not approve of their daughters having illegitimate children, but their attitude toward them was less harsh than the attitude of some of the women on welfare.

Most teenage girls who become unwed mothers in their junior and senior high school years do so because they are ignorant about birth control, and some because they want the welfare checks for their own "spending money." Even women who practice birth control themselves have difficulties teaching their daughters about it. One mother commented:

I've heard a lot of people say that it is, you know, that you are upholding this type of thing [premarital sex relations] if you tell your kids that you will give them birth control. But I am not upholding it, I just don't want to see it happen. I don't feel that the kids should go out and do it.

In some families the children are told that pregnancy can be prevented by means of birth control, but they are not told what type of birth control to use or how it can be obtained. In general there is little or no sex education in the home, and many Burgherside mothers themselves did not learn anything from their parents, including knowledge about menstruation.

The Economics of "Babies and More Babies"

A few teenage girls who know about birth control still become unwed mothers. Interviews with such teenagers and their parents reveal some economic motive on the part of the teenagers, not of their parents.

Teenage girls whose parents cannot afford to give "spending money" and who have tried unsuccessfully to get part-time jobs may see welfare payments to unwed mothers as the only alternative. Many teenage girls, from both welfare and nonwelfare families, are concerned with their immediate needs; they rarely think of long-range goals and consequences.

Contrary to the popular notion, most women on AFDC do not purposely seek to increase their welfare allowance by having more and more babies. Most welfare recipients argue that a woman does not necessarily gain financially by having many children, since expenses increase as the number of children increases. Why then do some women continue to have more and more children? (1) A woman may have had several husbands, each of whom insisted on having children. (2) Older women may lack knowledge about birth control. One woman said: *They didn't have it* [birth control] *in my time. And when they brought it out I began to take it. If it was there when I was coming up I would have been taking it like this every day. O-o-o! Every day!* (3) Women who are unable to find wage labor with adequate pay to support their families may be led to establish serial liaisons with men whose continued support is unreliable. A Burgherside woman who was once told by a Taxpayer that she had no excuse to have several children out of wedlock at the expense of Taxpayers explained that as a black woman without much education she could not get a good job to support her family:

> *The only thing she* [the black woman] *has is her body. So here comes another man that says, "I love you. I will take care of the other children as if they were mine." You know that you need his help to support your family. So you go with him because your body is the only thing you have. Maybe this man gives you two* [more] *children. He takes care of his children and the other two. Then after some time he leaves you.*

Case histories of Burgherside women receiving AFDC reveal a variety of reasons for their becoming welfare recipients, and show that they are not of homogeneous background, education, or capability. Many do not fit the stereotype described in the folk systems of Stockton. The "welfare cycle" as described in these folk systems does not exist in Burgherside. Teenage girls become unwed mothers, but this is not because of parental encouragement. The women receiving AFDC are no different from other Burgherside women in their concern for their children's education and the extent to which they "push" them.

How Beliefs about the "Welfare Cycle" Affect Education

Taxpayers and Nontaxpayers alike believe that Burgherside children are unable to learn in school because they come from families on welfare and are caught up in the "welfare cycle." As I pointed out earlier, Taxpayers think that in a place like Burgherside single-parent families (to which most welfare families belong) cannot raise their children to learn well in school. Furthermore, Taxpayers think that some parents on welfare deliberately discourage their children from doing well in school, so the children, too, grow up to become welfare recipients. A companion belief among Taxpayers is that people who are unemployed, especially the "hard core" unemployed, are likely to come from families on welfare. As children they have not learned the correct attitude toward school and have become dropouts; now as adults they do not have the correct attitude toward work. They make all kinds of excuses to avoid working, and thus continue to depend on welfare. They are those who have not learned to assume the responsibility of working to support their families and are caught up both in the cycle of poverty and the "welfare cycle."

These beliefs about people on welfare and the "welfare cycle" influence the attitudes of Taxpayers toward education in Burgherside and similar neighborhoods. I have already mentioned that most children selected for the headstart program (preschool) come from families on welfare, and, in fact, the Welfare Department is charged with selecting such children. The school problems of older Burgherside children are sometimes explained by pointing out that these children come from families on welfare and therefore have not been motivated to succeed in school by "their home environment." Taxpayers see a strong connection between the behavior of the "hard core unemployed," the "people caught up in the welfare cycle," and the behavior of children from Burgherside and Southside neighborhoods in school. One school official reported in 1968 that:

> . . . many of our students come from homes where little or no stress is laid upon assuming the responsibility on one's job (including the "job" of attending school), and taking it seriously enough to be there every day and on time. In short, we are up against a cultural block.

The belief that children from welfare families cannot learn or that those on welfare do not want to improve their conditions through education may be unfounded for the most part. I have shown that many people on welfare do want to improve their conditions in life and that they want their children to get good educations. Furthermore, life histories of women on welfare when compared with those of women not on welfare show that women on welfare are just as normal as others and are able to raise their children just as effectively. Finally, at least one study in Stockton shows that children from families on welfare are more likely than others from similar neighborhoods and ethnic background to do well in school. In a study of 190 girls from Burgherside high school who were failing one or more subjects in 1962, Fagley and Larsen found that 59 (31.1 %) of them came from "broken homes," and that only 21 (11.1 %) came from families on welfare. Fagley and Larsen concluded from this that it is "because of losing welfare checks for irregular attendance or for suspensions, [that] the majority of those who failed were not receiving welfare aid [Fagley and Larsen 1962:6]." This conclusion is not warranted. Could it not be that children from families on welfare are working harder in school because they don't like to be on welfare?

Guidance and Counseling as Mechanisms for Limiting Future Opportunities

The stated goal of the counseling system is to enable Burgherside children to succeed in school and eventually become Taxpayers. But in many respects the counseling system is actually one of the principal means by which the schools (and the wider community) limit the mobility of Burghersiders into the Taxpayer status. The way in which this is accomplished may be summarized as follows:

1. Burgherside children receive little or no orientation to counseling when they enter junior and senior high schools where these services are available.
2. Each counselor is assigned so many students that Burgherside children cannot receive adequate individual help.
3. The counselors, in addition to having a large number of students assigned to them, spend a high proportion of their time in what they consider "subprofessional kinds of activities."
4. The counselors have a tendency to redefine the academic problems of Burghersiders in clinical or psychological terms and this forces them to resort to therapy rather than educational counseling as a solution.
5. In general, Burgherside children are "programmed" into "deadend courses" that do not lead to their long-range educational and occupational goals.

Once Burgherside students enter the junior high school they are assigned counselors alphabetically. The only information about counseling they receive is contained in the student handbook, and it tells the students only about "programming." Upon entering the senior high school students receive slightly more information because the handbook here adds: "The student may make an appointment with his counselor when he has a problem concerning himself or his schoolwork. Your counselor's job is to *help* you; please take advantage of this [SUSD n.d.].

Some counselors say that they try to see their counselees during the first half of the year to explain to them what services are available, but in my discussions with Burgherside students I found that many of them had not been involved in such orientation. And one junior high school counselor pointed out: *With the heavy counseling loads now in reality, a counselor does well to see* the client *once a year.* It is a known fact that only the most seriously maladjusted students get in to see the counselor more than once or twice . . . and then when the teacher sends them in [emphasis added].

All counselors at the junior high school, except the head counselor, work part-time in spite of the large number of students assigned to them as Table 8.4 shows.

TABLE 8.4

The Number of Students and the Amount of Counseling Time Assigned to Each Counselor at the Junior High School Attended by Burghersiders[a]

Counselor	Amount of counseling time per day	Number of students per counselor
Head counselor	Full time	none (general duties, supervisory)
Mr. X	1 1/2 hrs.	300 (initials A–E)
Mr. Y	2 1/2 hrs.	450 (initials F–N)
Mr. Z	2 1/2 hrs.	450 (initials O–Z)

[a]Source: Stockton Unified School District 1967b: 8.

At the senior high school the counselors are full time but each has a counseling load ranging from 307 to 358.

The counselors complain not only of the large number of students assigned to them, but also of the use of their time for what they consider "irrelevant or subprofessional activities," as one report noted:

> As can be seen from the information in the body of the report the multitudinous demands on the counselor's time seriously detracted from the major function of the Guidance Services Office, which is counseling with pupils, classroom groups, conferring with teachers and parents, and supplying vocational materials to pupils who request them.

Quote from last year's report: "The result is three very fine, very conscientious, very capable counselors who are unhappy and discouraged because they do not have the time to do the work for which they have spent so much money, time and effort preparing themselves."

Seeing no chance of improvement they left this school, a school which desperately needs only top quality personnel with experience and understanding of minority problems [SUSD 1968a:43].

Because of the number of students assigned to each counselor and the use of counselors for "subprofessional activities," many students are not able to see their counselors for other purposes than for "programming," course changes, and preregistration for the next grade. It is because of the subprofessional activities that the counselors complain they are "literally overworked," as one informant explained below:

If a counselor has enough time to sit down and spend 45 minutes by himself in one day, he has almost too much free time. I don't believe that a counselor's time starts at eight o'clock in the morning and finishes when the school is over in the afternoon. And even when the school is out in June he's got work on his desk to be done. The only reason he gets out, leaves school, is because the kids are gone. But I worked at the school last summer in a different capacity. And every day there was a kid there waiting for me. This happened every day. Because as long as the children are there there's some counseling to be done because all of them have problems [emphasis added].

Unlike the functions of the classroom teachers, which tend to be more limited and specialized, those of the counselors are diffused. Counselors work with teachers, students, and administrators of their specific schools. They also work with the testing and research office and the pupil personnel office at the administrative center, as well as with parents and public agencies. Counselors complain of conflicts in the definitions of their role in the school system, and a recent study confirmed that administrators, teachers, and counselors have different conceptions of the job of counselors (SUSD 1969g). One counselor pointed out that counselors are *a buffer between the parent, the teacher, and the administration, and between the administration and the vice-principals.*

In a study of the relation between the administrative organization of the high school and the ways in which students are processed through it, Cicourel and Kitsuse (1963) observed that counselors tend to interpret students' academic problems in clinical terms, often seeking the explanation for poor schoolwork in terms of "motivation," "family situation," "peer adjustment," and so on. When students fail to respond to "psychologically oriented treatment," counselors and social workers may look for "deeper (i.e., clinical) problems," as the causes. The information that a student provides upon request about himself or his background may be taken as a confirmation of such clinical interpretation. Thus the attempt of the school to "help" the student solve his academic problems may result in redefining the "initial basis" of that problem. The authors suggest that this redefinition has important educational consequences (1963:18):

> One consequence of such an orientation of "help" would be to deflect school adminis-
> trations from examining the organization and methods of the school system, including
> the activities of counselors, as sources of academic problems. Another consequence
> of this orientation would be the creation of a population of students organizationally
> differentiated as clinical cases in need of therapeutic treatment.

The situation in Burgherside confirms these observations. But the clinical interpretation of the academic problems of Burgherside students is not only the result of the "bureaucratic counseling system" but also a reflection of the views held by Taxpayers that the problems of Burghersiders, whether these be school failures, unemployment, inadequate housing, or poverty, are primarily of a clinical nature. Counselors share the Taxpayers' views that the Burgherside environment is responsible for school failures in the neighborhood. They are also professionally trained to look for causes and solutions to academic problems in terms of "personal problems." The background of the counselors, therefore, does not prepare them to examine the activities of elements of the school system, including their own activities, as possible causes of school failure among Burgherside students. They probably regard as unimportant what they call "the routine educational counseling," although this may be what Burghersiders actually need. Only a few Burgherside students get such counseling, and these are said by the counselors to be those who know what they want, especially those who "have the potential to go to college." The counselors clearly distinguish between academic counseling and counseling for personal and social adjustment (i.e. therapy) and show a strong preference for the latter as their proper function.

My interviews with both parents and students suggest that in addition to seeing his counselor for the "routine sort of things"—programming, course changes, preregistration—a Burgherside student goes to see his counselor only if (1) he is sent there by his teacher as a behavior problem; (2) the counselor sends for him because he has a high potential that does not show in his schoolwork. Most Burgherside students, then, do not go to see their counselors for educational guidance on their own initiative. Furthermore, they tend to take their academic problems to their parents or their friends, the people least in a position to help them. Table 8.5 describes the persons with whom students in various grades discuss their academic difficulties on their own initiative.

TABLE 8.5
Persons to Whom Burgherside Children Most Often Address Their Academic Difficulties[a]

Person consulted	Total (96)	7th (9)	8th (12)	9th (24)	10th (28)	11th (12)	12th (11)
Parents	41.17	77.78	58.33	33.33	35.71	41.67	27.27
Siblings	12.50	11.11	8.33	20.83	7.14	25.00	—
Teachers	6.25	—	—	8.33	7.14	8.33	18.18
Counselor	9.38	—	16.67	8.33	7.14	—	36.36
Friends	26.04	11.11	16.67	25.00	35.71	25.00	9.09
Nobody	4.17	—	—	4.17	7.14	—	9.09

[a]Source: Author's interviews with Burgherside students.

The students were also asked if they had discussed with other people their educational goals and how they planned to attain these goals. The majority of them had not talked with their teachers or counselors. The eleventh- and twelfth-grade students consulted their counselors most because they had to obtain information about the requirements for high school graduation.

Most Burgherside students receive nonacademic counseling, that is, counseling dealing with "personal problems" as manifested in "problems with teachers (in the classroom) and on school grounds." All these problems are ultimately attributed to their environment as one counselor explains:

ANTHR.: *And what does your counseling consist of mostly?*

COUNSELOR: *Well, the counseling primarily deals with—for the period of time we have for counseling—you spend most of the time doing things other than counseling. But the time we do get into counseling we deal with social problems—problems in the classroom. Unfortunately this problem is referred to the counselor—not that the counselor would discipline them—but discipline problems occur in the classroom. And we are sort of liaison between the home, the students, and the teacher and try to work—whatever the situation is. And then the problems in the home that affect the school.*

ANTHR.: *What kind of problems are in the home?*

COUNSELOR: *Well, home-oriented problems in relationship to not wanting to settle down in the classroom, primarily, defiance of authority, you might say. I am not saying that it's all right to be so strict authority. But when you have a complete lack of cooperation in all respects—we've had a few cases of that nature; anything that was asked, requested or told to do is to refuse it. So this is the kind of situation that we have. And we have problems in relation to some of the students who could not get along with anyone and they always take offense with anything that is said—the teacher or the others. They're very tense kids and any-*

thing would offend them. And you have some that always carry a chip on their shoulders: nothing is right with the school; nothing is right with with anything—unless it is something that they want you to do. And anything that is against what they want you to do is wrong.

The counselor believes that the children are behaving that way because their parents failed to teach them the behavior appropriate in the school setting:

COUNSELOR: *I would say that these students do not see any relationship between their school and their future. Some never have, I believe. And when I say "Never," it's on the basis of the way in which they are. What happens to them outside of the context (of the school), that I don't know. But anyway, they can't see any relationship to school, between school and their life style—because their parents have not had the same kind of feeling. They themselves have not had the same kind of experience in school—from the time they get into the kindergarten. This can be blamed on some of the teachers who have no feelings for human beings. So therefore the child is completely closed off. And when they had almost all bad experiences, then the child sort of reinforces himself all the period of time. And when they come to a new experience they just assume it's going to be bad. And they sort of react to it before they actually had it. And this is it.*

Another counselor describes the effect of the environment on the children's motivation as follows:

Perhaps the most serious problem is that of motivation. Often we are working with youngsters from an environment where the people are suspicious of education and see no future beyond day-to-day existence; or those who find among their peers the reinforcements of success, acceptance, and mutuality of interests which they do not find among adults with whom they associate. These "adult models" with whom they are familiar are persons who have rejected them—often their parents, or, perhaps, teachers who have considered them failures and below normal or average individuals—or adults who have part-time, unskilled and semi-skilled jobs and dependent upon welfare agencies [emphasis added].

The definition of guidance needs of Burgherside children in terms of "personal problems arising from their environment" fits into the patron–client relationship between Taxpayers (including counselors) and Burghersiders. As in other aspects of this relationship, Taxpayers regard themselves not only as service-oriented but also as having the qualifications and responsibility to define the "needs" of their clients and the necessary "remedies."

The interpretation of Burgherside academic problems in psychological and clinical terms has led some counselors to adopt "group counseling." The purpose of group counseling is said to be helping

> *the students to work through their feelings and hopefully to understand why they feel as they do, so they can do something positive about it. It also can help them better understand their peers, their parents, and other authority figures in their lives.*

But group counseling is also a technique utilized by counselors to solve the problem of having to deal with a large number of students. It does not, however, work with all students, as one counselor points out:

> *I think group counseling seems to be about the most—I think it is the most positive. It depends upon the individual too. Some cannot function, cannot open themselves up in a group. It has to be a one-to-one basis. And some do function better in a group in terms of how they feel; they express themselves and relate to one another. But some of them just don't relate and so we have to find a way to get around it.*

Counselors who practice group counseling say they would like to see teachers included, since *many counseling needs grow out of teachers' relationship with students.* Some even suggest that teachers should be trained as *para-counselors who can handle minor counseling problems.*

The therapeutic treatment used in the group counseling or in dealing with individual cases consists of *showing interest in the student, by being patient, helping the student develop his own values, to know himself, which may even require the counselor developing the technique of "hearing" nonverbal communications, since these students have difficulty in verbalizing.*

One counselor described his role as follows:

> *Yes, I do group counseling. I have one group that we are involved a little bit about twice a week. And this primarily is dealing with students expressing their feelings so that everybody knows what their feelings are. Many of them are quite interested and if they are within their peer group they can begin to relate primarily and say what they have on their mind, and hopefully this will carry over to the classroom . . . I am not really sure. I have not set up any sort of evaluation device yet. But I am working on it now—so that I can measure what kind of progress has really been*

made. The only thing I am doing now is sending a form-note to the teacher to have them fill out and I have the students fill out a form at the beginning and they fill out another form approximately in the middle of the session and another at the end of the session; then in the end I will try to make some kind of evaluation, if I can. If it doesn't work then I will try something different in the next group.

By defining the problems of Burgherside children in school in terms of social and psychological adjustment, the counselors encourage the students in groups and as individuals to talk about their problems and work out their solutions. They regard such an endeavor as a prerequisite for Burgherside children to succeed in school. Burgherside students, however, do not appear to succeed in working out their solutions to these personal problems. Therefore they rarely reach the point where they can start to talk about and work out the solutions to their academic problems.

CHANNELING BURGHERSIDE STUDENTS INTO LOW ABILITY GROUPING

In Chapter 5 (p. 83) I pointed out that the courses actually taken by Burgherside students, especially at the senior high school level, are not those that can lead them to achieve their educational and occupational goals. Most students take courses regarded both by the schools and the neighborhood people as "dead-end courses." But they take such courses partly because of the counseling system, for the counselors tend to "program" the students into certain classes primarily on the basis of their previous performance on test rather than their future plans. When Burgherside students first reach the junior high they are assigned classes in the seventh grade on the basis of their records from the elementary school. I have already pointed out that these records do not represent their true ability because (*a*) teachers at the elementary school appear to grade Burgherside children on the basis of other factors than the actual work they do in the class, and (*b*) (as a result) these children do not learn by the time they leave the elementary school to associate working hard with making better grades. Failing to recognize these and other factors, counselors assign most Burgherside students in the seventh grade to "low ability groups" in the school's tracking system. One counselor explained their method of "programming" the children into "ability groups" as follows:

We were testing these kids and placing them in a tracking system. And this is why we need to have three tracks: X, Y, Z. X-track was the highest, with high scores, 7, 8, 9; Y-was the 4, 5, 6; and Z was the 1, 2, 3 group. Well, a large segment of these kids—mainly Negroes and Mexicans—I'd say, fall into this 1, 2, 3 group. And what we were doing was tracking them in a lower bracket on the educational scale.

Once Burgherside students are placed in these "low ability groups" they rarely advance above the "low" groups in subsequent grades. The response of the schools Superintendent to the "demand" of the Black Unity Council that tracking systems should be abolished appears to confirm this.

> Tracking is the title given to the organizational procedure of placing children into ability groups and assigning curriculum and learning sequences to match that ability. It has been a long-practiced procedure. It has some considerable merit if we are skillful enough to truly ascertain ability.[3] There is, however, much reason to question its effect on children. A child so placed in a low ability group has a serious problem in ever emerging from that category [SUSD 1968b:4251–4255].

As a result of the "demand" of the Black Unity Council the superintendent promised to ask the principal and interested faculty members of the senior high school to begin "untracking" their students in some academic areas in the fall of 1968. In-service training was to be organized to prepare teachers and administrators for this change and "heterogeneous groups" of students would be initiated, as personnel were trained or hired "who can create viable learning experiences" in such groups. When some of these things were eventually implemented it was found that those students who normally should be in the "low ability groups" did not fail their courses in the classes for "high ability groups." The counselor referred to above explained what happened when the low and high ability students were allowed to take college prep courses:

> *Well, after* [the sensitivity training] *some of us decided that we as counselors should make some changes because if you take a child's interest and personality and the drive that he has sometimes some of these will not be reflected in these test scores. So therefore we started channeling them into these other college prep courses. And the Social Science Department said, "Well, we will just eliminate tracking." And this is one area where the range of discussion can be broad and everything doesn't have to be read at the reading level. So therefore they opened it up.* [And they said] *"And we will accept X, Y, Z together on an integrated basis. And we are not going to count them even. We will just let the IBM scatter them into these classes." And it worked beautifully. Last year* [1969–1970] *those kids were placed on higher math and in algebra; some of them are now taking chemistry, senior biology.* And these are the basic subjects and they haven't been failing them. *So it tells me this: that we are putting*

---

[3]School officials, especially counselors, often present the case for tracking as if those considered poor students are the ultimate beneficiaries of the system. Consider the following statement made by a counselor during an interview on tracking in Burgherside schools:

a child in something where he is going to be challenged. And he sure has showed that he can improve and he can do some work.

In 1969–1970, when these changes were initiated, the number of chemistry courses in the senior high school grew from two to five. My informant reported that, *There were black and Mexican kids in all of them,* a situation that did not exist in 1968–1969 when I studied the courses taken by Burghersiders.

BURGHERSIDERS WANT ACADEMIC GUIDANCE FOR THEIR CHILDREN

School counselors distinguish between counseling and guidance. In guidance, according to them, the counselor tells the student what is expected of him; in counseling the student decides what he wants to do: He talks about his problems and works out their solutions himself. Burghersiders say that they prefer guidance to counseling for their children. They reject the definition of their children's educational difficulties in terms of personal maladjustment. They say they are poor, live under inadequate housing conditions, and do not have good jobs, but they are not "psychologically sick" or "lacking in motivation." The schools and counselors do not know that the parents tell children to "get all the education you can." How Burgherside parents feel about the school's interpretation of their children's educational problems as due to psychological problems can be seen from the following incident which took place in 1969.

A teacher reported to the principal that a young Mexican-American boy was being very disruptive in class. The teacher quoted the boy as saying he would either run away from home or kill himself. The principal sent for the mother, who did not understand English very well, for a conference. When

---

Let's take one area of Mathematics. There are certain hurdles that you must get over to go to the next hurdle in math. So we were taught first of all to add; then we learned how to subtract; then to multiply; then to divide. Now you take one step at a time. Then we went a little further and when we got up there we learned a simple arithmetic. Then we went into algebra and from algebra into geometry, and then into trigonometry. And then we went on to calculus and other higher branches of math. This is only one area. You're talking about a kid getting into a class that he wants. Right. We test our students and we have to see how they place on the stanine system. Now basically this is what it means: Here I am in the first three down here and I am going to take algebra. And I am not doing too well in algebra but I get by with a "C" or "D". Well, a "C" is possibly a pretty good grade and I didn't work too hard, I didn't work up to my full capacity. Therefore I go into Geometry and I make about a "C" or "D". All right, you're thinking whether I should get into Trig. These are hurdles you must go over. Right? Whether I should continue in Math? So really, if I haven't improved and I go into Trig. I'll possibly make a "C" or "D" too. But I should get the message after a while that this kid isn't doing too well and that too much math is going to hurt him.

the mother was told that the school psychologist had been invited "to look into the boy's problems" she became very angry and strongly objected to the school's classification of her son as a "psychotic."

Burghersiders say that the school should stress educational guidance because it will help the children find the school meaningful and get along with their teachers and with one another. Many parents recognize that they do not have sufficient background to help their children plan their educations and occupations, even though they know *how far* they want their children to go in school and what kinds of jobs they want them to have. They therefore expect the school—the counselors, especially—to provide their children with this type of guidance. Most students I talked with did not feel that their parents had *rejected* them; they felt, however, that their parents could not help them—that their parents were not capable of helping them.

We saw earlier that most Burgherside junior and senior high school students want to go to college, and that their parents also want them to go to college. But Burgherside students do not know (*1*) the requirements for getting into college, (*2*) how to apply for admission to college, (*3*) what it costs to have a college education, the possible sources of financial assistance, or how to qualify for the latter, and (*4*) how to relate their college aspirations to their vocational or professional aspirations. Neither do their parents provide them with this kind of guidance, because parents, themselves, do not know.

Many Burgherside parents described the following basic guidance needs of their children. (*1*) Counselors should show their children the connection between what they are doing in school now and their future lives as adults in American society. Parents imply that for them education for its own sake has little meaning. (*2*) Counselors should teach their children the relationship between the *effort* they are putting into their schoolwork and the possibility of getting the jobs they want when they "finish school." Burgherside children often realize too late in their educational careers that their lack of effort in school leads away from their desire for good and "clean" jobs, as this interview illustrates.

ANTHR.: *Do you think that in your schoolwork you are doing as well as you would like to?*

INFORMANT: *No. I don't think I am doing as well as I would like to. Last year I was goofing up too much like not going to school and cutting classes. I was goofing up with friends.*

ANTHR.: *Why do you allow your friends to take you away from school?*

INFORMANT: *I don't.*

ANTHR.: *All right, why do you goof off then?*

INFORMANT: *That was last year?*

ANTHR.: *Yes. But why? Why did you goof off last year?*

INFORMANT: *Because I really don't want to go to school. I didn't care about school.*

ANTHR.:   *You didn't care about school? Why not?*

INFORMANT: *I didn't care about going to classes last year.*

ANTHR.:   *When did you decide to go to college?*

INFORMANT: *This year.*

ANTHR.:   *What made you decide this year?*

INFORMANT: *Because you can't get a good job if you don't go to college.*

ANTHR.:   *When did you learn that if you don't go to college you won't get a good job?*

INFORMANT: *Because all my friends are out of school and they are just staying home; they are out of school and they are not working; because they didn't go to college. If you go to college you can get a good job.*

The students who "mess around" or "mess up" are potential candidates for "psychological counseling." Counselors say that they must first help the students find out "who they are and solve their problems." But Burghersiders say that when these children are "messing up" they need guidance, someone to tell them, "Stop doing this because you are hurting yourself."

The students "mess around" in many ways: cutting school, not doing homework, not taking the "right" courses, and so on. In the "ability groups," Burghersiders are at the bottom tracks which automatically channel them into the easiest—often "dead end"—courses. It is difficult for a student in the bottom track to move into the middle or high track. A student wanting to choose a course above his track level might be told that, *The course is hard.* The student usually responds: *Oh, no, not me. I won't take that.* In Burgherside this situation is known as "not taking the right courses." The right courses are described as "those that will enable you to continue your education"; the "right courses" are the opposite of such "low" and "dead-end courses" as shop, homemaking, work experience, or stagecraft.

Many students are thus "frightened away" from the "right courses," believing them to be "too hard." One twelfth-grade student said: *Yes, I have met many students who feel that they should not take classes that are hard. I felt this way myself. I guess everyone does—maybe because in an easy class one could get good grades easier than in a hard class.* Another student in eleventh grade said: *I think most students feel this way. Because most students like to take courses that are easy to pass. Very few students take the right courses because they feel they might not be able to pass them.*

Interviews with school counselors confirmed that the students are not taking the "right courses" as defined by Burghersiders. The counselors assign these students "low courses" because of (*1*) the students' test scores and (*2*) the students' avoidance of more difficult courses. One counselor describes the latter situation as follows:

We base our class assignment on his test scores. What he's done in the past. And I think in some cases we do a child injustice by doing on this.

But most of the children are honest with you. They will tell you, "Me, I didn't do too well in English. Don't put me in a hard class."

Now, if he's going to be honest with me, I've got to be honest with him and put him in the type of class where he could function and possibly have some success. And if I were to take a child out of the tenth grade with a ninth grade when he was making a low grade in English and give him English Literature which is a top subject—when they start reading Beowulf—well, he couldn't know what they were talking about.

So therefore, I better start him down there where it would be some benefit to him: plain grammar, plain writing, some of these things and reading will help this child and he will have steady goals and some success.

The same thing applies to any other field. But our basic subjects are Science, English, Math and Social Studies.

But Burgherside students do not necessarily do better in the "easy" courses. Some "go blank" because they are bored with unchallenging materials. Neither do they enjoy "plain grammar," as one student comments: *I don't care about how sentences are separated and cut into diagrams and parts of speech.* Another student also said: *You mostly sit down and read and write and answer questions from the book. It is same old thing every day and it gets boring till it goes in one ear and out the other.*

Burgherside parents believe that counselors should not assign students "low courses" just because of their past test scores. If students want to avoid "hard courses" the counselor should explain that they need such courses to continue their education. Parents do not know what courses their children need; counselors know. Some parents are not able to explain "real well" why they need an education; the school can. The point that the children need "a little talking to," educational guidance, is illustrated by the case described in the interview excerpt below.

ANTHR.: *So you believe that the main differences between the people of Northside and Southside are money and education?*

PARENT: *I feel it is money. The kids over here don't have nice houses and they don't have that much extra money to spend and they don't have nice cars. So what they end up is saying, "We are going to get one thing." And what is it? It is clothes. So they end up with a lot of clothes. You see, this makes up a little gap in a sense, that "we don't have a car, we don't have any money and when I come home Mama was drunk but that's all right, I got me a dress." So this makes the difference. But you are still not less smart, they are the same.*

ANTHR.: *Do the kids worry about their not having got good homes, good houses, to live in and they don't have cars or so? Do they worry about those things? They talk about them?*

PARENT: *The average black young man that I know talks about it. For instance, one little boy—this is his last year at Edison—and I was telling him, I says, "Why don't you go out to the University and make your student loans [if] you are going to go to the University?" And he says, "How much money will I get?" And I says, "Well, I don't know. My son was going to go to G——— University and I make out the budget for him and it came to $2,220." And I says, "That was away from home and he will be right out to the University." And I says, "To go here will cost maybe $1300 or $1500." And he says, "Oo-o! If I had that money I could buy me a car; I could buy me some clothes; I could buy me this." To him it sounded like a lot of money. And half of the kids I know that could go to college—at first time they get out of high school they get a little job making them $1.75 an hour. Oh! That's a lot of money!*

ANTHR.: *Suppose you gave some of the kids here some money, do you think they would prefer to use the money to go to college, or to buy a car?*

PARENT: *Buy a car—because this is something that they never had. They haven't really had the training over the years saying: School is what it is; you go to school and get education and you can buy yourself a car. You can buy what you want to buy. They would buy a car.*

I asked this same question of Burgherside students—and of the 68 students who answered the question, 13 said they would cars; 55 that they would use it to continue their educations. However, I think that if these students were given such money, most of them would not continue their educations because (*1*) they have no clear idea of what education beyond high school would bring to them and (*2*) they have received no adequate guidance and preparation for continuing their education beyond high school.

CHAPTER **9**

The Education Rehabilitation Movement: Taxpayers' Solution to the Problems of School Failure in Burgherside

Introduction

I have argued here that school failure in Burgherside is an adaptation to the limited opportunities had by Burghersiders to benefit from their educations. I have tried to show that Taxpayers, especially those making up the school personnel, see Burgherside environment as the main cause of school failure. School officials, like other Taxpayers, have interpreted the problem of school failure in Burgherside in psychological and clinical terms; they have also blamed it on Burgherside culture and language, which they argue are deficient (SUSD 1968b:4251-4255). Consequently, when Taxpayers decide to solve the problem of school failure in Burgherside, the solutions they propose deal mostly with "redeeming" Burghersiders from the effects of their environment, language, and culture. The policies and methods of the schools are left intact, except where changes are necessary in order to implement the new programs. Nor do the proposed solutions deal with the institutional barriers that limit the opportunity of Burghersiders to benefit from their educations—that is, those barriers mainly responsible for the evolution of the school failure adaptation in the first place, namely the social and economic discriminations that prevent Burghersiders from receiving full benefits from their educations.

Stockton Unified School District began in about 1963 to operate "remedial programs" aimed at improving the work of children in Burgherside and other Southside schools. This was a part of state and national efforts to increase the success of the children of the poor and ethnic minorities in public schools, especially in urban areas. These local and national efforts have many of the same characteristics as a social movement, and I am therefore calling them the Education Rehabilitation Movement. Here I follow Aberle (1966:315) in defining a social movement as "an organized effort by a group of human beings to effect a change in the face of resistance by other human beings." The Education Rehabilitation Movement is essentially a Taxpayers' movement designed to change Nontaxpayers into Taxpayers, and the resistance that Burghersiders and similar groups offer to the movement is often described by Taxpayers as "their apathy." On the other hand, Torch (1965) sees a social movement as a collective device by the members of the movement to solve their collective problems. This definition would not only exclude the Education Rehabilitation Movement but also missionary movements, the sole purpose of which may be to "save the souls" of people in other lands.

THE HISTORY OF THE MOVEMENT

The American belief in "equal educational opportunity" has been one of the main bases of the public school system. But as Coleman (1969) pointed out, in the history of the public school system the meaning of equal educational opportunity has changed several times, and in 1964 the concept meant

1. that all children in a given locality (like Stockton) have *access* to the same schools and the same curriculum, free of charge; and
2. that *the effects* of schooling should reflect this "equality of educational opportunity" (Coleman 1969:18).

Prior to 1964 it was known that all children did not benefit equally from the same curriculum open to them. For example, at the elementary school level groups of children attending the same schools learned more or less effectively, and in secondary schools different groups of children took different types of courses and also varied in their success. By the early 1960s the concept of "cultural deprivation" had come to be used to explain the failures of the children of the poor and ethnic minorities in public schools.

A national effort to solve the problem of school failures among such children began with the passage of the Civil Rights Act of 1964, which mandated the U.S. Commissioner of Education to "assess the lack of 'equal educational opportunity' among racial and other groups in the United States [Coleman 1969:18]." The U.S. Office of Education subsequently sponsored a study showing that "inequality of educational opportunity [existed] with regard to the effects of schooling" among the various groups, and that "the effects of schooling" depended partly on the family and neighborhood environment. Thus the conclusion of the study about the "cause" of school failure is very much like the folk theory of Taxpayers in Stockton about the "cause" of school failure in Burgherside. The study recommended some ways to increase the success of the children of the poor and ethnic minorities in public schools. For example, it argued that black lower-class culture influences black lower-class children in a way that makes them fail in school; whereas the white middle-class culture influences white middle-class children in a way that makes them succeed in school. The study, therefore, suggested that schools should devise "remedial" educational programs that would counteract the influence of black lower-class culture on black children. This would increase their success in school, although it would not necessarily make them do as well as white middle class children (Coleman 1969:23-24).

Coleman's Report had two important consequences relevant to the present study. First, it provided the justification for massive federal assistance to the public school system. In 1965 the U.S. Congress passed the Elementary and Secondary Education Act (ESEA) allocating $1.3 billion to assist the public schools to overcome the assumed negative influence of the family and neighborhood environment.[1] Second, the Report's explanation of school failures of the children of the poor and ethnic minorities was similar to the "cultural deprivation" hypothesis; the Report thus provided both empirical and "official" justification of the theory. The emphasis on the concept of "equal educational opportunity" in terms of "effects of schooling" provided the basis for Congressional appropriation of money to aid the public schools, and "cultural deprivation" became the theoretical basis upon which the public schools designed programs to be funded by the federal government in areas of curriculum, teaching techniques, and the like. Purcell lists more than 30 such programs under the ESEA grants (1969:412).

---

[1] It is possible that the findings of the study headed by Coleman were available to Congress and the Office of Education in whole or part in 1965. However, the findings were not made public until the Fourth of July weekend of 1966 (Mosteller and Moynihan 1972:5). In the present work I have relied on Coleman's summary of the findings published in 1969.

Education Rehabilitation Movement in Stockton

Before 1963 the concept of "equal educational opportunity" existed in Stockton in the sense that all children had *access* to the same schools in their neighborhoods, but the curriculum was not necessarily the same in all neighborhoods.[2] Some informants said that although it was well known that children from certain parts of the city and from certain ethnic groups were failing in school, no serious efforts were made to help them do better in school. Taxpayers and school personnel rationalized their inaction by saying that such children could not do well in school and that it could be proved by statistics. They made sure, however, that an equal amount of money was allocated to each child in all schools, so no one could attribute the school failures of these children to lack of equal funding.

After the passage of the State Compensatory Education Bill in 1963, known as the McAteer Act, the school district began to receive money from the state "to provide additional educational services to some disadvantaged children." Since the passage of the ESEA Title I in 1965 several federally funded remedial programs have been developed "**to overcome the shortcomings in the children from the disadvantaged areas** [emphasis added]." They include programs dealing with specific problems in reading, mathematics, language, self-concept, teaching techniques, curriculum development, and the like.

These programs were initially developed and supervised by some members of the district's central administration. When it was discovered that "there was no limit to the number of programs the district could request for funding," a Federal Projects Office was established, with a director and staff. In 1969, a group of teachers recommended to the school superintendent that he appoint a Compensatory Education Director, directly under his authority. The director was appointed in 1969 and the Office and Staff of Compensatory Education were created, and later the position was elevated to that of an assistant superintendent.

Individual remedial programs such as Pre-school/Headstart, Compensatory Education, Bilingual Education, also came to have separate offices, directors, staff, consultants, evaluators, and the like. The requirements for federal funding vary from program to program. Those like Bilingual Education are funded on a competitive basis, and therefore must be "innovative." Compensatory Education and Headstart programs are not funded

---

[2] At the time of the present study (1968–1970) informants insisted that there were differences both in kind and quality between the curricula of the schools serving Burghersiders and those serving Taxpayers. Unfortunately I was unable to obtain the figures for the number of "shop" courses in Edison Senior High (Burghersiders') and in Stagg Senior High (Taxpayers') to verify the accuracy of my informants' statements.

on a competitive basis and so need not be "innovative," according to one informant:

The ESEA Title I of 1965 provided funds to be used for the disadvantaged students. It is the titlement type of program which means that you have so much money set aside for a school district to use in the program that goes along with it. You are not competitive, in other words, you are not in a position in which you go through trying to write the best proposal to compete with other people. You just don't do that with ESEA. . . .

Most remedial programs of the Rehabilitation Movement are designed on the theory that there are *shortcomings in the children that must be overcome.* Like missionary movements, the Education Rehabilitation Movement is a "redemptive movement" that aims at "a total change in the individual" (Aberle 1966:317). Aberle (1966:320–321) states that

Virtually all redemptive movements, like the transformative movements, reject at least some of the features of the current society. They find evil in the world, not merely in the sinner. Although they put their energies into achieving a total change in persons rather than in societies, they also castigate the society.

One of the main goals of the Rehabilitation Movement is to "redeem" the "culturally deprived child" from "his environment."[3] As described in the programs this environment in Stockton has three components: (*1*) *the child's mother* (the father is almost never mentioned), who, it is said, "does not know" how to teach her child to succeed in school (for example, she does not reward her child for accomplishments); (*2*) *his home,* which is described as "disorganized" and not conducive to teaching the child the right values and positive attitudes toward school; and (*3*) *his neighborhood,* where, it is said, the residents have negative attitudes toward education. A child growing up in this type of environment comes to school at the age of five undeveloped in areas essential for success in school: language, reasoning ability, motivation, pride in achievement, perceptual ability, attention span, and feeling of self-worth. He also comes to school unable to adapt to authority and regulations.

As described by the Taxpayers, much resistance to the Rehabilitation Movement comes from the environment—from the apathy of the parents

---

[3]See exchanges between Austin (1965a,b) and Guthrie and Kelly (1965). In his criticism of the concept of "cultural deprivation" Austin asked its proponents: "From what is the child to be rehabilitated?" To this Guthrie and Kelly replied: "From undesirable behavior patterns acquired in the home and neighborhood."

and the community. The schools want parents to "become more involved" by attending PTA meetings and parent–teacher conferences. Some elementary schools in "target areas" like Burgherside persuade their teachers to visit parents at home. It is argued that more contacts between Burghersiders and "persons in positions of responsibility in the school system" will create more positive attitudes toward school. Taxpayers who favor "racial integration" of the school use a similar argument, namely that the negative effects of the Burgherside environment will be reduced if Burgherside children attend schools in Taxpayers' neighborhoods.

One "remedial program" not yet operating at the time of this study would intervene on behalf of the child as soon as he is born. The program is variously called "Happy Birthday," "Assisting Parent to Promote School Success," and the like. Mothers would be trained to "work effectively with their children immediately following the birth of the children," learning through "imitation of the aide and other resource persons." The program lists the following objectives in changing the mother component of the child's environment:

> 1. The importance of listening to the child, responding to his behavior, and anticipating his needs and actions will be repeatedly stressed. It is this type of behavior, of course, that the aide will illustrate with her own interaction with the mother.
> 2. The mother will be taught to emphasize, reward, and reinforce the behavior in the children which they find appropriate and will be urged to use disapproval and punishment techniques as little as possible.
> 3. The importance of conversation with the child will be stressed; mothers will be taught techniques to encourage the child to talk, ask questions, to be curious about objects.
> 4. The mother will be taught the value of helping the child to attend to objects, stimuli differences, similarities and groupings in the visual and auditory environment.
> 5. The mother will be taught strategies for regulating the behavior of her child which will then increase the level of conversation between them and will encourage the child to make choices and participate in the decision-making processes of the family.
> On these points and others, the focus will be upon showing the mother how to interact with another person rather than upon telling the mother what to do in a situation she did not have a chance to observe.

The descriptions of Burgherside and other Southside mothers given in the remedial programs and in interviews with Taxpayers are not based on any close study of these women in their homes and neighborhoods, but are based on Taxpayers' folk conceptions of Burghersiders. Such folk conceptions are reinforced by statistics about parents' education, unemployment, income, percentage of families on Aid to Families with Dependent Children (AFDC), and percentage of ethnic minorities in the neighborhood. These statistics lumped together invoke in the minds of Taxpayers the image of *a deplorable and depriving environment*, as one Taxpayer described Burgherside. Taxpayers therefore strongly believe that children who grow up in such an environment have a good many shortcomings "thrust upon them by the accident of birth."

The movement concentrates efforts on rehabilitating the child at school. Two main techniques are used. One, called "behavior modification technique," is directed toward "helping the child develop a sense of self-worth" and "positive attitude toward school."

The other technique of rehabilitation is the use of specialized instruction. The curriculum may be modified to make it "more relevant to the needs of the disadvantaged child." Courses, books, and other materials dealing with the various ethnic groups are used at all levels. Teachers participate in summer workshops to write companion texts on Black History, Mexican American History, Oriental History, and so on. The walls of history classrooms are decorated with posters of ethnic interest. Schools conduct in-service training "to help teachers understand the disadvantaged pupils more," but as I pointed out in Chapter 7, some teachers after going through in-service training become more confused about how to treat students.

Teachers are encouraged to be "innovative" in their instructional techniques. However, some remedial programs (e.g., bilingual education) come with built-in instructional techniques. The "experts" (often external consultants) who designed the program may insist on a particular teaching method. In the Compensatory Education Program the slogan is "individualized, diagnostic, and prescriptive approach."

> A basic approach or teaching strategy for this activity (reading) is its broad compensatory nature; a program that takes into account and is *designed to counteract those environmental factors which work against success for the child* [emphasis added]. The approach is pupil-centered and as individualized as possible. This individualization of the instruction program results from a comprehensive diagnostic analysis of each pupil's strengths and special educational needs. With such an educational diagnosis, the classroom teacher including other members of the instructional staff can better provide those learning experiences which will result in the greatest possible academic success [SUSD 1969a:18].

This approach essentially means that each child will receive instruction based on the analysis of his own specific learning difficulties. This is possible because there are teacher-aides and specialists to assist the regular classroom teacher, and it is hoped that this approach will help the children learn more. Some teachers in the Compensatory Education Program say they are much pleased with the idea of "individualized instruction."

Neither Burghersiders nor other groups for whom the remedial programs are intended participate in their development. Burghersiders are not consulted at the planning stages, and may never fully understand why and how these programs are supposed to increase the school success of their children. When the proposals for funding these programs are sent to Sacramento or Washington they are usually described as having been developed with the help of "a broad community-based committee," but such committees rarely include parents from the "target population." Their members are Taxpayers, some of whom may belong to ethnic minorities, and are usually teachers. These minority representatives may know about Burghersiders, but rarely consult with them about the programs.

The general procedure for "involving" parents whose children are in the remedial programs may be described as follows: Taxpayers design a program they think will solve some aspect of Burgherside's educational problems. If the program is funded, consultants are hired to implement it, and when it is in operation parents are expected to become involved in a program they may not fully understand. One informant reported that during its third year of operation an informal survey showed that many parents did not know what compensatory education programs were about:

> We went around in the Garfield and Van Buren areas, the Mexican families, for example. We asked them, "What do you know about the ESEA programs?" Because both schools were strictly ESEA schools. But they didn't know what ESEA was. They thought it was something that had to do with free lunches. They thought this was something that had to do with reading but no real idea what ESEA was.

Sometimes even teachers who are supposed to implement the programs in the classroom do not fully understand what it is about. My informant above continued:

> In fact, some of the teachers, they didn't know what ESEA was either. That's right. In fact, when ESEA first came in, we find that three years later we were of the opinion that ESEA would have done so much above and beyond in order to provide the real basis for learning. But in talking to the teachers we found that ESEA meant to them only that they would have smaller classes and more audiovisual things, you see. So this was what was actually going on because they didn't seem to be really confronted because nobody knew what was really going on. There was no real learning factor. What everybody got was the same dose that they [the students] were getting before, except in smaller groups.

Interviews with school officials confirm these statements. One informant pointed out that until recently the "target schools" were not at all involved in developing the "remedial programs":

> It was not until 1968 that we started involving the parents and teachers in deciding what types of programs within the ESEA guidelines would

be formulated. And now we have an active Parents' Advisory Committee and Teacher's Steering Committees. Prior to 1968 we had as much input as possible from the schools but we really wrote it out of the downtown office's program, not their program. When we went out to the schools and had them decide what to put into it then it became their program. And it became more effective.

However, such a voice has never been extended to Burgherside parents, and parents are not really involved.[4]

The Bilingual Education Demonstration Project:
A Case Study of an Education Rehabilitation Program

The bilingual Education Demonstration Project at Burgherside elementary school illustrates the way in which the Education Rehabilitation Movement programs are conceived, planned, and implemented by Taxpayers in Stockton.[5] In its first year the bilingual program operated in Burgherside only, but expanded to three other Southside schools by the time this study was completed. I will deal primarily with the situation in Burgherside.

---

[4]It does not really matter where one begins to investigate this problem. The general conclusion is that no one, except at the top, really understood what or how these remedial programs were supposed to function. The State Department of Education review in 1969 states:

> The consensus of the review team was that there was a good awareness and understanding and acceptance of the philosophy and objectives of the Compensatory Education at the top of the administrative level. However, this level of understanding did not always permeate the various echelons of line and staff positions. Compensatory Education, as an educational enterprise, planned to meet the specific needs of educationally disadvantaged children from poverty background, appeared not to be well understood by teachers, building administrators, and central office staff members. The concept of comprehensive programming to meet the multiple needs of children has not been accepted by the central office staff. Upon completion of numerous interviews and observations, staff members were of the opinion that Compensatory Education was or should be a partially fragmented program in remediation for children who were emotionally disturbed or had limited ability. Thus, the level of expectations seemed quite low. The Stockton Title I project was conceived, designed and implemented by the central office staff. A project writer, who is also the project director, wrote the design and submitted it to the Office of Compensatory Education. Classroom teachers, principals, members of the target area community and most central office staff members were essentially uninvolved and uninformed about the project [State of California Department of Education 1969:7].

[5]This section is not meant as a criticism of bilingual education *per se*. I am chiefly concerned with the role of Taxpayers and Burghersiders in its planning and implementation, and the implication of this for the expected result.

Some informants (Taxpayers) said that Mexican-American children were failing in school because they were not fluent in English. One school official suggested that a study of Burghersiders would show that Mexican-American children often fail their English reading and social studies because they cannot speak standard American English. The children who are not fluent in English do not participate actively in the classroom either, because they do not understand the lessons in English or they are afraid of being laughed at by their classmates for their accents. In addition, Stockton has a large number of children from transient migrant farm-labor families, who enroll in its schools for varying lengths of time. In the past, the school district had a program for teaching English to such children—but they did not study mathematics, science, social studies, or other basic subjects that were taught only in English. According to informants, it was illegal, until 1967, to teach a child in a language other than English in California public schools.

In 1967, the Curriculum Committee of the Stockton Teachers Association decided to develop a more adequate program for teaching the non-English-speaking children. This program would permit teaching English as a second language and teaching the regular school subjects in Spanish. The association discussed this with the superintendent at the Negotiating Council; he approved it and then appealed to the local state senator to introduce Senate Bill 53 to repeal the Education Code prohibiting schools from teaching in languages other than English.

The teachers who favored formulating such a program were mainly foreign language teachers. Mexican-American leaders (primarily teachers) who were involved in developing the program later convinced the school district to take the responsibility for it, rather than merely to leave it to the Teachers' Association.

The original program, according to a Mexican-American teacher, had two parts:

> The original concept of the thing was that, first of all, it would simply start with new people coming who knew no English but had some Spanish. And the idea was simply to give them a solid base in Spanish because we know that some of them—they knew Spanish but only enough to get along and not a solid base, and no English. They neither had a good English nor a good Spanish, so that one had almost schizophrenics. So the idea was to start them in science, and reading and writing and so on. And involving them in English, using the same thing but only taking Spanish as their basis so that when they came out they would actually be bilingual but they would also have been studying in other areas of the curriculum.
>
> And then the experimental part was to start with children in the

kindergarten class with probably a mixed group in which they would start learning both English and Spanish and train to be bilingual individuals. And they would be followed up in the following year in their first grade, then in the second grade, you know, year by year basis. But each year starting with a new group in the kindergarten, starting with the little ones, giving both English and Spanish. This would simply be a matter of evolvement.

A representative from the Teachers' Association and some people from the central office wrote and submitted the initial program to the state for approval in 1967, and then to the U.S. Office of Education area representative in San Francisco for funding. The program was funded for a planning period of eight months. The district then hired a Bilingual Program Director and dispatched emissaries to San Diego and elsewhere to consult with "experts" in bilingual education.

The program was funded on a more regular basis beginning in the 1968–1969 school year. Outside consultants were hired to implement it as suggested by the area representative of the U.S. Office of Education. A Bilingual Education Supervisor was also hired and local "competent bilingual teachers" were moved into the program. It was decided to start with Burgherside elementary school because of its small size: *The basic concept was simple—to begin with a limited number of people in order to be most effective in learning. And then it could be expanded into other ESEA schools on the Southside which get the most influx of people.* It was felt, too, that the "experimental part," that is, the teaching of kindergarten children of all ethnic groups in both English and Spanish, would encourage a strong community feeling in Burgherside:

> *The concept of having everybody turn bilingual would be a sort of integrationist idea in which everybody would be able to understand everybody, because the blacks here think that when Mexicans talk Spanish they are talking about them, you see. And conversely, if the Mexican does not understand English he is feeling that the black is abusing him in his own language. They feel something is going on because he doesn't understand Spanish. So that was the simple, basic idea of starting the bilingual program in the kindergarten—that at that stage all groups would be able to understand each other because there was no way they could be together.*

When the program began in the fall of 1968 there was a significant departure from this original concept. The part intended to provide "a solid base in Spanish" for the older non-English-speaking Mexican-American students was deemphasized; the experimental part, which was to start with the kindergarten class, was expanded to include the first and second grades, and the sixth-grade teacher "was encouraged to introduce Spanish lessons" to his class. A new element that was added to the program with a good deal of emphasis was the teaching of "self-worth" to the children. This part was designed "to enhance their self-perception and attitudes toward school," through a special "instructional program for developing the self-concept of Disadvantaged Children through Oral Language and Reading." This program is based on "theory and research in Child Psychology, Psychoanalysis, Educational Disadvantagedness, and direct observation of the children to whom it is intended to be applied"; it is also said to "constitute a positive, stable, and validly based concept of self, i.e., a continuing sense of personal identity." This aspect of the Bilingual Program was originally written for children in a Texas school, which is reported to have an enrollment of 100% Mexican-Americans. It was introduced into Burgherside elementary school, with 46.1 % Mexican-American enrollment, with practically no alteration to fit Burgherside's situation. The daily ritual in the "self-worth component" is for each child to stand before a full length mirror and recite certain statements about himself and his family. The model of the family in this part of the program is one in which both father and mother are present. If the school really believes that most Burgherside children do not have fathers, would this part of the program not increase their "negative self-concept"? Yet many school officials say that "the self-concept component is the best part of the program."

The "Problem of Parents' Involvement"

The bilingual program was developed and implemented without any consultation with the Burgherside elementary school principal and teachers. And when the school reopened in the fall of 1968, the entire Burgherside community was taken by surprise: Their school principal and the school secretary had been transferred, as had all but two of the teachers. The minority background of the new principal (appointed as a result of the school boycott organized by the Black Unity Council in 1967) did not necessarily compensate Burghersiders for the loss of their former principal, whom they had come to regard affectionately. It took considerable effort for the new principal to establish herself as the principal in the eyes of Burghersiders. Some of the bilingual teachers were also new to the district, and some of them felt that their first responsibility was to the bilingual program rather than to building a rapport with the community. Burghersiders, especially parents with children in the bilingual classes kindergarten through grade two, could not understand why all these things were taking place.

Four weeks after the program began, the Bilingual Education Director visited the school to explain it to the PTA. The meeting took place at 1:30 P.M. and was attended by only four parents. It began with some children from a bilingual class greeting the audience and singing in Spanish. This was followed by a movie of a bilingual demonstration class filmed in San Antonio, Texas. After the film the director explained how his program was different from another program (English as a Second Language) and that the present program included *all children*. He stressed the importance of the "self-concept component." The bilingual program, he said, would promote "self-worth" in the children. It would also promote intergroup relations: *because if everybody spoke to and understood everybody else, there would be no problems.* Burgherside children in the program would be bilingual by the time they finished sixth grade and the program would raise their academic achievement. The parents were told: *In Texas and New York, pupils who were considered as performing two years below normal showed at the end of their bilingual training that they had gained one year or two.* One parent pointed out that the program might create more problems for children who were already failing "in their normal schoolwork." The parent was told: *Whatever happens, the program will be good for them* because research shows this. When the meeting was over, the parents left hardly convinced that this was what their children needed. I know of no attempt to explain to Burgherside parents how the program would improve children's education, not even to the Neighborhood Improvement Association or to the Mexican-American members of St. Benedict's Church, who normally meet for movies and discussion each Wednesday evening and for religious worship on Sunday. One other attempt to tell Burghersiders about the program occurred early in 1969 when the funds for the program were threatened by Sacramento. As a part of the district's effort to mobilize a community-wide support to pressure Washington to continue funding the program, the Board of Directors of Burgherside Neighborhood Center was asked to write a letter and send a cablegram to Washington. The board was then told that the program was designed to help *all the children* in the neighborhood.

In the spring and summer of 1969 I made a survey of Burgherside parents to determine their attitudes toward the bilingual program. Of about 100 parents interviewed, 19 had not heard of the program after almost one year. The parents' responses are tabulated in Table 9.1.

Table 9.1, if taken at face value, shows that Burgherside parents were in favor of the bilingual program. However, such an interpretation is not entirely correct for several reasons.

(*1*) Burgherside parents, as I suggested earlier, tend to respond to questionnaire interviews according to what they think the interviewer wants them to say. Thus the same parents who responded "very satisfied" in the

TABLE 9.1

Attitudes of Burgherside Parents toward the Bilingual Program and the Neighborhood Elementary School[a][b]

Responses	Mex.-Amer.	Black	Other	Overall
How many of your children are in the bilingual program?				
Total	(46)	(18)	(11)	(75)
1	58.70	66.67	72.73	62.67
2	30.43	33.33	18.18	29.33
3	6.52	—	—	4.00
4 or more	4.35	—	9.09	4.00
How do you feel about Mexican-American children being taught their lessons in Spanish?				
Total	(58)	(29)	(11)	(98)
Very satisfied	55.17	69.00	27.27	56.12
Satisfied	34.48	27.59	72.73	36.73
Dissatisfied	3.45	—	—	2.04
No opinion	6.90	3.45	—	5.10
How do you feel about your own child being taught his lessons in both English and Spanish?				
Total	(57)	(28)	(12)	(97)
Very satisfied	59.65	67.86	16.67	56.70
Satisfied	29.82	25.00	58.30	39.96
Dissatisfied	1.75	—	46.67	3.09
No opinion	7.71	7.14	8.30	8.25
If your child is in the bilingual program, how do you feel about the kind of progress he is making in school?				
Total	(50)	(23)	(10)	(86)
Very satisfied	49.06	52.17	—	44.19
Satisfied	39.62	21.74	70.00	38.37
Dissatisfied	—	—	20.00	15.12
No opinion	11.32	26.09	10.00	15.12

[a]Source: Author's interviews with Burgherside parents.
[b]Values are expressed as percentages.

survey told the author during informal interview that they did not like the program. Some responded "very satisfied" because they did not understand what the program was all about. One parent summarized the problem of the "uneducated parents" as follows:

How can one question anything? We don't have this authority to go and question them [school officials] *about their judgment here.*

So talking about the bilingual program the Mexican people I know feel, you see, we were brought up with the idea that you respect the school and you respect the teachers because they're up there [making sign]. *They have education. They know what they're doing. You could put any program—a Russian program and if they think this is what is good for my children, well, "I'll go along with it," they say.*

Remember we talked about ignorance. Well, some of the people I know—not all, I don't know them all—but some of these I know feel they [school officials] *know what they're doing "Because I never had any school. And I want my child to get educated. So I sent him to school." They say, "Well, they're going to teach my child. They ought to know. You're a teacher, don't you know?"*

They're just like my mother. I see my mother and I see these mothers over here. They think the same. No matter what you put in there—the bilingual program or the Russian program—they can't definitely come out and tell you how they feel: *"Well, I like this or don't like that about it." And what do they even know or have seen about the program? They haven't come into the classroom to observe it. And they are not going to come just because you send them a letter* [emphasis added].

(2) Some Mexican-American parents like the program because they want their children to learn Spanish. These parents usually say: *Yes, I like it. I like my child to learn Spanish,* though they are not concerned with how learning Spanish will raise the child's academic achievement. They hope that it will promote communication between parents who do not speak English and their children.

(3) Some Mexican-American parents like the program because it teaches their "cultural heritage." One Stockton-born parent recalled that when she was very young people advised her to declare herself an Anglo or Oriental. That would enable her to *get somewhere, because there was discrimination against Mexicans.* But she refused. Now she is happy that the school is teaching her "cultural heritage."

(4) Similarly, most non-Mexican parents support the program because they think "it will help the Mexicans," not because it will raise the academic achievement of their children. The Neighborhood Association's support of the project, as demonstrated at the meeting in 1969 referred to above, was based on the idea that this is a program which would help the Mexican-Americans.

Some Mexican-American parents as well as others openly opposed the program but said they had no power to fight for its removal. In the following interview excerpt a Mexican-American parent who "campaigned for the program" in Burgherside describes the attitude of some parents.

PARENT: *It is a negative, negative attitude.*

ANTHR.:   *Do they talk about the bilingual program in the community? You know, like some of these people you've visited, do they talk about it?*

PARENT: *Well, it's negative* [laughing]. *They say they don't like it, "Well, what good does it do? My kids know Spanish already. What are you going to teach them in Spanish? He knows Spanish. It is English he needs." "Yes," I'd say. "He needs English."*

ANTHR.:   *But I guess that the school district feels that through the Bilingual Program the children will also learn English.*

PARENT: *Yes. That's what they say. And this self-concept, the image, you know.* [But] *the black mothers say, "My kids can't even read; he can't hardly write or can't hardly speak English and now they're trying to teach him Spanish."* [Laughs] *I say, "O.K., you feel that way. Come on the day that the Director is going to talk about it, come on over to the school. Ask questions, tell what you feel, what you want to know." And I say, "Come on into the school, why not? If you don't want to ask it I'll ask it for you." But you know the turnout we had, about four mothers.*

ANTHR.:   *It was, in my opinion, a sort of wrong time of day to hold such a meeting. They had it at one o'clock or something like that.*

PARENT: *Well, sometimes you don't know what hour is bad.*

It is difficult for some Burgherside parents to see how their children can improve in their schoolwork by learning Spanish. They do not understand the Taxpayers' logic regarding the program. One Mexican-American father told me that when his son goes to look for a job the employers will not ask him, "Can you speak Spanish?" but "Can you speak English?" *And if he no speak English he can't get nothing. Nothing.* This belief is widespread—that employers demand good knowledge of English, not Spanish. Even non-English-speaking parents feel that English should be stressed. The blacks, too, express similar feelings about teaching children "proper English." Some say that children should start learning "proper English" from Headstart. As one young man put it:

> *And don't have nobody in the Headstart class talking with slangs like this. Have somebody there who knows how to speak big words themselves, have large vocabulary. Don't have nobody in there, like I say, that uses slang words, you know. Have someone there that can communicate to their level, teach and understand them. I mean this is where I would start with Headstart.*

There are parents who feel that the Bilingual Education Program will actually slow the academic progress of their children. There are black parents, for example, who feel that their children have a different type of language problem that cannot be eliminated by teaching them both in English and Spanish. These parents feel that the school should concentrate on teaching their children English.

There are Mexican-American parents opposed to the program because it is teaching the children "Spanish" instead of "Mexican." In the fall of 1969, a clique of two Mexican-American women, two Anglo women and one black woman "lectured" me for more than an hour one day, complaining that their children were learning "Spanish" and not "Mexican." I once brought this to the attention of a school official who later explained to a PTA meeting that "Mexican" is a special dialect of "Spanish." A few days after the PTA meeting I visited a Mexican-American father who explained the difference between "Mexican" and "Spanish" as follows:

FATHER: *If the school wants the parents to read the message they send home it has to be written in Mexican. I am talking mostly about Mexicans, they can read it. They read Mexican very well.*

ANTHR.: *Isn't Mexican Spanish?*

FATHER: *No. Don't use Spanish. Don't be conflicted of being with your words "Spanish" and "Mexican."*

ANTHR.: *Are they different?*

FATHER: *Yes.*

ANTHR.: *Well, tell me more about that because I have heard some of our Mexican parents criticize the bilingual program at Washington School. They say that in the school we should teach* Mexican, *not* Spanish.

FATHER: *The Mexican is a—the Spanish—let us start with the Spanish. The Spanish is a dialect that comes from Spain. And their dialect is a little different than ours. Their words are spelled a little differently, pronounced a little differently, and they are Spaniards. They come from across the sea. And we are Mexicans from the Northern Hemisphere right here. And this is why we like to be identified as Mexicans. Mostly our writing are spelled and pronounced much differently than in Spain. I could not go further than this except that the words are different.*

ANTHR.: *And this paper here* [El Hispano] *that you were reading, do you think this paper is more Mexican than Spanish?*

FATHER: *More Mexican. If it were to become a Spanish paper there would be a lot of words different than these. They would use a lot of words differently, you know. And they mean the same thing but they are pronounced different and spelled different. And mostly—I tell you something else: A long time ago the white man was so afraid of calling Mexican* Mexican. *Then, to be polite, he used to call him Spanish. See?*

I did not interview the kindergarten or the first- and second-grade children in the bilingual program. However, their feelings about the program were studied informally, especially at interviews with their parents. Generally, children whose parents favored the program appeared to like it; whereas those whose parents disapproved of it appeared to dislike it. One parent reported that her second grade child did not want to attend school regularly because he did not want to participate in the program. Observations in the classroom showed that some children felt bored by the program; this was particularly true of the older children because those in the kindergarten and the first and second grades were sometimes using the same materials for their lessons. One informant described the situation as follows:

> *In one classroom this year every time I go in there they were still on the program, just about. And so the teacher asked me to come in and observe and get some of her group together and get them started to read. So I told her, "When are you going to get them started on the Reader," I said, "These children, some of these children, this is the first- and second-grade classes—I say, a lot of these children that you have got all these stuff you are using—this paper work like Latin kits, different kits," I said, "they got it in first grade classes." And I said, "They want a book. They are tired of this." And sure enough, while I was in there one day one little boy said, "Oh, no, not again." So that lets you know—that's one part of the problem of these kids. They are tired or bored. You can stay on something too long. Use a few minutes—15 to 20 minutes a day with the bilingual or fun program–whichever it is. I think you can wear the children out with it.*

Other children enjoyed the program. In one family a first-grade child was often eager to show her parents how many more new Spanish words she had learned at school.

Taxpayers implementing rehabilitation programs and educators in low-income neighborhoods often complain of parents' apathy and lack of involvement (Gordon 1968). This study of parents' involvement in the bilingual education program clearly shows that it is not simply "apathy" or "hostility" toward school that keeps parents from being "involved," but that, again, much of the problem lies in the "patron–client relationship" between Taxpayers and parents which prevents meaningful interaction between them because: (1) Taxpayers develop programs to solve Burghersiders' problems without consultation with Burghersiders; (2) Taxpayers impose the programs on Burghersiders and then expect them to "appreciate what is being done for them" by responding positively toward school; (3) Taxpayers in the Rehabilitation Movement are more concerned with "selling" their programs to local Taxpayers who are potential critics, to fellow members of the Movement, and to potential competitors for funds elsewhere than they are with helping "target area" residents understand the educational value of the programs. In the case of the Bilingual Program,

Burghersiders see themselves as merely experimental subjects. Any other "small school" would have served the same purpose. (4) Those Burghersiders who responded favorably to the program did so for reasons other than those intended by the Taxpayers.

In conclusion, a few additional remarks about the Bilingual Program are in order. Unlike other "remedial programs," it has a political overtone. Several informants have described it as "the only thing ever done for the Mexicans in this community." Since the program is "the Mexican thing" it is strongly supported, often emotionally, by a variety of spokesmen for the Mexican-American community. Many of these spokesmen are advocating that the Bilingual Program be introduced in all the schools in South Stockton, "that all children in South Stockton—from kindergarten through twelfth grade—should be taught all their subjects in both English and Spanish." Because of the political interests in the Bilingual Education Program and the fact that Stockton is now its national headquarters, I want to make the following observations: (1) Regardless of their ethnic background, most of the spokesmen and advocates for the expansion of the program into all South Stockton schools are Taxpayers whose children do not attend school in South Stockton. (2) None of these advocates, to my knowledge, has explained to Burghersiders the educational value of the program, and I am convinced that they will not explain its educational value to the residents in other neighborhoods. My general observation is that Southside spokesmen rarely seek mandates from those they claim to speak for. (3) Non-Mexican-Americans in Southside have so far supported the program for noneducational reasons. Unless the school district makes a serious effort to convince the Anglo, Black, Chinese, Filipino, Japanese, and other groups that the program can help their children educationally, a continued expansion of the program will meet with overt opposition. (4) Some teachers in Southside schools, especially the older ones, feel threatened by the program. As the program expands into more schools and higher grades, teachers who cannot retrain to teach the program may have to be replaced by those who can. Here, too, is a potential source of opposition.

Does the Education Rehabilitation Movement Solve the Problem of School Failure

It is difficult to say to what extent the Rehabilitation Movement has been successful in reducing school failures among Burgherside children. When I began my study in 1968, a school official said that the school district had tried everything to raise the level of achievement of the children but had not been successful: *We have reduced class size, employed specialists and*

*the latest teaching techniques, we have involved parents and the community.
But the children are still below grade level.* Later, another official told me:
*I am not sure we have done everything we can for these children. I believe
there is much more we can do but we just don't know what to do or where to
begin.*

Annual reports of individual programs usually describe them as "successful." In some programs the "success" is described in terms of higher test
scores by children. The compensatory education program begins each
year with explicit statements about the level of reading skill the children
participating in the program are expected to gain by a given period of time.
For example, in the fall of 1969 the goal for the sixth-grade reading program
was stated as follows: "By May 15, 1970, to raise the median gain of the
six-grade project participants in reading by 1.4 grade level." The children
were tested at the beginning ("pre-test") and in May ("post-test") and were
found to have made an overall gain of 1.2 grade level: "All of the [compen-
satory education schools] except [one] made more than month-for-month
growth for the period of instruction between the pre- and post-tests and
[one school] made more than two months of growth for each month of
instruction [SUSD 1970c: 14]. But the extent to which this improvement
shows itself in the regular classwork remains unclear. The same school
said to have made "more than two months of growth for each month of
instruction" in 1969–1970 did not show a significant improvement over
the previous year group in the state mandated reading test (3.8 in 1970,
3.8 in 1969).[6]

Anecdotal accounts are used to show that students, teachers, and parents
have developed "more positive attitudes." In programs in which test
scores cannot be used to demonstrate their success, "other improvements"
are usually described. In one program, for instance, "other improvements"
in 1969 included:

1. Attendance records have improved considerably and tardiness has
    become minimal.

---

[6]These are expressed in terms of "grade equivalent" which the school district defines as
follows: "This term (grade equivalent) is most easily explained by way of example. To determine
the definition third graders are tested using that test, and the average score for those students
on that test is defined as third grade equivalent. If the students were tested at the beginning of
the school year, the average score would be called 3.0 grade equivalent; if tested in the middle
of the year, the average score would be defined as 3.5 grade equivalent; and if at the end of the
year, the average score would represent 3.9 grade equivalent [SUSD 1970b: 3]." The scores
reported above are from tests given in the fall of 1970 and 1969 respectively. Notice that the
sixth grade in the 1970 test was the fifth grade in 1969, which is reported to have made 0.83
month's growth or gain for each month of instruction in the 1969–1970 school year (SUSD
1971: 22).

2. Children's participation in the classroom activities increased.
3. Parents have become more cooperative and attended PTA meetings and Parent-Teacher conferences more than usual.
4. Pupils have become adjusted better to school environment and their sense of self-worth improved.
5. Children's attention span improved.
6. The program generated interest in teachers and pupils as well as the general public.
7. General community attitudes toward school improved, etc.

I did not make a first-hand and careful evaluation of any of the "remedial programs." However, there are indications that in Stockton and other cities these programs are not as "successful" as usually claimed by the schools operating them. Rosenham's contention (1967) that these programs are sometimes marked as successful even before they are put into operation, is to some extent true in Stockton. [7]

Whenever a new "remedial program" is introduced into Southside or other schools the school district carries on extensive publicity directed primarily at Taxpayers, and intended to satisfy potential local critics. Press releases and feature articles in various papers describe the "uniqueness" of the program and how it will solve the educational problems of the "target area." Another form of publicity is directed toward interested parties in the region, state, and nation. The Bilingual Education Program,

---

[7] In his incisive observations about these programs Rosenham writes:

Some of those who believe that cultural deprivation does massively affect subsequent school behavior will argue that many demonstration projects, which were designed to compensate young children for the presumed deficiencies of their environment, have been "successful" and their success argues strongly for the utility if not downright correctness of the notions that spawned them. It may be useful to offer a *caveat* about demonstration projects. Demonstration projects are conducted with considerable fanfare. Often enough a group of students who have been neglected for quite a while are suddenly invaded by social scientists who are all ready to try something new. There are, to begin with, the enthusiastic teachers, who impart what they will impart with uncommon verve and vigor. With them are the social scientists, the measurers and observers, who, with their consultants, constitute quite a crowd. Mingling actively among these are the interested parties—members of the school board, and agency sponsors, and other curios. Finally, there is the press. Always hot for items of social interest, they are invited at the outset of the project, their cameras and pencils are evident throughout the project, and they come around for the closing party. All this is written up in the local papers, and a good deal of it makes the national magazines. The path to early fame is so well-paved that at least two projects we know of were announced as underway and successful before they were initiated [Rosenham 1967:41; in *Education for the disadvantaged,* edited by A. L. Miller, © 1967 by The Free Press].

through this type of publicity, attracted 177 "official" visitors during its first year from 23 areas throughout the nation to visit the three project classrooms and "this number does not include other visitors who came to observe the program without reservations [SUSD 1969f]."[8] It is conceivable that the claims made in these kinds of publicity and the "success" of the publicity constrain those who run the programs to describe them as "successful" in their annual reports (1) to avoid local charges of wasting Taxpayers' money; (2) to discourage competitors, including those who visited the program, from designing rival programs that threaten refunding; (3) to convince the Funding Agency that the program achieved its goals and deserves to be continued. This situation sometimes creates a discrepancy between "success" as seen by "internal" (local) evaluators of a program and "success" as seen by external evaluators.[9]

The Education Rehabilitation Movement, like a missionary movement, is not accountable to its "congregations in the field." The publicity directed to Burghersiders is merely in the form of an invitation "to be redeemed." The schools are not obliged to report to them the success or failure of their programs.

Since 1963, and especially beginning in 1965, the Education Rehabilitation Movement has influenced Burgherside education in some respects. I pointed out earlier that one consequence of the movement is the rise in ethnic consciousness among the blacks and Mexican-Americans, and that this is directly in response to the hypothesis that these people are "culturally deprived." The new pride in ethnic identity has in turn increased their desire for more and better education. Stockton as a whole, Taxpayers and Burghersiders alike, is doing better today in the state-mandated tests than it was doing previously. But Burghersiders have not achieved any significant improvement relative to the schoolwork of Taxpayers. The data on their schoolwork reported in this study do not reveal any great improvement.

However, these programs unintentionally alter the structure of particular schools, and that of the entire school system, to some degree. In the 1968–

---

[8] The annual report of Burgherside Elementary School in June 1969 listed the number of "officials who visited the three bilingual education classes during 1968–1969 by place of origin: Stockton (64), Sacramento (25), Merced (3), Berkeley (1), Lodi (2), Cutler Orosi District (18), San Diego (1), Tulare (1), Texas (4), Manteca (2), Los Angeles (3), San Jose (unspec.), Linden (1), Palo Alto (1), Modesto (4), Arizona (1), Brentwood (2), Oklahoma (1), Richmond (7), ABC District (6), Carpinteria (2), Washington, D.C. (5).

[9] See *Status Report on Stockton Unified School Districts ESEA, Title I Project,* by the Bureau of Program Development, Division of Compensatory Education, State Department of Education, Sacramento, California, February, 1969; esp. General Findings, Applicable to the District Base Title I Project, p. 1.

1969 school year, the introduction of the Bilingual Education Program in Burgherside Elementary School resulted in the replacement of almost the entire staff, the appointment of a principal from a minority group, and the introduction of an additional criterion of teacher evaluation. In another Southside elementary school with 1,000 students the Compensatory Education Program in the 1969–1970 school year brought in additional staff of 1 instructional specialist, 3 reading specialists, 3 mathematical specialists, 1 counselor, 1 intergroup relations specialist, 1 librarian, and 14 instructional aides. The staff directly involved in particular "remedial programs" has therefore affected the structure of the school system primarily through increases in the bureaucratic organization. When a program is considered important and relatively permanent it becomes a separate unit in the school bureaucracy.

The "remedial programs" are also responsible for the rapid increase of minority school personnel (see Table 9.2). The number of minority teachers rose from 21 in 1961–1962 to 231 in 1968–1969. Furthermore, minority groups often base their demands for greater roles in decision

TABLE 9.2

Changes in Percentages of Ethnic Composition of Newly Hired Certificated Personnel in Stockton Unified School District, 1946 to 1970, Showing a Rapid Increase in Hiring of Members of Ethnic Minorities after 1965 When the Education Rehabilitation Movement Began [a]

Year	Total new teachers added	Percentage of teachers hired per ethnic group				
		Anglo	Black	Mexican-American	Oriental	Other
1946	?	100.00	—	—	—	—
1947	44	97.73	2.27	—	—	—
1950	88	95.45	1.14	1.14	2.28	—
1955	61	88.52	1.64	1.64	8.20	—
1961	160	88.13	6.88	1.25	3.75	—
1962	127	90.55	3.15	—	5.51	—
1965	?	?	?	?	?	?
1966	?	?	?	?	?	?
1967	140	83.57	11.43	—	2.14	2.86
1968	33	−30.30	15.15	30.30	24.24	—
1969	39	−15.38	33.33	41.03	−2.56	25.64
1970	46	−45.65	60.87	19.57	17.39	2.17

[a]Sources: (1) *Employment of Certificated Personnel of Ethnic Minority Groups in Stockton Unified School District, 1947–62*(Sandelius 1963); (2) Stockton Unified School District.

making in the school system of the "remedial programs." The following is a part of a petition sent in 1969 to the superintendent by one organization asking for more say in decisions affecting "remedial programs":

We recommend that you select the administrators, teaching and para-professional personnel with the following rationale being given top priority:

(a) Since all of the District's Compensatory Education programs, including ESEA, serve a significantly large percentage of ethnic minorities, efforts should be made immediately for the 1969–1970 academic year to include "qualified persons" from those groups at every level for the project operations. Specifically, our concern is with the obvious lack of ethnic representation at the decision-making level. This includes the position of project director, the assistant directors for elementary and secondary components of the program, the project school principals, and, in some schools, the resource teachers;

(b) In addition, it is recommended that the para-professionals be recruited from the project area with preference being given to the parents of project participants. Such qualified persons are presently available to fill these positions [Letter from the Black Teachers' Alliance to the Schools Superintendent, March 1969:2].

Thus, since 1965 the number of ethnic minority people who are both classified and certified school personnel has increased markedly. Several of them now hold such administrative positions as principals, deans, and project directors; and one is an assistant superintendent in charge of the secondary schools. Members of ethnic minorities were elected to the school board in 1965; at the moment, three of the five board members are from ethnic minority backgrounds. A coalition of some Taxpayers and Southsiders, including Burghersiders, recently got the city charter amended to elect board of education members by districts rather than citywide. Will these structural changes eventually reduce school failure in Burgherside? Perhaps they will, but only to a limited extent, for school-failure adaptation in Burgherside is not only caused by the organization and control of the schools, but also by the lack of opportunities beyond the schools.

CHAPTER 10

The Silent Minority:
What Burghersiders Think of
Taxpayers' "Solutions"

Burghersiders Look at the "Solutions"
Proposed by Taxpayers

The "remedial programs" are essentially products of the beliefs and efforts of Taxpayers. Burghersiders are invited to participate in the programs
when they are already in operation in the classrooms. What do Burghersiders think of those "solutions" proposed by Taxpayers to reduce school
failures in the neighborhood? Burghersiders are skeptical that these "remedial" programs can solve their problems. They reject the Taxpayers'
contention that the programs are not very effective because of the negative
attitudes of Burghersiders toward school, and argue instead that Taxpayers do not understand their problems and therefore cannot design
programs that will solve them. Some say the solutions do not work because
Taxpayers cannot "think poor." That is, Taxpayers are rich people and do
not understand how the poor think and live.

One informant told the following story to illustrate the argument that
Taxpayers do not understand Burghersiders' problems. The informant
said that her Aunt Mary Lou had moved to New York from Arkansas

with her parents at the age of 16. When her parents died, soon after their arrival, she dropped out of school and got married. At the time of the interview Mary Lou was a widow for the second time and, with nine children, she was subsisting on welfare (Aid to Families with Dependent Children). A few years ago, one of her former high school teachers, now a wealthy lawyer, persuaded Mary Lou to go back to "finish school," promising her financial assistance as long as she was in school. He suggested that by finishing school she would be able to get a good job and support her family, and also set a good example for her children. My informant pointed out that when Mary Lou accepted this advice her problems got worse. She was no longer able to take good care of her family, and her adolescent children soon got into trouble with the police. She had no hope that Mary Lou could ever qualify for a job good enough to support her family. She concluded by saying: *Do you see what I mean? In the case of my aunt her going back to school was wrong. Now this is what I have been trying to prove to you—it has did more harm than it did good.* She said that Mary Lou should have refused the advice but she felt obliged to accept it. The rich lawyer, she said, *was thinking good but not thinking poor:*

> *How I think he felt? He thought he was doing—this rich lawyer thought he was doing much good. But he is a wealthy man and so really can't think poor. He was thinking good but if he would have thought this way: "Instead of the mother I would get the daughter," he would have been doing better. See? Because the daughter was coming up. He would have said, "I am going to send Sandra to school," or "I am going to send Frank to school." He would have did better than sending the mother to school, or, then talked the mother into going to school.* He should have been on the child.

In discussing some of the remedial programs Burghersiders often comment: *We don't think that they* [the Taxpayers] *can really see the whole problem and the causes of the problems.* One Burghersider asked me, *Wouldn't you say that people that live in poverty know better how to solve these problems than people from Northside?* Some call the "remedial programs" placative: *Because they will say that they will try to help us but then they are really for themselves. They want to keep us off their back.* Burghersiders feel that if Taxpayers really wanted to help Burghersiders solve their problems they would begin by asking Burghersiders what they need, (because it is the poor who know the problems of the poor) then, using this information, they would work together with Burghersiders in developing the "remedial programs."

Burghersiders' Version of the "Cultural Deprivation" Theory

Official documents of the school district no longer designate children from Burgherside and similar neighborhoods as "culturally deprived" but as "culturally disadvantaged" or simply "the disadvantaged." However, many Taxpayers, including some school personnel, still refer to them as "culturally deprived." Burghersiders almost never use the terms "culturally deprived" or "culturally disadvantaged" to describe themselves, and they do not like other people to thus refer to them.

Throughout my research in Burgherside, I heard Burghersiders use the term "culturally deprived" only two or three times. The first time was at a meeting of the Board of Directors of the Burgherside Neighborhood Center in December 1968, when the center's director, a non-Burghersider, read a letter he had sent to thank some Taxpayers for "providing donations for a Halloween party for the culturally deprived children of Burgherside." Some board members murmured but did not openly protest. The next day when I met one of the parents who was at the board meeting she asked me what I thought about the center director's saying that *these children here are deprived.* She said it made her feel *real angry* and added: *He* [the director] *just thank his God the president* [of the Neighborhood Association] *was not there.* Had the president been there, she explained, he would have told the director to apologize to the people for saying that their children were "culturally deprived."

I heard the term again when some friends from Burgherside were visiting my apartment. When I asked why Burghersiders were not doing well in school, one youth said: *Don't you know* they said *we're culturally deprived?* But he himself did not know what was meant by "cultural deprivation."

Burghersiders reject the Taxpayers' designation of their children as "culturally deprived" and do not accept this as the reason their children are doing poorly in school. However, they admit that Taxpayers "push" their children more than Burghersiders do because Taxpayers are more educated than Burghersiders. It is said that since Taxpayers are professional people—teachers, judges, doctors, business people—*this is all they* [Taxpayers' children] *hear most of the time and it rubs off on them,* that is, the children learn about these professions and how to go into them. These are the advantages that a Burgherside child lacks: *His parent is not educated, and if your parent is not educated you're lost.* Wealth, like education, also makes a difference. It is said that when a Burgherside child *comes home from school their parents may be drunken and saying whole bunch of dirty words.* A Northside child may also find his parents drunk when he comes home from school, but

If they get drunk over there they can come along and say, "Here's ten or five dollars and go play." And you wouldn't care if she [your mother] got sloppy drunk. And this makes a difference.

When I introduced the concept of "cultural deprivation" at interviews, Burghersiders replied with their own version of deprivation: (*1*) their children are deprived of good education by the schools; (*2*) Taxpayers deprive them of opportunities to "upgrade" themselves.

We saw earlier (Chapter 5) that Burgherside parents say that they are a lost generation because they are uneducated. They want their children to do well in school and to "finish school" so that they can get good jobs. When talking about school dropouts, Burghersiders say that their children are being "pushed out" of school by Taxpayers. They say, too, that they had much hope the Pre-school/Headstart program would teach their children the Three "R"s early in their school career, but they now feel disappointed that the school is emphasizing "how to get along." Burghersiders do not usually accept the schools' explanation of why Burgherside children do not learn to read. They say that their children cannot read because the schools did not teach them to read during their early school years, and instead emphasized "cultural enrichment" and "how to get along together."

Burghersiders also say that they are "deprived" because Taxpayers deny them opportunities to improve their homes and the physical appearance of their neighborhoods. And they are denied good jobs. They would like the neighborhood to look as beautiful as those of Northside but they have no money to improve it. One Mexican-American high school student said:

I don't know if you have gone through Southside, especially this Burgherside or Crumbling Alley as they call it. You know I have gone through all these neighborhoods since I lived here most of my life on the Southside with all the poor housing. You compare it with the place they've got Montgomery Ward and all that new model homes and all that.

In the following interview excerpt two informants explain what they understand by "cultural deprivation" in Burgherside: inability to get a loan to improve their homes, inadequate government and other services to Burgherside, and so forth.

ANTHR.:   *Well, I was explaining to you what Taxpayers mean by "cultural deprivation." Do you feel that Burghersiders are culturally deprived?*
FIRST INFORMANT: *Live where? Burgherside?*
ANTHR.:   *Yes.*

SECOND INFORMANT: *In what?*

FIRST INFORMANT: *Yea. In just about everything.*

ANTHR.: *They're culturally deprived, aren't they?*

FIRST INFORMANT: *This is the way I feel: Money, yea, knowledge about the black man, they don't know nothing, they don't know nothing about the black man.*

SECOND INFORMANT: *We in Burgherside are deprived. We are not only deprived, we are very deprived. Do you know why? I went down to Charter Way, and I bet you—within the last two years they have tarred up and re-tarred that street, within the last two years. Look at Burgherside, look at the streets.*

ANTHR.: *Well, Burgherside is in the county.*

SECOND INFORMANT: *You are not asking whether county kids are better than city kids. You are asking whether they are deprived—and this is where it comes to the adults: they are being deprived. And even if it is a family that has been wanting to upgrade their house, they are deprived. Do you know after I put in for a loan for my house, do you know how long it took me to get it—in another city?*

ANTHR.: *No, I don't. Why?*

SECOND INFORMANT: *I live in Burgherside. I am deprived because Burgherside is not fit for anybody in San Joaquin County to give you a loan. So I don't care if you live in the city or in the county, when they say "pay taxes" you still pay it.*

FIRST INFORMANT: *You pay taxes to the white man because the white man is going to fix the whole thing.*

SECOND INFORMANT: *And this is the truth. This is deprivation.*

I once asked a Taxpayer about the difficulty Southsiders, including Burghersiders, faced in getting loans to improve their homes and for business purposes. The Taxpayer said that banks are reluctant to give loans to these people for fear that they might get into trouble with the law and be sent to jail, and therefore be unable to pay the loan. Furthermore, he said the city is expanding northward and many Southside houses and shacks are going to continue to decrease in value.

BURGHERSIDERS ARE SKEPTICAL THAT SCHOOLS CAN CHANGE THE ENVIRONMENT

The school system partially attributes the failures of Burgherside children in school to the effects of "their home environments." It wishes to reduce these effects. It wants also, if possible, to change the environment (for example, by changing the parents through "remedial programs" like "Happy Birthday" described previously). Burghersiders think otherwise.

One informant said: *You really can't do anything about the environment until you get the child educated.*

But the environment the schools want to change is not the one Burghersiders speak about, though both have their origins in poverty. For Burghersiders, the environment has two aspects, the material and the nonmaterial. The material aspect includes the general physical appearance of Burgherside neighborhood—poor housing, rough, littered streets—all the things that make the neighborhood "Crumbling Alley." It also includes unemployment among adult residents. All these factors affect the education of their children. For instance, as we have seen, children sometimes have to go to work to supplement the family income, and they often have to "work in the fields"—the last place they really want to work:

> *We don't like to work in the fields because, I mean, in picking tomato you soon get tired. You want to do something else that won't make you tired. You know that sometimes we were working 14 hours a day. Most of time 12 hours. We used to make more than $100 a week.*

Burghersiders argue that the school cannot change the physical and economic characteristics of the neighborhood; similarly, it cannot change the "uneducated parents." What the school can do is to educate Burgherside children "out of the environment." The environment itself cannot be changed because the factors that produce the environment of poverty are still there.

Burghersiders do not accept the school's argument that parents must develop positive attitudes before children can learn. They argue that they do not have negative attitudes, although they may be uneducated. They also reject the school's argument that their children are not doing well in school because they, the parents, are not involved. In Chapter 8 I suggested that some teachers may be using good grades to reward children for their parents' interest and cooperation, and poor grades to punish children whose parents they consider "uninvolved and uncooperative."

Burgherside parents who are on their way up—"the para-professionals" in the school system such as teacher-aides and teachers' corps, as well as a few PTA activists—usually support the schools' contention that "parents' involvement is the crucial factor." One para-professional said:

> *Once you get a parent and the kid knows this teacher had talked to the parent, I think you are going to get a better reaction from the child. If he sees that his teacher has dropped in to see his parent he's going to become more alert you know, start something.*

The same "magic of contact" argument is used by the schools and the para-professionals to encourage teachers to visit parents at home. Sometimes it is said that the teacher will be able to learn more about the "child's problems" by visiting his home. Parents say they cannot stop teachers from making home visits, but they are skeptical that such visits will improve their children's schoolwork. Some parents think home visits are a good idea because then they no longer have to visit the school.

Will School Integration Reduce School Failure in Burgherside?

In 1969 the most controversial issue in the Stockton public school system was "racial integration." Most Taxpayers opposed the proposal submitted by the schools superintendent to the Board of Education to integration by voluntary busing by a vote of 16 to 1. In the October the Board of Education rejected it by a vote of four to one in July, 1969. That summer Stockton parents were polled by the board and rejected integration by voluntary busing by a vote of 16 to 1. In the October election to the Board of Education, a slate of three antibusing candidates "scored an easy victory" over prointegration candidates.

Taxpayers were unevenly divided on the larger issue of school integration. The majority opposed it and regarded the election of antibusing candidates as a vindication of their position. However, a small group of Taxpayers supported the superintendent's proposal "on legal, moral and educational grounds." After their slate of candidates lost, they decided to move the issue into the law courts. In a meeting following the election one speaker declared:

We have some type of a moral obligation to demonstrate that as middle class citizens—whatever, that is—to the indigent people of the community that we are as concerned as they are about integration.

Supporters of the superintendent's proposal had hoped that school integration would help to break down the "cycle of poverty" that character-ized Southside neighborhoods, basing their argument implicitly on the "cultural deprivation" and "cultural disadvantage" concepts. At a public hearing on the proposed integration in June, 1969, one supporter said:

As it is now, poverty leads to environmental and cultural obstacles. These lead to poor health and inadequate education, limiting earning potential, which leads to poverty. It's just one continual circle. We must break this circle.... The average poor child who attends school where a substantial majority of the children come from more advantaged homes will perform at a higher level than a poor child similarly situated in all other respects but attends [sic] school with a majority of poor children.

Taxpayers opposed to integration were more explicit in stating that Burghersiders and other Southsiders were "culturally deprived," but their solution was different. In public hearing in June, 1969, one representative of the Taxpayers' Action Committee read the following prepared statement:

> In an effort to upgrade the present school system and to mix the environment of the culturally deprived, the following proposals are offered for consideration.
> 1. Provide enrichment materials in the home such as subscriptions to *Weekly Reader* and *Humpty Dumpty*.
> 2. Provide educational tools and toys, such as coloring books, papers, scissors, paints, clay, and so on.
> These materials will benefit all pre-school and school age children who come from culturally deprived homes. Enriching the school by providing school assemblies which provide music, both instrumental and vocal, puppet shows, field trips; now use the buses already in operation to visit the seashores, the markets, industrial plants and so on. Provide at least once a year a dinner using table cloths, napkins, proper place setting, forks, knife and spoon. More interaction with the school with emphasis on sports. The home environment will determine his academic ability. Home should become a continuation of school rather than a bleak environment with nothing there to give the child a touch of cultural heritage.

Both the proponents and opponents of school integration attribute Burgherside's children's failures in school to some version of the "cultural deprivation" theory, but they propose different solutions.

Burghersiders did not participate directly in the debate on school integration in 1969. Few, if any, attended the public hearing, and none of them made a public statement on the issue. Moreover, no one sought to find out what Burghersiders thought about the proposed integration or about school integration in general. Even those who were speaking for Burghersiders sought no mandate from them; these spokesmen felt convinced that Burghersiders could not object to what they said on their behalf: that Burghersiders desired integration because it was good for them.

At the suggestion of Burgherside Elementary School's principal, I interviewed several Burgherside parents on the school integration issue in the spring of 1969. Table 10.1 describes some of their attitudes toward the integration of schools. As the table shows, Burghersiders did not strongly support school integration. Less than half of them believed that it would improve their children's school work, and some even believed it might have adverse effects. As I pointed out earlier, Burghersiders tend to agree in a questionnaire with what they regard as the official position; they must have felt very strongly about school integration to express as much dissatisfaction as this table indicates. The usual reason given by those supporting integration was that "it is good for different races to mix together," not that it will help their children to learn more.

TABLE 10.1

Attitude of Burgherside Parents toward School Integration and toward Busing the Children to Achieve Racial Balance in Schools[a][b]

Responses	Black	Mex.-Amer.	Other
Overall effect of integration			
Total	(29)	(60)	(12)
A. Good	34.48	48.44	58.33
B. No difference	55.17	26.67	25.00
C. Bad	—	6.67	8.33
D. No opinion	10.34	18.33	8.33
Effect of children from other neighborhoods			
Total	(29)	(60)	(11)
A. Good	34.48	43.33	63.64
B. No difference	55.17	41.67	27.27
C. Bad	—	10.11	—
D. No opinion	10.34	5.00	9.09
Attitude toward busing to achieve integration			
Total	(30)	(59)	(12)
A. Very satisfied	6.67	11.86	33.33
B. Satisfied	23.33	33.90	8.33
C. Dissatisfied	46.67	38.98	50.00
D. No opinion	23.33	15.25	8.33
Attitude toward busing into Burgherside neighborhood			
Total	(30)	(56)	(12)
A. Very satisfied	13.33	12.50	33.33
B. Satisfied	36.67	30.36	25.00
C. Dissatisfied	20.00	30.36	33.33
D. No opinion	30.00	26.79	8.33

[a]Source: Author's interviews with Burgherside parents.
[b]Values expressed as percentages.

The point here is that in the issue of school integration, as in other areas of education in Stockton, Burghersiders and Taxpayers see things differently. I once tried to explain to a Burgherside parent that advocates of school integration believed it would improve their children's education. This woman quickly replied:

Yea. What's special about going to school with white people? I mean, this is why I can't get that. I wondered about that, you know, when I read all the controversy. Why should they want to be with white people?

Burghersiders, then, do not associate integration with "steps toward quality education." One Mexican mother who favored integration said: *Yea. I am for integration.* BUT *I would want them to give my kids a better quality education.* A black father said: *No. I don't care if they integrate the schools.* BUT *I want them to give my kids a better quality education.* To Burghersiders *quality education* can be achieved quite apart from integrating the schools. One black parent explains:

> *I really don't go for integration. As far as the child being educated I don't feel that this is really the most important thing. I feel that all schools should be equal wherever they are; and a child should learn just as much in one school as they learn in other schools. I don't think this is where it really is at. Should kids, you know, be moved from one place to another so that they will be integrated? So what? I don't care if my kids never see a white person, you know. If they are well equipped, you know, when they go out seeking a job or whatever they want to do just as they know as much or educated as well.*

When asked about the effects of integration on his children's education, a Mexican-American father replied: *Well, I don't see no benefit. I can't see it.*

Most of the junior and senior high school students questioned felt the same way as their parents: They want better quality education, not busing to achieve integration. A Mexican-American high school student said: *Well, one thing that I would say—they should give us a better education.* He then explained what he meant by a better education.

> *A better education, they should give us accordingly Mexican-American teachers and black teachers. They should also have a club for each one of them. That is because the ones who are racists are having trouble now. And what I'd say is that they should look toward more of our problems than anybody else's problems. It is these races that I am talking about. They should try to do more for us because of* the Anglos, they got it made already. *They say, "Why should we help you people?" you know. They can't make anything of us by busing to integrate. The way I think is that they should give us better education over here, the same as they got toward Westside or Northside at Stagg or Lincoln. Because right now they say that Lincoln and Stagg have better education than all Southside, Franklin and Edison, and all the junior highs that are over here. The junior highs over there got better education, better teachers. And here it seems like leftovers.*

It is important to recognize the effects of the subjective comparison that Burgherside parents and children make between their education and that of Northside. The usual conclusion is that Burgherside has inferior education and that their teachers are not very interested in teaching them well. For example, the following excerpt shows that some students feel that their teachers do not recognize them as "academic materials" but "only good for sports," and therefore do not make much effort to teach them.

ANTHR.: *Do the students want the busing?*

STUDENT: *No. They don't want busing. What they want is better education. Because the school I am going right now I don't think they can give us better education.*

ANTHR.: *Why not?*

STUDENT: *Because for one thing I think most of the teachers at my school are prejudiced. That is the way I put it. Because I notice lots of them looking towards the Mexican-Americans and the Negroes with the attitudes, you know, they think that they won't make it. You know, the prople that are on that football team, especially Negroes, they can play better than any other group. Right now we've got a good team at my school. [And the students] think they have it made just by playing in the sports. But that's wrong.*

ANTHR.: *Do the students think this way?*

STUDENT: *Yes. They think because their names come on in the paper, you know. They think that they're going to make it with this but that's wrong. They need more than just that. That's why the teachers look toward him and say, "Oh, he's only good for this," you know. "If he comes into my room he isn't going to do nothing. But when he goes out to play he can do great out there." This is the way I put it.*

A few Burghersiders said integration would improve their children's education because the Northside had "better schools, better teachers, and better education," but not because their children would be associating with Taxpayers' children. I once tried to explain to a Mexican-American parent that some Taxpayers believed that Burgherside children would do better in school if they had more contact with Taxpayers' children. The mother then asked me, *You know what? If you have a black or white or brown child together in the same classroom, what do they learn directly from each other? They learn more from the instructor, don't they? And from the facilities they have to learn with?* Some Southside parents therefore send their children to Northside schools because they think that Northside has better schools, rather than because they like integration. A Southside parent who sent her daughter to a Northside high school said:

I am not satisfied with the schools in Southside, the way they teach them here. So this is why I moved my child across town because if white child get education I know mine will get education, just by being there with them, you know. And the things that they need to learn more or less in the schools here they [i.e., teachers] *stick strictly to just the books, you know. They never—take for instance in English—ask a child what he would like to do, what he will like to be like, "Well, can you write out something about your life?"*

Another informant supported integration because: *There would be a greater chance that teachers would pay more attention to Mexican-American children with the rest of the white faces in the class.*

Burgherside parents, like Taxpayer parents, opposed to integration, want their children to attend the neighborhood schools because they fear for their safety and do not want to waste much of their time waiting for buses to pick up or bring home their children. As one informant explained:

Most parents want their kids to be close at home, especially when they are younger. So if anything does happen to them they can be close to them and they can go and get them or something. They want to be able to walk to school or walk back from lunch. They want their kids in their neighborhood schools close to home. They don't want to worry about waiting down for the buses and spending the time it takes to get there and the time it takes to get back.

Burghersiders also opposed busing because there were rumors that parents would have to pay the bus fares. Burghersiders said they could not afford to pay the fares and that Taxpayers' children should be bused because their parents can pay.

Others said that busing their children to Northside schools might have adverse consequences, since children from poor families might become prejudiced against Taxpayers' children who have more material things. One father said:

I will go along with a writer who wrote once here in Stockton Record *not too long ago. He said "If my child comes from a poor family and I dress him as well as I can and give him money for his lunch, send him across town to the Northside, then he is going to see his friends, his friend better dressed,* [with] *better shoes, while he has a little car to go to school and all that." He says, "How do you think that is going to help us when he comes back to that neighborhood?" You might say, "Well, yes, he's going to work himself out of that neighborhood because he doesn't like that neighborhood." But will it be that way? Or will he start building a prejudice concience, saying "You rich son of a gun, how come you've got all these and I haven't got them?"*

Such exposure could also create problems for Burgherside parents because their children might start making demands they could not afford. The same informant went on:

> *Actually, it will be a good thing for the rich man to come over to the poor section so he can learn how the other side lives. This is actually what they should try to do, see. It is good for him because he has it already. But do you think that it is going to work the same way for one who hasn't to see one who has? Well, your child is going to go home and say, "Daddy, how come I haven't got this?" and "Daddy, how come he's got it and I haven't got it?" You see. So what are you going to answer?*

Taxpayers and Burghersiders, then, differ significantly on the educational values of school integration. The latter do not believe that their children learn more by association with Taxpayers' children. One mother sums up:

> *I think that my child goes to school to learn and I fail to see how integration will make much difference to his ability to learn. He doesn't learn by who sits next to him; he learns by what he and his teacher put into it. The ability to learn is not transmitted just by mere presence of the other. I don't believe it matters where a person my child sits next to lives.*

Burghersiders reject the idea that Taxpayers' children are "smarter" than Burgherside children. What their children need, they argue, is "better education." *It is not so much the kids we are talking about,* said a black mother. A Mexican-American father said: *I believe that instead of busing the children the teachers should be rotated to different schools.* And a black father added: *And I want the children to get a* better *education—no matter where.*

The Role of Improved Communication

Stockton school officials believe that the problems of Stockton schools, particularly Southside schools, would be greatly reduced "if there were no communication problems." After the high school crisis of 1969 some officials said that the crisis would not have occurred if there had not been a breakdown of communication. Some of the "demands" and "recommendations" presented by the students, they said, were already being implemented. One official said: *We just don't know how to get the information to them.*

The school system tends to view home–school communication as essentially concerned with giving out factual information to students and parents, telling the people what is being done for them and what is expected of them. In the fall election of 1969 some candidates for the Board of Education made the "breakdown of communication" one of the central issues in their campaign. One candidate told a Burgherside audience: *It is quite obvious that there is a real problem of communication. It follows from this that there is a breakdown of communication not only between the administration and the board but in the school system as well.* The incumbent candidate promised to continue "attempts to find solutions" to the communication problems. He went on:

> *Other issues concern students' unrest. This is one in line with communication. It is important that we establish some lines of communication between the central administrators and the principals, principals and teachers, and teachers and their staff, then staff and students and parents. Somehow we have failed in this little task but we hope this problem of communication can be solved; and, hopefully, it will keep us aware of the types of problems we are going to be facing. Attempts to find solutions before they are brought to us can be continually exercised.*

This type of communication—giving out factual information—flows continually from the central administration office to the public through press releases, to the principals and teachers of various schools through memos, the weekly bulletins, and various meetings. One para-professional who was impressed by the one-sidedness of the communication in the school said:

> *Like the faculty meeting here, it is no faculty meeting. It's a principal's meeting. Well, the principal talks all the time. Well, call it a faculty meeting, and then talk all the time. We just sit and listen and the principal tells us what to do.*

One aspect of the problem of communication in Burgherside is obviously its one-sidedness.

But there are also cultural barriers and difficulties created by the social distance and mutual self-definitions discussed in Chapter 7. Burghersiders recognize these "cultural differences" but, they ask, why should it be they and not the teachers and other Taxpayers who learn an alien culture to cross the communication barrier? They feel that teachers, for instance, should learn Spanish in order to talk with non-English-speaking Mexican parents, and not expect parents to learn English to help the teachers. Furthermore, since Burgherside English differs from Taxpayers' English, teachers should learn Burgherside English. Some Burgherside parents say they are "completely turned off" by the fear that *they* have to speak "perfect English" when they go to the schools. One informant said: *And they think we're dumb. It's just that what they're talking about we don't relate to it, you know, when they're talking about perfect English. You don't know perfect English here. So it's kind of foreign.*

Burghersiders are sensitive about these language differences. Some say that they don't know the verbs and vowels "real well." Some Mexican-Americans stay away from meetings with teachers because: *They are ashamed of their difficulties to communicate in good English. The teacher will use better English and words you will not understand. And half of the time you will say, "What?" and he has to explain what the word means and he has to come down to where you are at.* Teachers, too, do not understand what Burghersiders are saying, so Burghersiders have to try to explain to the teacher in the teacher's own language (i.e., standard English), and that is discouraging, as one black informant pointed out:

> *The parents feel that they won't be able to get through to the teachers because the teachers wouldn't know what they were talking about, you know. Like you and I are talking and I say, I want to ask something. I would say "garbage can" and maybe you say "container." Teachers use this term, we use different terms than teachers use. And sure, they don't understand what we're talking about. And parents just feel rejected. Or, maybe the teachers use words which we don't know the meaning of it. Instead of getting the context—many parents here are not educated enough to get the meaning from the context.*

Two Filipino teenagers jokingly suggested that the solution to the communication problem would be for each teacher to live with a Burgherside family for a week or two each year. In that way, *Teachers would learn faster about Burgherside than they can from all the books they read about poor people,* their mother agreed. At the moment Taxpayers do not know enough about Burgherside to communicate with them through either verbal or nonverbal means: *Teachers think they know the community but they don't really know it. They know our names but they don't really know how we feel.*

This lack of understanding between the community and the school may be illustrated by the reaction of Burghersiders to a principal's policy of talking to parents behind closed doors in his office. They felt that this particular principal *talked to but not with them.* He was particularly criticized because he always had his office closed when he talked with parents. One informant said:

> *What kind of feeling does that give you if you're a parent? You go and sit in this chair, you know, to talk to the principal behind closed doors! It is the authority attitude that principal had. He wasn't like the other*

principal, that one would never do it, unless it was a confidential that he had to talk to a parent or a kid. Then he would close it. And then it's open again—and we all respected him, and the kids respected him, and the kids respected the building. You never saw no broken windows and no vandalism.

This former principal one day shocked some parents who were selling cake to raise money for the PTA when he bought a piece of cake for a dime: *He brought his dime, ten cents, and he bought a piece of cake. And this aggravated us because if he wanted a piece of cake we will give it to him. Or, why not give us a dollar? Give us five dollars. This* [the principal] *was an administrator.*

Some teachers will never learn to talk with Burghersiders, according to informants: [Those teachers] *may be smart and know their subjects—but still won't make it.* They are also the teachers and administrators who "go by the book." They never learn to understand Burghersiders—the way they live, talk, and feel. But there are some teachers and administrators "who know the people," who are able to relate effectively to parents and children and to communicate with them, and these are the people "who will make it" in Burgherside schools. They are neither too permissive nor too authoritarian. When they talk the children listen and hear because they usually talk at the level of Burghersiders. The following excerpt illustrates those "who will make it" and those "who will not." Here informants describe an incident they witnessed in one school:

FIRST INFORMANT: *Well, you know I went to a meeting when the kids were worrying about wearing their pants. And out of all those people they got up there and really talked it was only one and I'll say he'll make it—if he doesn't change. That is Mr. S., he'll make it because he talked to those kids what they really wanted to hear.*

Oh, they were really getting J. up and down. One side up and down the other. And even A., they were getting up his one side and riding down the other. So you can't really say that they were downing the white because they had the black person, they were downing her too.

SECOND INFORMANT: *These administrators didn't understand what the kids want.*

FIRST INFORMANT: *Yes. They came—here was speaking A. as an educator you know, speaking big words. Then came J., sitting and putting on her big front black.*

But S. came up and say, "Now, look, we are going to get you down to the nitty-gritty. You can wear pants. I think we can get together. I don't want you to wear them kind of skipped at the back." And he talked to them in their language. And one girl tried to raise her voice and S. said, "Now you shut up and let me get through what I got to say and then it is your turn." But he was down to their level and you can hear a pin fall. And he was really telling them identical things.

SECOND INFORMANT: *Their language.*

FIRST INFORMANT: *The identical thing that J. and A. was telling them—but S. was down to their language, you know. He was with them. And the biggest trouble-maker over there he just told him, "You just shut up a minute. You talk black shit. Shut up!" Now, what if A. had told them to shut up?*

ANTHR.: *Yes, there could have been trouble?*

FIRST INFORMANT: *A. and J. had been telling them to be quiet. They were saying, "Anybody who wants to talk raise their hands." And they were all talking.*

A. was saying, "I have nothing on my desk that says you girls can wear pants." And one girl got up and said, "Oh yes, you do. You are standing there telling a lie." This was her administrator. She didn't have no respect for him. You have to respect yourself and gain respect before someone else will respect you.

But when S. got down to their level he says, "Now, I'm going to see that you girls get what you want." A. had been sitting there for about one hour telling them, "Write out what you want and put them on my desk." And they were really ripping him off at the mouth. Now S. says, "If you want to wear short pants I don't want them all cut up in the back and I don't want no blue jeans. I want that stuff and I want you to put on girdles." And when somebody wanted to speak he says, "Shut up and let me tell you what I want to tell you." S. said, "When you finished put it on my desk in the morning and good night. And I want you to go home." And they said, "All right" [imitating the girls].

He [S.] was [acting like] a poor man that's talking to them. He was concerned. If you don't feel concerned, I don't care who you put over there, he won't make it.

Some black and Mexican-American teachers and administrators, known as "Oreo cookies" and "Tio Tacos," respectively have as much difficulty as some white teachers and administrators in talking with Burghersiders. Burghersiders define the "Oreos" or "Oreo cookies" as "people who are black on the outside but white on the inside," and a "Tio Taco" is *"brown por fuera y blanco por dentro"* ("brown on the outside and white on the inside"). Both the "Oreo cookies" and the "Tio Tacos" are described as "those who don't care about the progress of their own people," especially the progress of poor blacks and Mexican-Americans. One informant characterized the "Oreo" as follows:

An Oreo is one that if a black kid's hair is out of place he turns his nose. When he could encourage a black child he sits back and views him the same way as if he was Anglo-Saxon. And in teaching process, instead of saying: "You black kids, I am going to see that you get this work done; I expect this of you because it's going to be harder for you than for whites"—he sits back just like Oreo. He says, "If you are in this class you know you better learn." He doesn't know how to communicate at their level.

The older generation of Burghersiders tolerated the "Oreos" and "Tio Tacos" and some even tried to become like them. Now, however, the situation is different: *This new generation sees through all of them* and rejects them. And Burghersiders say that the problem is becoming more complicated because the Taxpayers prefer to promote the "Oreos" and "Tio Tacos" to positions of authority over poor blacks and Mexican-Americans. When pressured to appoint more blacks and Mexican-Americans to administrative positions, the school district may hand-pick people who do not understand and cannot communicate with Burghersiders and Southsiders. The schools may even appoint such people to the office of school–community relations where they act as the "go-betweens."

Burghersiders do not feel that teachers are willing to learn their language and way of life so as to communicate more effectively with them. They therefore suggest that in addition to the "go-betweens" in the community-relations office there should be some "in-betweens" in the schools. The "in-betweens" are people slightly more educated than Burghersiders, but not as educated as teachers and administrators. Such people, they hope, will be able to talk with both the educated people in the schools and the "uneducated parents" of Burgherside. At the moment, teacher aides are said to be the nearest thing to the "in-between" persons proposed by informants; but the aides are not effective channels of communication between teachers and parents for some reason.

"A Real Change Must Start at the Bottom"

Since Burghersiders do not accept the Taxpayers' analysis of their educational problems and are often skeptical of the programs developed by Taxpayers to solve them, I asked Burghersiders what could be done. What should be done to reduce school failures among their children? I often phrased the question about change as follows:

They say, "Here is Burgherside. What are its problems in education? We want these children to get ahead. We want something done about their educational needs." Now we ask you *to try to do something in this regard. What would you do? Where would you begin?*

Burghersiders say they would begin at the bottom. By "bottom" they mean Headstart/Pre-school. One mother said. *If a man came with billions of dollars and is going to do something about education in Burgherside, all right, if this were me, this is where I would start. NOT with the adults, NOT with the parents. The Headstart is where I would begin: Like I told you, I would start at the bottom.*

Burghersiders say that a good foundation for a successful school career is laid in the earliest years of schooling. Children who learn the basic skills—reading, writing, and arithmetic—in the early primary grades will do well throughout their elementary school careers. They are also the ones who will do well in junior high school and senior high school, and who will eventually "go to college and make it." This is why the Headstart/Pre-school program appealed to Burghersiders initially, and why they feel so disappointed by what they consider a departure from its main purpose of teaching the basic skills. Since they do not accept the Taxpayers' label of "culturally deprived" or "culturally disadvantaged," they also reject the theory that in order to learn, the learning faculties of their children must first be stimulated through play. They say that teaching, not play, is the key to a proper foundation of school learning. Headstart teachers should be "qualified," according to Burghersiders. They should "talk correctly," not "talk with slangs" like Burghersiders. Burghersiders also want something done about the "middle," about students in the junior and senior high schools. However, the proper place to start is at the bottom. *How can you start at the middle?*

What should be done about teachers? Burghersiders reply that although some black and Mexican-American teachers are "Oreo cookies" and "Tio Tacos," they appear in general to care more about the academic well-being of black and Mexican-American students than white teachers do. Following the Edison High School riot of 1969 both the Black Students Union and Chicano Students Association "demanded" "more Black and Brown teachers," counselors, and administrators. Some Black and Mexican-American teachers demonstrate that they "care more" by representing what they consider to be the educational interests of Southsiders before the school board, the school superintendent, and other officials. In fact, in 1969 two teachers' organizations, the Black Teachers Alliance and the Mexican-American Educators Association, arose with the explicit goal of working toward the improvement of the education of black and Mexican-American children within the school district. It should be pointed out that some white teachers share and articulate the same concern for Southsiders.

The community debate on racial integration of schools and the crises in some Southside schools in 1969 probably raised the value of black and Mexican-American teachers for Burghersiders. Particularly after the crisis at the high school, a significant number of Burgherside children began to feel that they "would do better in school" if more of their teachers were of their own races (see Table 10.2).

TABLE 10.2
How Well Burghersiders Do When Teachers Are of Their Own Ethnic Groups [a][b]

Response	How did you do when you took a course given by a teacher of your own race (i.e., before crisis)? (65)	How do you think you will do if more of your teachers were members of your own race (i.e., after crisis)? (70)
Better than usual	18.46	42.86
Same as usual	69.23	54.57
Worse than usual	7.24	2.80
Never had one	4.62	

[a]Source: Author's interviews with students.
[b]Values expressed as percentages.

There are several kinds of curriculum changes Burghersiders say are needed. One change, which has already been discussed, would put more emphasis on reading, writing, and arithmetic and less emphasis on play activities. A second type of change would make the curriculum reflect more the cultures of black and Mexican people, and the books the children read in school would deal with life styles familiar to them. When a parent was told that the schools were ordering books on black and Mexican people she replied: *Yes—that's just this year (1969). Were they there last year?*

Some Burghersiders support the bilingual program, as we mentioned above, because it is teaching their children their "cultural heritage." Burghersiders say that children should start learning their "cultural heritage" very early. One young man complained that the white man is *always changing things around in the books* so that the white man is always the hero in the stories. I pointed out that black and Mexican-American people are now writing books about their people and are "telling it like it is." He would discover this as he advanced in his education. His mother said he should learn his "cultural heritage" from his early years. It is too late to teach it to him at the junior high school, high school, or college because by that time he is already "bitter and militant."

Parents feel that the school curriculum should stress both training for college and training for good jobs. For Burghersiders the main function of the schools, the essence of formal education, should be training children to get good jobs when they grow up. School or education would be meaningless to most of them outside this context. Going to school should essentially be a preparation for jobs. When asked how the school should be improved, a Burgherside parent replied:

> *I would like to see subjects introduced in the lower grades pertaining to the vocational needs of our time—such as introduction to IBM programming, typing, fundamentals of geometry, algebra, principles of salesmanship.*
>
> *I feel that even at this grade level counseling should begin toward future vocation—to motivate the child to see some idea of the foundation he has to lay for a job in the future. Children need to begin this before they reach high school. They begin to drop out in the first and second grades unless they realize why they are in school. Best learning years are 1 to 12 years.*[1]

A Mexican mother would eliminate all the "extra things" in order to teach the children the basic reading, writing, and arithmetic. She added: *I prefer the old method because right now they've so many new things to learn.* And she concluded: *Promotion should be based on grade, not age.* Fully aware of their own lack of ability to provide effective educational guidance for their children, Burgherside parents expect the school to provide their children a good foundation in the early years. But the early foundations that they want are not those stressed by the current school programs based on the theory of "cultural deprivation."

The "Educational System" Is Changing, But School Failures Remain

Burghersiders feel that some changes are taking place in the school system but that these are mainly political and structural ones. Young people are primarily responsible for these changes. *What the younger generation are doing: protest, screaming, howling, "Why am I here? I like to be there. I want better things of this stuff and that stuff."* That is the breaking point. Black youths are constantly praised by the Mexican-American informants for their "new boldness." One woman said that the Mexican people should "be more aggressive" in view of the magnitude of their problems in school: *We should come to the school in anger and make demands. Unfortunately, when we come to the school we come without hats in our hand as humble people. This doesn't get us anywhere.*

Other Burghersiders are "not sure" that "Mr. Charlie" (the white man) is sincere in his concessions to those who are "demanding change." At the

---

[1] This woman told me recently (1971) that the family transferred their junior high school child to a private school where she "will get a better preparation for life."

Annual Burgherside Parade in June 1969, one black father discussed with me for half an hour his misgivings concerning "Mr. Charlie's" intentions. He said "Mr. Charlie" was leading the black man to a point where he would hurt him most. Another black man invited me to spend the night with his family because he had so many questions to ask me about "Mr. Charlie" that *we might talk all night.* When I got there the only question he asked me was whether I thought "Mr. Charlie" meant what he was saying— that he was going to change things.

Burghersiders say that among black, Mexican-American, and white people there are those who do not want change. These primarily include people who fear that the "new militancy" of the youth threatens their jobs or material security. According to one black informant: *They do not want to rock the boat. They feel, "I've gotten this far and I am doing all right." But it gets to the point that "all right" isn't good enough, you know. I think, you know, that most of them have gotten into that slot, "I'm doing all right, so why make all this noise?"* A Mexican-American informant said that the older people have difficulty accepting new things:

> *Well, that is like any other habit: they have been in the habit for so long for going along; and most of the ones I've talked to feel that this is a terrible thing. They don't think about the reasoning behind it. They just think that they are doing all these bad things just to be militant, you know, to be different. But I don't think they really think too much about the reasoning behind it. They've got a lot of reasons to do those things that they are doing. Some of them will eventually accept it but right now many of them I don't really think they will accept it.*

Burghersiders fear in particular that "Oreo cookies" and "Tio Tacos" in their opposition to the "new generation" may sabotage the changes taking place. Furthermore, they feel that minority people in positions of authority who are interested in helping their people do not usually have real power. The white man is: *always telling a minority person what to do. You will get up there and you will have been given a little bit of authority, yea. On the outside you say you are for your own people. But you might be hurting them more. Yet you'd go back and tell your friends you're for your own people.*

It is also said that some white people are not ready to accept the fact that changes are needed in the schools and society. *Some do. But I think there is a majority who don't,* according to one black informant, *The majority still don't accept it.* A Mexican-American informant said that white people are shouting "law and order" in order to stop changes being made:

> *Well, if they can create a police force like the Gestapo so they can scare people, that they think they haven't got to change and to stop them, then*

they can use a backlash to stop them. But otherwise, as you can see, that is not even going to stop them. It is too late for that. No, no, no. They can use the excuse of "law and order" but that will never stop them. It is too late now, it is flowing; like I said, the river is flowing and every person identifying himself with it, asking what he is.

Burgherside parents criticize "the system" and their criticisms often focus on specific aspects of the system: teachers, new programs, and the like. They have some well-developed ideas about certain changes they think desirable. Although they do not have a fully developed program, they know what ought to be done but not necessarily how it can be done. Individuals talk about changing "the system" but there is little organized effort to do this. Furthermore, they rarely conceptualize change in terms of the overall structure of the school system. For example, although some Southside "spokesmen" were talking about community control of schools in 1969, Burghersiders never mentioned community control to me. When I asked how they would feel if the School District granted them control of their own neighborhood school, nearly 50 % said they would be dissatisfied or had no opinion. Some informants later told me that they did not want community control because nobody would ever give it to them. The older people, then, do not believe that they have the power to effect change. So they are amazed at the changes the young people have brought about.

During the mid-1960s many parents were active in both the Fire Department and the Neighborhood Association, but at the period of my research, much of this was history. Except in periods of crisis the regular meetings of the association are usually attended by the same handful of residents— less than 10 on any given occasion. Many parents feel that it is no use to try to organize meetings: *They feel powerless and so will just talk about the problems. If you mention getting together in a meeting of all the residents they say, "It's not going to do any good."* Their past experiences suggest that "it's not going to do any good."

Burgherside Association continued to be the only organized group in the neighborhood concerned with education. It was instrumental in organizing Burgherside Pre-school in 1966; it introduced a tiny tots program in 1967, and it has co-sponsored study halls with the PTA. But it, too, has not often been successful. During the fall of 1969 the Regional Office of the OEO asked the Neighborhood Center to work out their priorities, reporting that there was money available for any program they wanted. Burgherside residents decided on education as their most important priority, and they planned to hire an "Education Assistant" to help Burgherside pupils in the community. They submitted their proposal for funding, but were told that there was no money for such a program.

CHAPTER 11

The Next Generation and the Meanings of "Equal Educational Opportunity"

Treating the Symptoms of the Problem

In the decade of the 1960s American social scientists, more than ever before, began massive efforts directed toward increasing the educational success of the children of the poor and ethnic minorities in American public schools. These social scientists were partly responding to the "social conscience" of the period about the social and economic conditions of the poor and of ethnic minorities. Like their fellow citizens, many of them had come to believe that poverty and inequality should not exist in the midst of affluence and that social science could contribute to the elimination of these problems by showing how the poor and ethnic minorities could achieve better success in public schools. Thus their increasing theoretical and research activities in the field of education have been generated by practical rather than intellectual considerations. Differences exist among different schools of thought about the causes and cures of school failures; but the various points of view have generally been directed toward influencing social policies on how to solve the problems of poverty and inequality through education.

The three competing explanations reviewed in the first chapter of this

252

book state that school failures are due to (a) cultural deprivation, (b) inferiority of the schools attended by the children of the poor and ethnic minorities, and (c) genetic inferiority of some ethnic groups, particularly the blacks. In general American social scientists, including those who blame the schools, tend to assume explicitly or implicitly that the main cause of school failures lies in the background of the children. That is, they assume that the children of poor and ethnic minorities fail in public schools because of those background characteristics that distinguish them from middle- and upper-class children. These distinguishing characteristics may be biological, cultural, linguistic, psychological, or social, depending on the dominant interest of the social scientist. Once a particular difference is postulated, the main task of research is to determine the nature and extent of the difference. Data so compiled are correlated with children's achievements at school and this connection is taken as proof that the particular explanation of why the children of the poor and ethnic minorities fail being proposed is correct. This preoccupation with the characteristics of the individual child and his background arises inevitably because American social scientists share the American belief that the individual is responsible for his own success or failure in life (Cloward and Ohlin 1960:125; Sexton 1970:19). It is also due to the disproportionate influence of psychology on American educational research (Kimball and McClellan 1962). This bias has prevented social scientists from fully exploring the structural and cultural factors in the wider society that may lead to high proportions of failures in some segments of the society. It has also led those concerned with reducing failures to design remedial programs that treat failures as individual problems, the histories of which begin at birth. For the most part the programs have not succeeded in solving the problems because they are based on false assumptions about the causes of school failures.

In order to examine the historical, cultural, and structural factors that lead to school failures in Burgherside it was found necessary to define the population studied more precisely. All children from a background of poverty do not fail in school; nor do all those who fail come from such a background. Similarly all children from an ethnic minority background do not fail; nor do all those who do not come from such a background succeed. I suspect that white children from a background of poverty fail in public school for different reasons from those that cause school failures among minority groups. I have also made a distinction between *immigrant minorities* like the Chinese and Japanese, and *subordinate minorities* like the blacks and Mexican-Americans. The former are characterised by high success in school whereas the latter are marked by failures. The present study has dealt mainly with the problem of school failures among the subordinate minorities.

The explanation for school failures among subordinate minorities reviewed in this book tends to ignore historical factors except those that begin at the birth of the individual. I have tried to show that a major source of the inadequacy of these theories is their essentially ahistorical approach to a problem that has its roots in history. The inadequacy of this approach for explaining the situation in Burgherside came to my attention early in my study. I had begun my study thinking that the problem of school failure in the neighborhood could be explained through a careful analysis of the contemporary life styles of Burghersiders. However, after my initial survey of more than 100 households and some intensive interviews I realized that there were two types of historical factors influencing education in Burgherside in significant ways. The first had to do with urbanization, the second, with the experiences of the subordinate groups in American society.

My household survey showed that many Burgherside parents and other adults are first generation urban residents from the rural South and rural Mexico. Therefore, any realistic explanation of their present behavior must take into account their patterns of adjustment to urban ways of life, including their adjustment to the urban education system. It would be erroneous to analyze the behavior of Burghersiders simply as that of "low-income people" in contrast to the white middle class. As the analysis presented in the preceding chapters shows, Burghersiders sometimes relate to the schools on the basis of their experiences in the rural South and Mexico, not simply as lower-class people. Furthermore, although Burgherside parents often lack the educational backgrounds of middle-class parents which give the latter advantages in helping their children with their schoolwork, it is erroneous to explain their behavior as socially, psychologically, and clinically abnormal.

A more fundamental historical factor in the school failures of blacks and other subordinate minorities is the basis of their association with the dominant white group and the adaptation that they have made to the institutions of American society because of their historical experiences in these institutions. I have argued, for example, that the initial association of subordinate minorities, like the blacks, with the dominant group was neither voluntary nor motivated by the drive for economic self-improvement, as in the case of the immigrant minorities. Furthermore, after their emancipation, blacks were legally and ideologically led to expect equal treatment with whites in education and the benefits from it; but in practice they have been systematically denied this equal treatment. Historically, they have been given inferior education and those among them who managed to receive good educations have been excluded from the social and economic rewards awarded to whites. That is, they have been denied the opportunity of getting good jobs and receiving good wages commensurate with their education. It is therefore my contention that blacks responded, more or less unconsciously, to this limited postschool opportunity partly by reducing their efforts in school tasks to the level of rewards they expected as future adults of American society. In the past this mode of adaptation, which results in a high proportion of school failure, served some needs of blacks as well as those of the dominant white society. For blacks it reduced the painful feeling that they worked as hard as whites in school for fewer rewards from society. Blacks, as was pointed out in Chapter 1, developed an elaborate belief system with which they rationalized their school failure. The adaptation also served the needs of the dominant white society because it ensured that most blacks qualified only for those social and economic roles considered appropriate for blacks. The dominant society, too, developed its own elaborate belief system that both reinforced black school failure and rationalized their low social and economic position in society.

The present study examined three ways in which school-failure adaptation is maintained in Burgherside. First, there is "a lag" in the efforts of Burghersiders to achieve their stated goals in education. Parents, students, and peer groups behave in ways that contribute to the stability of the adaptation, that insure that they will fail in school. For example, the children are frequently absent from school and their classes; when in class they seem to lack seriousness about their work. Not only do they believe that they "will not make it" (i.e., succeed) but also *they do not try to make it*. This is not because the students do not know what to do in order to succeed; they are fully aware that the Chinese and Japanese students in their schools do well in their classes "because they make the effort." The loss of the desire to perform or compete effectively in their school work is the result of their adaptation to the limited opportunity to benefit from their educations. And lack of competitiveness insures that they will not do well in school, that many of them will fail. Similarly, although Burgherside parents tell their children that it is important to get good educations, they also tell them directly and indirectly that they are not likely "to make it in the white man's world" even if they have good educations. This reinforces the lack of desire on the part of the children to compete effectively in school. The peer groups, as I have shown, pull the children away from whatever educational goals they may have.

Second, it is shown in this that school-failure adaptation is maintained by the way in which teachers interact with Burghersiders. The people who call themselves Taxpayers include teachers. They insist that Burghersiders are a different type of people; they are Nontaxpayers who do not bear their share of the responsibility for financial support of the political, educational, and other community institutions. Since some Burghersiders receive public assistance (welfare) they are also looked upon as financial burdens to Taxpayers. The latter feel strongly that Burghersiders should assume their full responsibility as citizens by becoming Taxpayers and that they can achieve Taxpayer status through education. Teachers are therefore hired as professional people to enable them to become Taxpayers, but their attitudes and approach to Burghersiders tend to defeat this purpose. Like other Taxpayers, teachers insist on relating to Burghersiders as their patrons. They neither accept Burghersiders as equals nor interact with them as they do with parents who are Taxpayers. As for Burghersiders, their attitudes toward education and the effort they make in school are greatly influenced by their experiences with teachers and other Taxpayers. The two groups, teachers and Burghersiders, do not agree as to what constitutes the "problems" of Burgherside education, their causes, and their cures. Thus the relationship between them contributes to maintaining the school-failure adaptation in the neighborhood.

Third, the school system contributes to maintaining school-failure adaptation in Burgherside by defining its educational problems in psychological and clinical terms. Taxpayers contend that the purpose of educating Burghersiders is to make them into Taxpayers. They point out that they themselves have good jobs, good wages, and live in good neighborhoods (things which indicate that they are Taxpayers) because of their educations; and they say that Burghersiders can do the same if they work hard in school. But they fail to point out that Burghersiders face special problems as subordinate minorities in their attempt to achieve the status of Taxpayers. They are judged not as individuals but on the basis of their ethnic membership for jobs, wages, and residence, even when they have reached the same levels of education as Taxpayers. In fact, the community seems to use its schools to control the rate at which Burghersiders achieve Taxpayer status, which is not very high. Many children either drop out of school or graduate from high school with "dead-end courses" on their records that do not qualify them for those jobs that lead to Taxpayer status. This situation is reported to be changing as a result of the Fair Employment Practices Act and other measures taken by the state and federal governments to reduce discrimination against members of ethnic minorities.

Let me reiterate that the stated intention of the schools is to help Burghersiders become Taxpayers. The school system plans its activities in order to achieve this end. But the assumptions about Burghersiders inherent in these activities, and the methods by which they are expressed more or less defeat their purpose. For example, there are three myths about Burghersiders existing in the schools as well as the wider community that support the psychological and clinical definition of the academic problems of Burghersiders, and that, in turn, ensure that Burghersiders continue to fail in school. These are: that community or parent "involvement" promotes school success, but Burghersiders are not involved; that Burgherside households are female-dominated and such households in a place like Burgherside simply cannot raise children to succeed in school; and that Burghersiders are caught in the endless cycle of welfare and poverty. These beliefs influence the way the school system treats Burghersiders. The counseling system, as I have tried to show, is one mechanism by which the schools limit or control the mobility of Burghersiders into Taxpayer status.

Failure to recognize this type of group adaptation continues to create some misunderstanding about the educational needs of Burghersiders. For example, teachers and other Taxpayers in Stockton often imply that Burghersiders ought to be working harder in school than they are because it is good to make good grades in school, and hard work will show that they value education. But Burghersiders (like other Stocktonians) do not value education or making good grades for their own sakes, *but as a means to good jobs, good wages, and so on.* On this particular point, Burghersiders differ from many contemporary critics of the education system. Some critics, for example, argue that schools are obsolete or "irrelevant," and others take even a more nihilistic view that formal education is not necessary for people like Burghersiders. Burghersiders themselves *insist that they need formal education,* although what they usually mean by this is that they wish to be given a preparation for employment in good jobs. As a corollary to this, they feel that they should be given the opportunity to get such good jobs with good wages when they achieve good educations. They point out that in the past there were people among them who worked as laborers although they had good educations. They generally complain that they are "getting a dirty deal." What my informants repeatedly implied is that they have not been adequately rewarded for their educational accomplishments. It seems to me that it is for this reason that Burghersiders (as well as blacks and Mexican-Americans in Stockton and elsewhere in the U.S.) have developed the types of attitudes that prevent them from actually competing effectively in school. This adaptation developed as a collective response to a situation they faced as a group rather than as individuals; it is a collective response to the problem of the discrepancy between what they believe they should receive from society and what society actually gives to them. Although it is manifested in the behavior of individual children, as expressed by how they perform in school, it is not an individual phenomenon but one of group adaptation, which is passed on from one generation to the next.

Subordinate minorities continue to have a high proportion of school failures because the factors that produced this form of adaptation still exist. These are:

1.   Inequality of educational rewards; this has not changed, and subordinate minorities still regard their "struggle for equality" as a priority over hard work at school.

2.   The folk and scientific definition of subordinate minorities as mentally inferior or culturally inferior to whites, both in school and in occupational placement, remains an important element in American culture today.

3.   The schools have not changed their treatment of subordinate minorities because their actions are determined by the ideas and policies of the dominant group.

Two Meanings of "Equal Educational Opportunity"

The present study shows that the concept of **equal educational opportunity** has received only a **partial definition** in American social science. As presently used it refers to those efforts made to enable each child to study in school under favorable learning conditions. That is, "remedial educational programs" are designed to overcome whatever educators and social scientists see as the "educational handicaps" (e.g., language, health, hunger, parental attitudes, and so on) of a particular group of children (Coleman 1969:24). But the concept has another meaning: It refers to the ability of the individual and of groups to benefit from their educations on an equal footing with the dominant group once they leave school. People do not succeed in school simply because they have high IQs, favorable attitudes, or come from affluent family backgrounds (Cloward and Ohlin 1960); but how they expect to use their education in the future strongly influences how they behave in school. The latter is what some psychologists call a problem of **incentive motivation** (Hull 1943). By this type of motivation is not meant giving children candy in the classroom so that they will learn their alphabets. Rather it refers to the willingness of society to distribute without discrimination those occupational, monetary, and other rewards that it claims to distribute to its citizens on the basis of educational qualification. **Equal educational oppurtunity** therefore refers to both **equal favorable learning conditions for all children** and to **the equal enjoyment of the benefits or rewards of education by individuals and segments of the society according to their educational achievement.**

Equality of educational opportunity cannot be achieved by reforming the school alone, no matter how far reaching or how well intentioned such reforms may be. It cannot be achieved by abolishing the traditional form of school organization or abolishing formal education altogether. It cannot be achieved by mounted efforts to change subordinate minority children and their environments no matter how plausible the "behavior modification models" or schemes may appear. It cannot be achieved by turning subordinate minority children over to business firms to teach. It cannot be achieved even if all schools are racially or ethnically "balanced." Some of these efforts will benefit some children; but they cannot alter the adaptation described here for subordinate minorities. Burghersiders and similar groups will increase their efforts, and therefore their success in school, when the two meanings of the concept of equal educational opportunity become a reality to them.

There is, however, the problem of "cultural lag." I believe that those who initiated and operated the compensatory education (remedial) programs in the 1960s were surprisingly naive in their thinking. In Stockton, for instance, these people's explicitly stated goal was to change in a period of eight months the attitudes and behavior patterns that have been developed and transmitted over several generations. The same thinking probably led Jensen and others to conclude that since the compensatory education programs did not solve the problem of school failures among subordinate minorities in a period of from four to five years (1965–1969), the problem must be hereditary. The present study does not suggest that Burghersiders and their problems would fit into this simple scheme of "stimulus–response." In attempting to change the adaptation described in this book, it would be unrealistic to expect an instant result. If the two meanings of equal educational opportunity stated above were to become a reality in Burgherside today, Burghersiders' attitudes and behavior would not change immediately. It would require some time for Burghersiders to develop a new set of beliefs that assures them that the barriers to equal opportunity have been removed. It would require time for them to develop new attitudes toward competing for success in the classroom and time to develop new work habits.

School-failure adaptation will remain in Burgherside as long as the concept of equal educational opportunity receives only a partial definition, no matter what remedial programs are developed to change Burghersiders' beliefs about themselves, about school, and about school work. This study has shown further that the real source of the school-failure adaptation lies in the wider community. The schools—administrators, counselors, teachers, pupils, and so on—are merely playing the roles that the community assigns them.

Bibliography

Aberle, David F.

    1966   *The Peyote religion among the Navaho.* New York: Wenner-Gren Foundation.

Austin, Ernest H., Jr.

    1965a   Cultural Deprivation—a few questions. *Phi Delta Kappan* **46:** 67–70.

    1965b   A parting shot from a still skeptical skeptic. *Phi Delta Kappan* **46:** 74–76.

Ausubel, David

    1964   How reversable are the cognitive and moturational effects of cultural deprivation? Implications for teaching the culturally deprived child. *Urban Education* **1:** 16–39.

Baratz, Stephen S., and Joan C. Baratz

    1970   Early childhood intervention: The social science base of institutional racism. *Harvard Educational Review* **40:**29–50.

Berg, Ivar

    1969   *Education and jobs: The great training robbery.* Boston: Beacon Press.

Berger, Peter L., and Thomas Luckman

    1966   *The social construction of reality: A treatise in the sociology of knowledge.* Garden City: Doubleday.

Bernstein, Basil

    1970   A sociolinguistic approach to socialization: With some reference to educability. In *Language and poverty: Perspectives on a theme,* edited by Frederick Williams. Chicago: Markham Publishing Co.

Berreman, Gerald

    1972   Race, caste and other invidious distinctions in social stratification. *Race* **23:** 385–414.

Black Teachers Alliance

    1966   Letter to the Superintendent of Schools, Stockton Unified School District. March, 1969.

260

Bohannam, Paul
 1957   *Justice and judgment among the Tiv.* London: Oxford University Press.
 1965   The differing realms of the law. In *The ethnography of law,* edited by L. Nader.
        American Anthropologist **67** (Special Issue): 33–42.
 1968   Gluckman's "The Idea of Barotse Jurisprudence": A review. *Kroeber Society
        Papers,* No. 36:94–1010.
 1969   Enthnography and comparison in legal anthropology. In *Law in culture and society,*
        edited by L. Nader. Chicago: Aldine.
Bordua, David J.
 1960   Educational aspirations and parental stress on college. *Social Forces* **38**: 262–269.
Brookover, Wilber B., and Edsel L, Enckson
 1969   *Society, schools, and learning.* Boston: Allyn and Bacon.
Brookover, Wilbur B., and David Gottlieb
 1964   *A sociology of education.* New York: The American Book Company.
Burma, John H. (Editor)
 1970   *Mexican-Americans in the United States: A reader.* New York: Schenkman Pub-
        lishing Co., Inc.
Callahan, Raymond E.
 1962   *Education and the cult of efficiency.* Chicago: Univ. of Chicago Press.
Cicourel, Aaron V., and John I. Kitsuse
 1963   *The educational decision-makers.* New York: Bobbs-Merrill.
Clayton, Thomas E.
 1965   *Teaching and learning: A psychological perspective.* Englewood Cliffs, New Jersey:
        Prentice-Hall.
Cloward, Richard A., and A. Jones
 1963   Social classes: Educational attitudes and participation. In *Education in depressed
        areas,* edited by A. H. Passow. New York: Teachers College.
Cloward, Richard A., and Lloyd E. Ohlin
 1960   *Delinquency and opportunity: A theory of delinquent gangs.* New York: The Free
        Press.
Cohen, Elizabeth G.
 1965   Parental factors in educational mobility. *Sociology of Education* **38**: 404–425.
Cohen, Yehudi A.
 1971   The shaping of men's minds: Adaptations to the imperatives of culture. In *Anthro-
        pological perspectives on education,* edited by Murry L. Was, Stanley Diamond, and Fred O.
        Gearing. New York: Basic Books.
Coleman, James S.
 1965   The adolescent subculture and academic achievement. In *The schools and the urban
        crisis: A book of readings,* edited by August Kerber and Barbara Bommarito. New York:
        Holt.
 1969   *Equal educational opportunity.* Cambridge Massachusetts: Harvard Univ. Press.
Cooper, Bruce
 1971   *Free and freedom schools: A national survey of alternative programs.* Washington
        D.C.: U.S. Govt. Printing Office.
Crossland, Fred E.
 1971   *Minority access to college: A Ford Foundation report.* New York: Schocken Books.
Deneberg, Victor H.
 1970   *Education of the infant and young child.* New York: Academic Press.
Deutsch, Martin
 1967   *The disadvantaged child,* selected papers of Martin Deutsch and associates. New
        York: Basic Books.
Durkheim, Emile
 1951   *Suicide: a study in sociology.* Glencoe, Illinois: Free Press.

Eysenck, H. J.
  1971   *Race, intelligence and education.* New York: Library Press.
Fagley, Gladys, and M. Larsen
  1962   *A Study of 190 at Edison High School who failed one or more subjects during the first or third quarter of the 1961–1962 term.* Mimeo.
Foster, George M., Jr.
  1961   The dyadic contract: A model for the social structure of a Mexican peasant village. *American Anthropologist* **63**:1173–1192.
  1963   The dyadic contract in Tzintzuntzan, 11:Patron-client relationship. *American Anthropologist* **65**:1280–1294.
  1967   *Tzintzuntzan: Mexican peasants in a changing world.* Boston: Little, Brown.
Frost, Joe L., and Glen R. Hawkes
  1966   *The disadvantaged child: Issues and innovations.* Boston: Houghton Mifflin.
Ginzberg, Eli
  1956   *The Negro potential.* New York: Columbia Univ. Press.
Ginzberg, Eli
  1967   *The middle class negro in the white man's world.* New York: Columbia Univ. Press.
Goldstein, Bernard
  1967   *Low income youth in urban areas: A critical review of the literature.* New York: Holt.
Glazer, Nathan, and Patrick Moynihan
  1963   *Beyond the melting pot: The Negroes, Puerto Ricans, Jews, Italians, and Irish of New York City.* Cambridge, Massachusetts: MIT Press.
Gordon, Ira J.
  1968   *Parent involvement in compensatory education.* Urbana, Illinois: Univ. of Illinois Press.
Gordon, Milton M.
  1964   *Assimilation in American life: The role of race, religion, and national origins.* New York: Oxford Univ. Press.
Grant, Madison
  1970   *The passing of the great race in America.* New York: Arno Press and the New York Times.
Guthrie, James W., and James A. Kelly
  1965   Compensatory education—Some answers for a skeptic. *Phi Delta Kappan* **46**:70–74.
Guthrie, James W., George B. Kleindorfer, Henry M. Levin, and Robert T. Stout
  1971   *Schools and inequality.* Cambridge, Mass.: MIT Press.
Harvard Educational Review
  1969   Environment, heredity, and intelligence. Reprint series No. 2.
Henry, Jules
  1971   Education of the Negro child. In *Anthropological perspective on education,* edited by Murry L. Wax, Stanley Diamond, and Fred O. Gearing. New York: Basic Books.
Hentoff, Nat
  1966   *Our children are dying,* New York: Viking.
Herrnstein, Richard
  1971   IQ. *The Atlantic Monthly.* September, 1971, pp. 43–64.
Hertzberg, Alvin, and Edward F. Stone
  1971   *Schools are for children: An American approach to open classroom.* New York: Schocken Books.
Hey, Robert P.
  1972   An F for inner-city school experiment. *Christian Science Monitor* **64**:1.

Hill, Winfred F.
    1963 *Learning: A survey of psychological interpretation*. San Francisco: Chandler Publishing Co.

Hillson, Maurie, Francesco Cordasco, and Francis P. Purcell (Editors)
    1969 *Education and the urban community: Schools and the crisis of the cities*. New York: American Book Company.

Hollingshead, A.
    1949 *Elmtown's youth*. New York: Wiley.

Hostetler, John A., and Gertrude Enders Huntington
    1971 *Children in Amish society: Socialization and community education*. New York: Holt.

Hull, C. L.
    1943 *Principles of behavior*. New York: Appleton.

Hunt, J. Mc. V.
    1964 The psychological basis for using preschool enrichment as an antidote for cultural deprivation. *The Merril-Palmer Quarterly* 1:209–248.
    1967 The psychological basis for preschool cultural enrichment programs. In *Social class, race, and psychological development*, edited by M. Deutsch *et al*. New York: Holt.
    1969a Has compensatory education failed? Has it been tried? *Harvard Educational Review* 39:278–300.
    1969b *The challenge of incompetence and poverty: Papers on the role of early education*. Urbana, Illinois: Univ. of Illinois Press.

Huizar, Tony
    1969 La voz de la juventad. *El Hispano,* August 19, 1969, p. 5.

Hutchinson, Edward W.
    1965 *Stockton Church Metropolitan Strategies: Parish Studies Report* 1: Appendix A: Characteristics of the Stockton metropolitan area. Mimeo.

Hyman, H. H.
    1953 The value systems of different classes: A social-psychological contribution to the analysis of stratification. In *Class, status and power*, edited by Reinhardt Bendix and S. M. Lipset. Glencoe, Illinois: The Free Press.

Illich, Ivan
    1970 *Deschooling of society*. New York: Harper.

Inkeles, A.
    1966 A note on social structure and the socialization of competence. *Harvard Educational Review* 36:265–283.

Inner London Education Authority
    1967 The education of immigrant pupils in primary schools. *ILEA Report, 1959.* London.

Janssen, Peter
    1972 OEO as innovation: No more rabbits out of hats. *Saturday Review,* 55:40–430.

Jensen, Arthur R.
    1969a How much can we boost IQ and scholastic achievement? *Harvard Educational Review,* Reprint Series No. 2., pp. 1–123.
    1969b Reducing the heredity-environment uncertainty. *Harvard Educational Review,* Reprint Series No. 2, pp. 209–243.

Kahl, Joseph
    1953 Educational and occupational aspirations of common man's boys. *Harvard Educational Review* 23:186–203

Katz, Irwin
    1967 The socialization of academic motivation in minority group children. *Nebraska Symposium on Motivation,* pp. 133–191.

Katz, Michael
    1971   *Class, bureaucracy, and schools: The illusion of educational change in America.*
    New York: Praeger.
Kimball, Solon T., and James E. McClellan Jr. (Editors)
    1962   *Education and the new America.* New York: Vintage.
Kohl, Herbert
    1967   *36 Children.* New York: New American Library.
    1969   *The open classroom.* New York: Random House.
Kozol, Jonathan
    1972   *Free schools.* Boston: Houghton Mifflin.
Kraus, Michael
    1966   *Immigration: The American mosaic.* Princeton, New Jersey: Van Nostrand,
    Reinhold.
Leacock, Eleanor B.
    1969   *Teaching and learning in city schools. A Comparative study.* New York: Basic Books.
    1971   Introduction: The concept of culture. In *The culture of poverty: A critique,* edited
    by Eleanor Burk Leacock. New York: Simon and Schuster.
Little, Arthur D. and Associates
    1964   *The Metropolitan Stockton Economy: Analysis and Forecast.* The Department of
    City Planning, Stockton, California.
    1965   *Stockton Community. Renewal Policies and Program.* The Department of City
    Planning, Stockton, California.
Lynd, Helen, and Robert Lynd
    1937   *Middletown in transition.* New York: Harcourt.
Macias, George Azcarate
    n.d.   Mexican, Mexican-American, and Chicano. In *A Chicano speaks out,* Part Two,
    p. 2. Reprinted from *The Sacramento State Hornet.* Mimeo.
Martin, V. Covert
    1959   *Stockton Album through the Years.* Stockton, California.
Meer, Bernard, and Edward Freeman
    1966   The Impact of Negro neighbors on white homeowners. *Social Forces* **45:** 11–19
Merton, Robert K.
    1957   *Social theory and social structure.* Glencoe, Illinois: Free Press.
Miller, Harry L. (Editor)
    1967   *Education for the disadvantaged.* New York: The Free Press.
Model City Correctional Project (MCCP)
    1967   *Socio-Economic Investigation of San Joaquin County* (Appendix Report). Stockton:
    Institute for the Study of Crime and Delinquency. Mimeo.
Moore, G. Alexander
    1967   *Realities of the urban classroom.* Garden City, New York: Doubleday.
Mosteller, Frederick, and Daniel P. Moynihan
    1972   *On equality of educational opportunity.* New York: Random House.
The Newson Report
    1963   *Half our future.* London: H.M.S.O.
Purcell, Francis P.
    1969   The disadvantaged child and the culture of poverty. In *Education and the urban
    community: Schools and the crisis of the cities,* edited by Maurie Hillson, Francesco
    Cordasco, and Francis P. Purcell. New York: American Book Company.
Reimer, Everett W.
    1971   *School is dead: Alternatives in education.* Garden City, New York: Doubleday.
Riessman, Frank
    1962   *The culturally deprived child.* New York: Harper.

Rist, Ray C.
    1970   Student social class and teacher expectations: The self-fulfilling prophecy in ghetto education. *Harvard Educational Review* **40**:411–451.
Rempson, Joe L.
    1967   School-parent programs in depressed urban neighborhoods. In *The Urban R's: Race relations as the problem in urban education,* edited by Robert A. Dentler. New York: Praeger.
Rosenham, David L.
    1967   Cultural Deprivation and Learning: An examination of method and theory. In *Education for the disadvantaged,* edited by Harry L. Miller. New York: The Free Press.
Rosenthal, R. and Lenore Jacobson
    1968   *Pygmalion in the classroom.* New York: Holt.
Sandelius, Stanley E.
    1963   Employment of Certificated Personnel of Ethnic Minority Groups in Stockton Unified School District, 1947–1962. Unpublished M.A. Thesis, University of the Pacific, Stockton.
Scarr-Salapatek, Sandra
    1971a   Unknowns in the IQ equations. *Science* **174**. No. 4015.
    1971b   Race, social class, and IQ. *Science* **174**. No. 4016.
Sexton, Patricia Cayo
    1961   *Education and income: Inequality of opportunity in the public schools.* New York: Viking Press.
    1970   *The American schools: A sociological analysis.* Englewood Cliffs, New Jersey: Prentice-Hall.
Siemans, L.B.
    1965   The influence of selected family factors on educational and occupational aspirational levels of high school boys and girls. In *Low income youth in urban areas: A critical review of the literature,* edited by Bernard Goldstein. New York: Holt, 1967.
Silberman, Charles
    1970   *Crisis in the classroom: The remaking of American education.* New York: Random House.
South Stockton Parish
    1967   *A Statistical Study of South and East Stockton.* Mimeo.
State of California, Department of Education
    1969   *Status Report on Stockton Unified School District's ESEA, Title 1 Project.* Sacramento, California.
State of California, Department of Human Resource Development
    1966   Clearance Unit No. 5. Sacramento, California.
    1969   Monthly Labor Bulletin, Stockton Metropolitan Area.
Stein, Annie
    1971   Strategies for Failures. In *Harvard Educational Review,* Reprint Series No. 5, *Challenging the myths: The schools, the blacks, and the poor,* pp. 133–179.
Stockton Record
    1971   Contract teaching system not a major remedy. Dec. 14, p. 5.
Stockton Unified School District (SUSD)
    1967a   *Annual Report, Washington Elementary School*
    1967b   *Student Handbook, John Marshall Junior High School.*
    1968a   *Annual Report, John Marshall Junior High School.*
    1968b   *Records of Board of Education Minutes.*
    1969a   *A Compensatory Education Program,*
    1969b   *Records of Board of Education Minutes.*
    1969c   *Annual Report, John Marshall Junior High School.*

1969d *Racial and Ethnic Distribution of Employees: Certificated Personnel.*

1969e *Annual Report, Edison Senior High School.*

1969f *Annual Report, Washington Elementary School.*

1969g *Report on the Status of Pupil Personnel Services in the Stockton Unified School District.*

1970a *A Demonstration Bilingual Bicultural Education Project, Title VII Grant Application.*

1970b *Report on the State Testing: Results for the Year* 1969–70. Mimeo.

1970c *Compensatory Education Comprehensive Report.*

1971   *Report on the State Testing: Results for the Year* 1970–71. Mimeo.

     n.d. *Student Handbook, Edison Senior High School.*

Taba, Hilda

    1967   Cultural deprivation as a factor in school learning. In *Problems of children and youth in modern society,* edited by Gene R. Medinnus, Harold Keely, Karl Mueller, and Eldred Rutherford. New York: Selected Academic Readings, Inc., College Division.

Thompson, Frank V.

    1920   *Schooling of the immigrant.* New York: Harper.

Torch, Hans

    1965   *The social psychology of social movement.* New York: Bobbs-Merrill.

University of California Extension, Stockton College

    1957   *Community Analysis for Adult Education X187AB.* Winter 1957. Mimeo.

Valentine, Charles A.

    1968   *Culture and poverty: Critique and counter proposals.* Chicago: Univ. of Chicago Press.

Warner, W. Lloyd, Robert J. Havighurst, and Martin B. Loeb

    1944   *Who Shall Be Educated?* New York: Harper and Row.

Webster, Staten W. (Editor)

    1966   *Knowing the disadvantaged child.* San Francisco: Chandler.

Whitten, Norman E., Jr.

    1965   *Class, kinship, and power in an Ecuadorian town: The Negroes of San Lorenzo.* Stanford, California: Stanford Univ. Press.

Index